NOSTALGIA

AGNES ARNOLD-FORSTER

NOSTALGIA

A HISTORY OF A
DANGEROUS EMOTION

PICADOR

First published 2024 by Picador
an imprint of Pan Macmillan
The Smithson, 6 Briset Street, London EC1M 5NR
EU representative: Macmillan Publishers Ireland Ltd, 1st Floor,
The Liffey Trust Centre, 117–126 Sheriff Street Upper,
Dublin 1, D01 YC43
Associated companies throughout the world
www.panmacmillan.com

ISBN 978-1-5290-9136-6

1 3 5 7 9 8 6 4 2

A CIP catalogue record for this book is available from the British Library.

Typeset in Perpetua Std by Palimpsest Book Production Limited, Falkirk, Stirlingshire
Printed and bound by CPI Group (UK) Ltd, Croydon, CR0 4YY

Visit **www.picador.com** to read more about all our books
and to buy them. You will also find features, author interviews and
news of any author events, and you can sign up for e-newsletters
so that you're always first to hear about our new releases.

For Nye

CONTENTS

LIST OF ILLUSTRATIONS

Photographic credits are shown in italics.

1. Swiss physician Johannes Hofer coined the term 'nostalgia' in his 1688 dissertation. *Photo: Dissertatio medica de nostalgia, oder Heimwehe/[Johann Hofer].Wellcome Collection.*
2. Twentieth-century diagram of the four qualities, elements, humours and temperaments. *Photo: The four qualities, elements, humours and temperaments. Drawing, 19--.Wellcome Collection.*
3. The Soldier's Dream of Home by Currier & Ives. *Photo: Michele and Donald D'Amour Museum of Fine Arts, Springfield, Massachusetts Gift of Lenore B. and Sidney A.Alpert, supplemented with Museum Acquisition Funds. Photography by David Stansbury.*
4. Captain Henry W. Howgate, from an 1883 publication. *Photo: Impress/Alamy Stock Photo.*
5. Drawing of an Inuit village near Frobisher Bay. *Photo:* Arctic Researches and Life Among the Esquimaux: Being the Narrative of an Expedition in Search of Sir John Franklin in the Years 1860, 1861, and 1862 *by Charles Francis Hall (1865), New York: Harper and Brothers.*
6. Engraving of a British soldier writing letters home from a foreign battlefield, circa 1880. *Photo: Lakeview Images/Alamy Stock Photo.*
7. Boy 'putter' drawing a coal truck along a 24-inch-high seam in Halifax,Yorkshire, 1848. *Photo:The Print Collector/Alamy Stock Photo.*
8. Entrance to the Berlin Zoo in 1930. *Photo: Pictures Now/Alamy Stock Photo.*

INTRODUCTION

THE GOOD OLD DAYS?

I was a very nostalgic child. Melding fairy tales with *Horrible Histories*, I spent hours imagining myself transported back in time to invented and romanticized versions of the seventeenth, nineteenth and early twentieth centuries. I was an avid reader of Enid Blyton's novels and begged my parents to divert me from my 1990s London primary to a boarding school in 1950s Cornwall. My pleas went unanswered, so I went to my uniform-free state school every single day in pleated skirts and white blouses, desperate to return to a world I'd never even inhabited. Somehow, I still managed to make friends. As an adult, however, I cut these emotional ties to history and developed a new, much more cynical relationship with the past. I did a history degree, then another, and then another. I became hardened to history, a steely academic who rejected sentimentality. In my personal life, I also ceased to be nostalgic. Instead, I enjoyed the present and looked to the future. I like to think of myself as progressive, and I'm certainly an optimist. But, despite these political and temperamental tendencies, here I am writing a book in defence of nostalgia. Or, at least, a book that treats the feeling and phenomenon with respect and attempts to do justice to its complexity, power and remarkable ability to shapeshift.

If you consult a dictionary, nostalgia's definition is relatively straightforward. It is an emotion, 'a wistful or excessively sentimental yearning for return to or of some past period or irrecoverable condition.'[1] Psychologists have a similar understanding of the term, and, while they acknowledge its complexity, they consider it a stable scientific category. It is 'a complex emotion that involves past-oriented cognition and a mixed affective signature'.[2] Or, in lay terms, a bittersweet feeling in response to the past. It's prompted when you think about, reminisce over or dwell on a memory. And, usually, we're not just talking about any memory, but a fond, personally meaningful one. You might view this memory through 'rose-tinted' spectacles, but it also might provoke a feeling of sadness or grief: you miss, long or lament for a lost moment in time. You might even wish to return to it. The joy of reminiscence is jumbled up with a sense of loss, regret or pain.

Nostalgia is, then, about much more than just remembering the past. After all, memory is fallible, unreliable even. Nostalgia is an emotional state – we are nostalgic for moments in time that we invest with meaning. Some periods of history – whether personally or collectively experienced – are made to carry more significance than others. We might deliberately or unconsciously manipulate our own pasts, consolidate memories of very different times and places, and reconstruct that information to align more closely with our current values, ethics or sense of self. Nostalgia is part of that reconstruction. It takes things that happened and suffuses them with feeling, glosses them in gold and bathes them in rose-tinted light.

While there are generic, general definitions of the emotion, nostalgia also takes various forms. There's the nostalgia for things you yourself have experienced. You might feel wistful about your own childhood, teenage years or university days. And there's the nostalgia, like mine, for a time before you were born or can recall – an urge to travel back to a distant period of the past. Depending on who you ask, which experts you consult, nostalgia might be deeply personal – an individual emotional experience. Or it could be a collective one, something prompted by rituals and shared experiences, written about in the press and cultivated or exploited by politicians, for example. This collective version of nostalgia is just as often a genuine feeling as it is an abstract concept. When you read newspaper articles that wax lyrical about a very different past, the author might not be in the throes of nostalgia themselves at the very moment of writing. Maybe they weren't experiencing the feeling at all, but knew the effect that writing about nostalgia might have on their readers.

But, even if we focus, just for a moment, on nostalgia as an emotion experienced by an individual, it – indeed, like all human feelings – is more complicated than it might first seem. Today, most scientists of emotions locate them firmly in the mind. Pioneering work conducted in the nineteenth and twentieth centuries suggested that emotions are related to a group of structures in the centre of the brain, called the limbic system.[3] Emotions, for many neuroscientists and psychologists, are thought to be innate, biologically bound and recognizable across cultures and communities. Much like the Disney/Pixar movie *Inside Out*, we are all governed by the joy, fear, anger, sadness and disgust that inhabit our brains. These 'basic' emotions are distinguishable from an individual's facial expression and in their physiological processes, like when our hairs stand on end or our hearts race.[4]

For the past fifty years, this concept of emotions has been championed by the psychologist Paul Ekman. Certain emotions, according to Ekman, appeared to be universally recognized, regardless of time, place or cultural context. Deviating slightly from Pixar's model, Ekman first proposed six basic emotions: anger, disgust, fear, happiness, sadness and surprise. Later in his career, he suggested that more universal emotions may exist beyond these six. Other psychologists have suggested amusement, awe, contentment, desire, embarrassment, pain, relief, sympathy, boredom, confusion, interest, pride, shame, contempt, relief and triumph. Basic emotion theory is, however, less about the precise number or identity of the universal emotions, and more about whether or not feelings are standard across history, cultures and species; whether or not they're inherited and evolutionary; and whether or not they are physical responses to things that happen to or around us.[5] This brain model of how we feel and communicate – the idea that emotions are hardwired into our neurotransmitters – is now widely shared in medical, scientific and psychological circles. But it isn't uncontested. What emotions are, and what they mean, has changed dramatically over time, and varies according to who is doing the analysis and investigation.

Many historians, for example, are broadly opposed to basic emotion theory, partly because it takes a relatively reductive approach to the subtleties and varieties of feeling.[6] In his recent, expansive history of human emotions, Richard Firth-Godbhere isn't convinced by Ekman's theory: 'his six basic emotions . . . came from a small set of American faces, which he then imposed as a framework over the expressions seen in the rest of the world.'[7] Basic emotion theory, as he points out, distils the grand diversity of human behaviour, styles of expression and feelings to a short, restrictive list.

And it isn't just historians who are sceptical. Science writer Leonard Mlodinow's book on the psychology and neuroscience of emotion, Emotional: The New Thinking About Feeling, discusses the limitations of Ekman's general ideas. Contradicting the older notion that feelings are 'innate hardwired responses to a set of archetypal stimuli', he cites the emotions researcher James A. Russell, who instead claims that 'different languages recognize different emotions. They carve up the domain of emotion differently.'[8] Various studies of anger exemplify this point. In 1970, the anthropologist Jean L. Briggs published her ethnography of an Inuit community. Briggs found that the community – the Utku people – not only rejected what she and her American compatriots called 'anger', but had no equivalent term or concept.[9] More recently, the psychologist Lisa Feldman Barrett has argued that anger is not a single, internal instinct, but rather a 'diverse population of experiences and behaviours'. Both Feldman Barrett and Russell take a theoretical approach to emotions as psychological constructions.[10] In other words, the great variety of language, culture and personal experience shape 'core' feelings into many different forms. 'The varieties of anger,' Feldman Barret writes, 'are endless.'[11] To what degree emotions are biological or cultural is still very much up for debate in psychological circles (and, to an extent, in historical ones too), but, as Mlodinow puts it, science has not yet identified 'truly objective criteria to reliably determine whether a person or an animal is in one emotional state or another'.[12]

But, to step away from these academic debates for a moment,

it's clear that the language we use to describe emotions does tend to be imprecise and individual. Feelings are subjective and we do not know what one person's anger feels like to them and how much it has in common with our own experience of rage. It is also possible to distinguish between expressions of feeling that take widely recognizable forms (a scream of terror, or floods of tears) and a feeling state that is internal and profoundly personal. Our emotional language is also expansive. Rage, anger, fury and ire all describe something, but do they all describe the same thing?[13] The rich vocabulary of emotions hints at the often incommensurate variety of human feeling.

Nostalgia, like anger, has many related terms. It is associated with memory, but also yearning, homesickness, reminiscence, longing and regret. While most English-speakers will have an intuitive sense of what nostalgia means, that sense might not be shared by people encountering the term in other languages and from different cultures. Nostalgia also has some cognate words in other dialects. *Sehnsucht* is a German noun, roughly translated as longing, desire, yearning or craving. It's a feeling about the imperfect and unfinished elements of life, paired with a yearning for an ideal alternative – a kind of strange backward utopianism. C. S. Lewis called it an 'old ache', or the desire for 'our own far-off country'.[14] German also has *Ostalgie*, a nostalgia specifically for aspects of life in communist East Germany (see Chapter Eight: Political Nostalgias for more on *Ostalgie*). It is a portmanteau of the German words *Ost* (east) and *Nostalgie* (nostalgia). Portuguese's *saudade* is similar, an emotional state of melancholic longing for some much-loved thing or person. It is felt especially acutely when the object of desire is either unreal or does not reciprocate the intense feelings. The Welsh word *hiraeth* means a deep longing for something, especially one's home or homeland, and specifically in the context of Wales or Welsh culture. Emotions are intricately intertwined with the language we use, and different words have different meanings, however subtle. It is almost impossible to translate these words precisely. Many of these terms have no exact parallels in any other language, and, as a result, neither do these feelings have identical twins in other cultures.[15]

In the same way, the English word *nostalgia* captures something both geographically precise and culturally specific. This makes writing a biography of nostalgia, one that at least attempts to look beyond the anglophone cultures of Britain and North America, tricky but not impossible. I have had to do more than simply follow the appearance of the word in texts of different languages, but look instead at what the term is taken to mean or imply, and pay close attention to the context and specificity of circumstance. Even between two countries that share a common language, like Britain and the United States, nostalgia can mean quite different things, and is shaped by their respective societies, political dynamics and cultural norms.

The word *nostalgia* also captures something historically specific. Because, if emotions and the language we use to describe them can alter according to place, then they can also shift across time. The past is a foreign country, after all. Nostalgia is perhaps the best example of how malleable emotions and their terminology have been, but other feelings have also shifted. The Regency heroines of Jane Austen novels were frequently 'vexed', but how many of us experience the same sense of vexation today? Some emotions are new. How about FOMO, or 'fear of missing out'? It only entered the dictionary in 2014 and means the feeling of anxiety we experience when we think an exciting or interesting event may be happening elsewhere; it is often aroused by posts seen on social media. One hundred and fifty years ago, 'depression' referred to a mood, not a mental illness. In the early fifth century, monk and theologian John Cassian wrote about an ancient Greek emotion called *acedia*. A mind 'seized' by this emotion is 'horrified at where he is, disgusted with his room . . . It does not allow him to stay still in his cell or to devote any effort to reading.' He feels both an intense 'bodily listlessness' and a 'yawning hunger'. Cassian and other early Christians called *acedia* 'the noonday demon' and it arose from the spatial and social constrictions of a solitary monastic life.[16]

The comings and goings of different emotions and the words we use to describe them presents a problem. What is the biographer supposed to do with descriptions of nostalgia (as we know it) before the word began to be used in the modern sense? Because before the twentieth century, 'nostalgia' did not mean the kind of historical longing we now know. Does that suggest people's internal lives were different too? Back in the eighteenth century, for example, did people feel a longing for the past in quite the same way as they do today? And, if so, did they call it something else? As discussed, historians and some psychologists agree that modern emotion words do not name universal or natural, biologically bound entities. Modern-day 'anger', for example, probably wasn't felt by ancient Greeks and Romans (who spent a lot of time describing exactly what different feelings felt like to them), because they lived in very different worlds. Their overarching 'mental and moral frameworks', as the historian Thomas Dixon puts it, 'differed so fundamentally from ours'.[17] For example, Aristotle described a passion he called *orgē*. While key components of modern-day anger, according to philosopher Martha Nussbaum, are physical or bodily – including elevated heart rate, raised temperature and enraged facial expressions – *orgē* was all about thoughts.[18] Specifically, the belief that someone has been wronged, combined with an intense and overwhelming desire for revenge. Like anger, the history of nostalgia is one of radical variety and change. To paraphrase Dixon, there is no one thing in the world, either past or present, to which the English word nostalgia invariably refers.[19] There is not one, but many nostalgias to investigate.

Emotions have a history, even though the study of that history is only a relatively recent undertaking. But it is incredibly difficult to fully understand the internal workings of people's emotional lives, especially the feelings of those long dead. There are plenty of emotions in the written traces individuals leave behind, but they do not provide us with unmediated access to their feelings. Instead, they offer us insight into how people chose to craft their emotional personas. I am not suggesting, when people sat down to write a furious letter or record their sorrow in their diary, that they were being deliberately artificial or writing with future historians in mind. But, rather, that we are all subject to the emotional codes of conduct implicit in our societies and influenced by cultural standards and

modes of expression. This book is, therefore, an account of nostalgia's social, political, cultural and scientific life, not an exercise in
collective psychobiography.

*

While all emotions have their own histories, there are few feelings
as ubiquitous, and as tricky to pin down, as nostalgia. One of the
reasons for its elusiveness is that nostalgia can't seem to sit still.
Perhaps more so than other feelings, it is always changing and has
undergone a particularly radical transformation. Just a hundred years
ago or so, it was not merely an emotion, but a sickness, something
that afflicted servants in seventeenth-century Switzerland, attracted
the attention of medicine's finest minds in eighteenth-century
England and killed American Civil War soldiers in their thousands.
Today, things are different. Nostalgia no longer affects the body, only
the mind. Nostalgia is no longer a fatal diagnosis. In the twenty
years between the First World War and the end of the Second World
War, it changed from being a sickness acquired by a yearning for a
distant *place*, into a relatively benign longing for a bygone *era*. Now,
for many people, it is little more than a fond feeling for the past
– a mostly harmless condition experienced by antiquarians and
sentimentalists.

What, then, was the nostalgia of yesteryear? How did it differ
from the feeling we know today? When did it change and why, and
what does this shift tell us about the history of the world? After all,
as a bit of London graffiti acknowledged in 1974, 'Nostalgia isn't
what it used to be.'[20] These questions are at the centre of this book.
To answer them, I've taken a broad chronological sweep. And I've
had to write not just a biography of an emotion, but a biography
of a disease, with a bit of science writing, cultural commentary and
political analysis thrown in as well. The narrative ranges widely,
from the wild-flower-covered slopes of the Swiss Alps in the seventeenth century, to the ships that carried enslaved people from West
Africa to the Caribbean, to the ports and barracks of nineteenth-
century Egypt, to interwar sprites and spirits on the Isle of Man,
to Jewish refugees in wartime New York, to Lebanese psychoanalysts

in the Swinging Sixties, to the Nazi revival of 1970s Berlin and to the election campaigns of Donald Trump, America's forty-fifth president.

Nostalgia's story begins in the seventeenth century, when, in 1688, the Swiss physician Johannes Hofer coined the term.[21] Derived from the Greek *nostos*, or homecoming, and *algos*, or pain, Hofer first identified it as a disorder afflicting European mercenary soldiers fighting far from home. Sufferers experienced acute longing, a kind of melancholia, and were desperate to return to a familiar but distant object or place. The Swiss milking song, 'Khüe-Reyen', was a particular trigger and its impact so debilitating on the armed forces that its playing was punishable by death. Young women who left home to work as domestic servants, men in their twenties and children sent to the countryside to be nursed were all susceptible to this acute form of homesickness. It plagued the Alps and spread through Europe – an emotional pandemic with prominent peaks in autumn when the falling leaves prompted melancholics to think of the passage of time and their own mortality.

In nineteenth-century Europe, it was one of the medical profession's most studied conditions. This mysterious disease caused lethargy, depression and disturbed sleep. Sufferers also experienced bodily symptoms – heart palpitations, contusions and dementia. For some, the illness proved fatal – its victims refused to eat and slowly starved to death. In the 1830s, for example, one Paris resident died, suffocated by the despair of having to leave his cherished home. He succumbed to a 'profound sadness' and a 'raging fever', just hours before his house was due to be demolished.[22] Nostalgia, the sickness, was widespread throughout Europe and travelled via the ships carrying enslaved Africans to North America. At this point, it had not yet acquired the positive association with trivial self-indulgence that it has now. Instead, it had the power to kill and disable, and it was treated with gravity.

And yet, nostalgia was not just something experienced by individuals. It was a social and political condition, vulnerable to misuse, one that reflected the anxieties of the age. Nineteenth-century French doctors were intensely and perhaps bizarrely concerned by nostalgia.

They considered the disease a product of the country's peculiar preoccupation with the past. This made sense for a nation undergoing radical change. Like in many other European countries, canals, telegraph cables and railways were wrapping France in a new net of communication. Peasants were now working far from home and travelling to big cities distant from the humble villages of their birth. Wars fought abroad were fostering a new sense of national identity and a commitment to land and territory. It is not surprising that the French felt adrift, disconnected from their past and increasingly wistful about a rapidly disappearing culture and community.[23]

One of the most confounding things about nostalgia is not just its transformation from disease to emotion, but also its slow conversion from something associated with place, to a feeling connected to time. In 1680s Switzerland and in 1830s Paris, nostalgia and homesickness were approximate synonyms. But, towards the end of the nineteenth century, the two parted ways and began to mutate. They shed their medical associations and, as a result, were taken much less seriously. This tells us a great deal about what was going on in this period of global history.[24] The divorce of nostalgia and homesickness, and the degradation of their shared severity, were products of capitalism, colonialism and international warfare.

The decades either side of 1900 were a period of mass migration. Colonial soldiers set off from London, Paris and Brussels seeking wealth and making homes in distant, tropical places. Refugees sought solace from war, genocide and pestilence. And migrants travelled far, searching for new places to set up shop, find friends and make families. But with travel came homesickness. In the late 1930s, Kathe Kupferberg was one of about 20,000 Jewish women who came to Britain from Nazi-occupied territories on a domestic-service visa. In her diary, she described how, on her day off, she would go on long walks down strange streets, feeling desperately alone: 'Suddenly a terrible wave of homesickness constricted my heart and I burst out in tears. I felt ashamed to be crying there out in the open, but I had nobody I could pour my heart out to.'[25] In the nineteenth century, homesickness was a noble condition because it demonstrated a commitment to your family and your deep emotional roots. It was a virtue, a sign of sensitivity. But, as the twentieth century got underway, homesickness became increasingly infantilized and trivialized. An emotion that tied people to the place they were born no longer worked in an increasingly global world – one with porous borders that relied on a mobile workforce.

The early twentieth century also witnessed nostalgia's transformation from a disease into a relatively benign emotion. In the first few years of Queen Victoria's reign, two new words entered common English parlance: 'emotion' and 'scientist'. And, by the end of the nineteenth century, human emotions – including nostalgia – were objects of scientific study. In 1898, an American psychologist, Linus Ward Kline, conducted a study of 176 people.[26] A four-year-old boy moved with his parents to a new neighbourhood. Before they had even unpacked their belongings, their son was struck by an acute bout of nostalgia. 'Let's take the cows and go back home,' he implored. Unlike his medical predecessors, Kline interpreted this less as a sickness and more as a relatively normal emotional response to change. In 1900, the *American Journal of Sociology* made the first known use of 'nostalgia' in its modern sense: 'It is reason and convenience that lure him from the time-hallowed; it is nostalgia that draws him back. A little novelty charms, but a general invasion of the new makes the world look bleak and dreary.'[27] And as the twentieth century progressed, more and more psychologists and psychoanalysts took up the scientific study of nostalgia, taking over from physicians and, in the process, slowly transforming it from a deadly sickness to the much more benign feeling with which we're now so familiar. The 1964 edition of the *Concise Oxford Dictionary of Current English* was the first to define nostalgia as a 'sentimental yearning for some period of the past'.[28]

By the 1970s, nostalgia was everywhere. No longer a threat to body and mind, it became something of a fad. Writers from across Europe and North America worried about what the journalist and businessman Alvin Toffler called a 'wave of nostalgia'.[29] This 'wave' travelled across the Atlantic, flooding France, Britain and Germany with old-fashioned films, 1950s music, and journalists wringing their hands over the state of society. In the seventies and into the eighties, nostalgia continued to plague the West. It dominated the airways, transformed the way people dressed and decorated their homes, and altered people's professional and political lives. And, as companies and cultural producers cottoned on to its commercial power, they began to exploit the emotion's seductive qualities. Just because nostalgia was no longer deadly, it did not mean that it was no longer complicated.

Nostalgia started cropping up in television adverts in the 1970s, when household names like Hovis and Cadbury's ran innovative campaigns designed to remind people of a simpler time and evoke a rapidly vanishing world. This kind of marketing strategy remains popular. From 'Keep Calm and Carry On' posters to retro kitchen scales, nostalgia still has selling power. Etsy stores sell online browsers a rose-tinted vision of the past by way of knick-knacks, vintage clothes and trinkets. Some of the most popular television programmes from the last few years have capitalized on viewers' fond feelings about the 1980s, complete with references to *Ghostbusters*, My Little Pony and The Clash. Advertising executives argue that nostalgia works in this way because it makes people feel good. It is, they believe, a grounding force, something that calms our nerves and makes us part with our money.

Nostalgia has the power to make you buy things, but it can also change the world you choose to live in. For some, nostalgia is more than just a passing feeling. It prompts people to remake their surroundings, to take themselves back in time and live as their predecessors did, complete with Victorian dress, 1940s appliances or 1970s wallpaper. From the couple who went viral for living as though they were in the nineteenth century (see Chapter Seven: Reinventing the World), to the 'mummy bloggers' posing in Regency dress, to the people who re-enact famous battles, the past has a powerful allure – an attractive quality that reshapes personal and social lives, and transforms the landscape and infrastructure of towns and cities worldwide.[30]

In the late twentieth century, nostalgia was taken up again by psychologists and neuroscientists. They studied it in laboratories, conducted surveys of chronic nostalgics and watched when bits of their brains lit up on MRI scans. They used portraits of friends, old postcards and evocative smells to make people feel nostalgic, and then studied the effects of this emotion on their mood and behaviour. Some psychologists have devoted a lifetime to the exploration of this elusive emotion. These scientists claimed (and still do) that they could 'see' nostalgia on brain scans and in questionnaires. It was counted and categorized, and people have made whole careers out of its study. Unlike historians, most psychologists now say that nostalgia is felt by pretty much everyone, regardless of when or where they live, and that it is an overwhelmingly positive experience. It serves a range of emotional functions. It boosts people's mood and increases their sense of meaning and purpose. It raises self-esteem and enhances experimental subjects' optimism for the future. It can improve perceptions of friendship and social support, nurture sentiments of protection and love, lower anxiety and prompt friendly behaviour.

Luckily, some of this scientific work found a useful application. In the world of business, the idea that feelings of nostalgia are pleasurable means that organizations' human-resources departments can also use the emotion to cultivate community. In recent decades, companies have deployed nostalgia to foster commitment and belonging, encourage staff loyalty and boost workplace well-being. Some of this is done cynically by organizations who use cheap emotional tools to soothe employee stress instead of offering better pay, improved working conditions or increased autonomy. If you can make your staff feel nostalgic by reminding them of the good old days, then they're likely to stay longer, put up with lower pay and feel better about their working lives (or so the management consult-ants say . . .). Nostalgia is also a benign by-product of places like hospitals, railway stations and coal mines – places where employees have spent many years, built up a lifetime of experience and watched the working world change around them. Unlike many other work-places, hospitals, railways and coal mines have traditionally been centres of the local community – industries and organizations that employ the majority of a village's or a town's residents. People have historically invested strong, positive feelings in the places where they work. After all, while nostalgia might be bittersweet, it is usually more sweet than bitter.

But, if nostalgia is pleasurable for the individual experiencing the feeling, its reputation as an influence on politics and society is not so honeyed. Despite all its changes, it still carries its own emotional baggage and, even after it lost its capacity to kill, nostalgia continues to be blamed for a range of perceived sins. Some left-wing commentators have criticized recent populist movements for their nostalgic appeals to a mythic bygone age. From Brexit to Donald Trump's attempts to 'Make America Great Again', nostalgia persuades, deludes and charms people into making electoral decisions. Even the EU chief negotiator, Michel Barnier, blamed Brexit on Britain's 'nostalgia for the past'.[31] For many, it is a fundamentally (small-c) conservative emotion, one held by people unwilling to engage with modern life – the proverbial ostriches with their heads in the sand. It is, according to sociologist Yiannis Gabriel, 'the latest opiate of the people'.[32] Populist movements worldwide are repeatedly criticized for their use and abuse of nostalgia. The images these movements paint of the past are often condemned for being overly white and overly male. However, nostalgia is not just a condition of the Right. The Left is also accused of an emotional and nostalgic commitment to things like the Paris Commune, the Soviet Union and the United Kingdom's National Health Service (NHS). Nostalgia is indeed a political engine. It powers people – on both sides of the political spectrum – to vote in certain ways, advocate for certain services and protest certain policies. And, perhaps most intriguingly, the politics of nostalgia seem particularly potent today.

In the twenty-first century, nostalgia has been dogged by associations with populism and intellectual vacuity. But perhaps it needs some rehabilitation. Nostalgia not only offers us a crucial and illuminating case study of how the meanings and experiences of feelings mutate over time, it also acts as an alert system. When we see it in a public and political debate, we should pay attention. What do we find when we really look at nostalgia? What experiences is it being used to long for and lament? What does its deployment and expression tell us about what society and individuals value at any given time? And can we move away from seeing those with a tendency towards nostalgia as sick, sentimental or stupid?

Nostalgia is everywhere, a source of both pain and pleasure, and it explains so much about modern life. This book, therefore, uses one emotion as a lens to consider the past and present of science and medicine; the changing pace of society; our collective feelings of regret, dislocation and belonging; the conditions of modern and contemporary work and industry; and the politics of fear and anxiety. Expressions of nostalgia are one way we communicate a desire for the past, dissatisfaction about the present, and our visions for the future. In this way, this is not only a history of a dangerous emotion, but an analysis of what we are doing now, how we feel about it and what we might want to change about the world in which we live.

CHAPTER ONE

MILKMAIDS AND MERCENARIES

In 1788, a student from Bern – one of the thirteen cantons of the Old Swiss Confederacy – moved to Göttingen in present-day Germany to study medicine.[1] Göttingen's university had been founded in 1734 and had already established some quaint traditions and quirky customs. When students were awarded their doctorates, for example, they were drawn in handcarts from the university to the Gänseliesel fountain that stands, to this day, in front of the old town hall. There, they had to climb the fountain and kiss the statue of the Gänseliesel ('goose girl'). Sadly, the Swiss student studying abroad never quite made it to graduation. Almost as soon as he arrived at university, he took to his bed, convinced that his aorta was about to burst. No one could convince him otherwise, and he remained bed-bound, supine with misery and fear. Finally, his father sent for him to return home. The student leapt from bed and ran all over the city, fizzing with joy and anticipation. He said goodbye to the few friends he had made in his short time in Göttingen and set off. Just days earlier, he had been unable to move – stricken with nostalgia, sick with melancholy. But it did not take much for him to recover, just the mere thought of returning to Bern was enough to reinvigorate the young man.

The Old Swiss Confederacy (or the Republica Helvetiorum) and its constituent thirteen cantons existed from the time of the Thirty Years' War (1618–48) until Napoleon's invasion in 1798. This was an ancien régime, a place where aristocrats and oligarchs ruled with unimpeachable authority, except for the occasional economic or religious revolt. At the Treaty of Westphalia in 1648, the Swiss Confederacy gained legal independence from the Holy Roman Empire. Then, as France grew into a great European power, the Confederacy turned to this affluent neighbour for trade, protection and cultural inspiration. But Switzerland retained its own identity and its own national character. This was a rural landscape and its inhabitants depended on its trees, soil, mountains and rivers for their sustenance and sense of self. Visitors to the Old Confederacy wrote lengthy passages in travel volumes about pleasant valleys covered with vineyards and orchards, and small walled towns nestled beneath mountains that were treacherous to climb. The plains around Geneva and Savoy were planted with walnut trees – great multitudes of them – and tourists described how, on every autumn Sunday, the locals would go out to walk among the trees, harvesting the nuts and celebrating the season of plenty.

The roads to Basel were flanked by vertiginous peaks, and the country's central cantons were crowded with mountains of great scale, some as high as 12,000 feet above the surface of the sea. It was to this extraordinary altitude that the country owed the fineness and subtlety of its air and atmosphere. One visitor recalled that, whenever the Swiss were abroad, however 'bold and hardy' they might be, they felt a kind of anxiety and uneasy longing for the fresh air they had inhaled since birth.[2] This reputation for refined atmospheres propelled doctors to send the sick and infirm from across Europe to recuperate among the wild-flower meadows and pine forests of the Swiss mountains until well into the twentieth century. Even today, the worried wealthy spend their money and time in luxurious spas, bathe in spring water and inhale the sweet Alpine air to cure them of their ailments. The country has long had a reputation for attracting the affluent, and, in the eighteenth century, it was, in general, a wealthy place. Roadside inns offered travellers feasts of trout, carp, beef, veal, fowl, pigeon, butter, cheese, turnips, apples and peaches, together with good wine, and all at a very reasonable price.[3]

Even the peasants who lived in the present-day capital, Bern, were relatively well off. The city's houses were mostly made from white stone, and grand piazzas branched off the main streets. The gables of shops and houses provided walkers with ample protection from wind and rain, and visitors remarked how easy and pleasant it was to stroll along the broad pavements.[4] According to local legend, the city is named for a bear. On the day that Bern was founded, in 1191, the Duke of Zähringen had vowed to name the city after the first animal he encountered while hunting. The beast appears on the city's coat of arms and, since the fifteenth century, bears have been kept in two enclosures filled with tall trees to distract them from their captivity. Bern's historic old town is now a UNESCO World Heritage Site, and it still has its bears, although they have been moved to a more humane enclosure closer to the city's perimeter. From Alpine meadows full of flowers to its well-nourished and occasionally bear-infested cities, early modern Switzerland was, by all accounts, a place you would miss if you spent too much time away from home.

The young student who was so anxious about his health had only just embarked on his medical degree, so he might not have understood much about his own condition. And yet nostalgia as a medical diagnosis was widely known in eighteenth-century Europe. Sufferers experienced intense and debilitating longing, a kind of melancholy, and were desperate to return to their families or place of birth. The condition spread across Europe, eventually setting sail aboard ships to the early colonies in North Africa, South Asia and the Americas. And yet it was specifically Switzerland, the stricken student's much-missed home, that had, a century before, been the birthplace of nostalgia.

The sickness was first identified by the doctor Johannes Hofer. Born in Mühlhausen in present-day Germany on 28 April 1669, Hofer undertook almost the reverse journey of the homesick student who would set off to study in Göttingen over one hundred years later, leaving home to attend university in Basel and graduating in 1688. His final thesis was a dissertation on nostalgia, or homesickness, completed at the end of the summer term, in June.[5] Having identified the disorder among Swiss mercenary soldiers, Hofer was moved by the stories of afflicted youths who (unless rapidly returned to their native land) 'met their last days on foreign shores', and devoted his studies to their mysterious ailment, which he called *La Maladie du Pays*.[6] As he saw it, nostalgia was a kind of pathological patriotic love, an intense and dangerous homesickness (or *Das Heimweh* in Hofer's native German). It was an illness associated with being uprooted, a sickness of displacement, a kind of sadness or depression that arose from the desire to return to one's home. Writers and physicians observed the powerful pull exerted by the family and particularly by one's parents. Sufferers lamented the geographical distance between themselves and their mother's kitchen, and they grieved because they had been 'abandoned by the pleasant breeze of their native land'.[7]

Hofer was concerned that this dangerous, even fatal, disease had not yet received sufficient attention from medical experts. He endeavoured to describe and detail the condition, and to identify its causes, characteristics and possible cures. He defined nostalgia as a disease of the imagination, a mental or emotional disturbance. Victims held a constant vision of their native land in their mind's eye – they were obsessed with sweet but painful memories. Signs of imminent nostalgia included sad and wistful wandering about, scorn for foreign habits and foods, distaste for strange conversations, a natural tendency towards melancholy, and repeated displays of passion for their homeland. Symptoms of the disease ranged from continued sadness, thinking only of the fatherland, disturbed sleep, either 'wakeful or continuous', 'stupidity of the mind' and a low tolerance for cruel jokes or even the slightest injustice, to depleted strength, diminished sight or hearing, fevers and a lack of interest in food or drink.[8] It was these last two symptoms that most often led to the patient's eventual death.

Victims of nostalgia, as Hofer identified, were primarily young people and adolescents sent to alien lands, regions and cities. Constitutionally timid people were particularly vulnerable and were more likely to be overcome by their memories of the 'sweet father-land' and a loathing of foreign climates. These sensitive youths did not know how to get used to strange manners and foods. Students – due to their age and intellectual disposition – were at greater risk. They were so vulnerable that they did not even have to leave Switzerland to succumb to nostalgia. Hofer described the case of another young man from Bern who spent his youth studying in Basel. Throughout his time at university, he suffered from sadness and was afflicted with a continuous burning fever. The family with whom he lodged feared the worst, anticipated his death and uttered public prayers for his eternal salvation. Eventually, he was taken to a doctor who diagnosed him with nostalgia and instructed him to return home immediately. Upon embarking on the return journey, he already seemed improved. With every mile travelled away from Basel and towards Bern, his strength increased and his symptoms abated. Almost as soon as he arrived, the half-dead patient began to draw breath more freely, engage in conversation more easily and show a 'better tranquillity of mind'.[9]

Even trips to the local hospital or neighbouring village could provoke nostalgia in flighty or highly strung young men and women. In his dissertation, Hofer recounted the case of a country girl who, in 1688, was clambering over a rocky outcrop, halfway up an Alpine slope, when she slipped and tumbled down several feet. Seriously injured, she was carried away to hospital, where she lay, unconscious, for many days. Physicians plied her with remedies and performed surgeries, and gradually she healed. Once better, however, she awoke and sat straight up in her hospital bed. Realizing that she was no longer in the mountain village of her birth, homesickness took hold. She spat out her foods and medicines and wailed, '*Ich will Heim; ich will Heim* (I want to go home, I want to go home).' She said nothing else, turned listlessly to the wall and responded to no one. Eventually, her parents came to collect her. Almost immediately, her mood and condition improved and, within a few days back in her own home, she returned to full fitness, entirely without the aid of further medical care.[10]

*

This version of nostalgia – one that posed a serious threat to people's health and survival – is very different from the one we live with today. Nostalgia no longer affects the body, just the mind. We no longer call it a malady of memory or attempt to treat nostalgic patients with brisk walks and bloodletting, and it is no longer a fatal diagnosis. Nostalgia has obviously changed, but so has the world around it. People in the past inhabited a different internal universe. A sharp distinction between mind and body is a relatively recent invention, and in the seventeenth and eighteenth centuries the boundaries between sickness and 'the passions' (as emotions were then known) were blurry and easily crossed. Much more so than today, early modern doctors worked at the intersection between the physical and the psychological.

Throughout the long history of medicine, practitioners have grappled with this question of the relationship between mind and body. Today, we might speak of emotional health or well-being, and doctors acknowledge that feelings might affect our mental health or even provoke mental illness. This relationship between emotions and the physical body is an increasingly prevalent part of today's medicine and culture. Self-help books and academic studies suggest that feelings like stress and anxiety increase mortality rates and even play a role in the onset of heart failure.[11] But, in Hofer's world, emotions were seen as particularly dangerous, posing a potentially acute threat to healthy physical function. Take anger, for example. In early modern medical texts, the emotion is discussed as a key component of health and disease, and it had the capacity to mutate from an infuriating mental state into something bodily. Spanish physician Alvarez de Miraval (who died in 1598) warned patients against the damaging effects of anger on physical health.[12] He stressed that rage could cause heart palpitations, make people spit or cough blood, and produce fevers and epilepsy. In contrast, the English medical writer William Corp recommended anger as a potential *treatment* for disease, particularly if those illnesses were the product of excessive cold or a depressive state of mind.[13]

Medical texts in the seventeenth and eighteenth centuries urged their readers to suppress their pride, rage, envy, malice, grief and fear because an overemotional state could weaken the body and provide the perfect conditions for disease to fester. Any excess of passion or emotion was thought to deplete the body's reserves. One author reminded readers that they should avoid 'wrath, anger and envy,' and that they even needed to, 'use mirth moderately.'[14] It was not just negative feelings that could cause ill effects; anything that could send people over the emotional edge was a potential cause for concern. Some people were predisposed to intense feeling. Those born in April or November were thought to be hot, dry and choleric – prone to pride and boldness, and quick to 'mock, scorn, quarrel, game, drink and wench, and sometimes steal'.[15] Their heightened emotional state put such people in particular danger of falling ill and was thought to lead to fevers and debauchery. The sins of passion could even cause a person to go insane or succumb to an early death.

This interpretation of the emotions relied on a very different understanding of the body. Early modern medicine depended on a reworking of ancient Greek and Roman theories. In this system, all diseases were explained by imbalance – by bodily substances or fluids out of kilter with each another. In antiquity, Hippocrates and his follower Galen combined craft knowledge with ancient science and philosophy to produce a systematic explanation of the behaviour of the human body in times of both sickness and health. Key to this explanation was the role of the four 'humours': black bile, yellow bile, phlegm and blood ('humours' comes from the Latin for fluid or liquid). The various combinations of these humours in different people determined their 'complexions' or 'temperaments', their physical and mental qualities and their dispositions: 'It cannot be denied but our minds are affected by our humours.'[16] The ideal person, in a state of ideal health, had an evenly proportioned mixture of the four, and a predominance of one produced a person who was sanguine (from the Latin for blood), phlegmatic, choleric or melancholic. Each complexion had specific characteristics, and the words carried much weight that they have since lost. For example, a choleric man was not only quick to anger, but also yellow-faced, lean, hairy, proud, ambitious, revengeful and shrewd.

The humours also dictated disease. An excess of one fluid or another could explain someone's symptoms. Cancer, for example, was an excess in black bile congealing in a certain part of the body, amalgamating into a malignant tumour. Each humour had its own characteristic or complexion: hot, cold, wet and dry. Curing an illness involved identifying the imbalance in humour or complexion and rectifying it. A cold injury or illness must be treated with a cold remedy and vice versa. These ideas still circulate today. People might be described as 'hot headed' or they might 'catch a cold' from the temperature of the air or the changing season. When these humours were in balance, health prevailed; when they were out of balance, disease took over. People and their physicians collaborated to keep the humours in check and restore equilibrium by adjusting diet, exercise and the evacuation of bodily fluids.

Most early modern doctors had to undertake a university degree to practise medicine, and would study for a similar length of time to physicians today. However, the degree involved a broad education and only a fraction of the time was spent learning actual medicine. They were also taught ethics, Greek, natural philosophy and law. This broad, gentlemanly education was supposed to turn the phys-ician into a well-rounded and scholarly man – fit for polite society. After all, most of his patients would be drawn from the upper echelons, the only ones who could afford his services. Most of the medical component of his training was book or lecture based, with students reading and hearing about the ancient humoral theories of Galen and Hippocrates. Until the nineteenth century, physicians received very little practical education (whereas surgeons have always learnt mostly by apprenticeship).

Some of the early modern doctors' tenets chime closely with our own. It was just as important to them to prevent illnesses as it was to cure sickness. They tried very hard to keep the body in balance by regulating rest, diet and the environment.[17] But, if prevention failed and disease took hold, then physicians had a broad arsenal of potential remedies at their disposal. They recommended moderation, advised gentle exercise, championed a balanced diet and urged their patients to get enough sleep. Medicine in this period was a protracted, voluble affair, with friends and relatives, doctors, divines and other healers lingering over how patients ate, slept and defecated.

Compared with the hectic schedules of today's doctors, time spent with sufferers was ample. Physicians were, however, realistic about how much use they could be in cases of severe ill health. They saw themselves as acting in partnership with patients and their bodies. Diseases were – according to this way of thinking – often self-limiting and possessed their own internal logic. The doctor's job was just to guide biology in the right direction. The humours would go awry, the body would display troubling symptoms and then order would return. Humans had a remarkable ability to return themselves to health – even without clinical assistance.

It is not all that surprising, then, that the physician's role was primarily to assist the body's own healing power in the resolution of disease. The medical man must – in most cases – allow 'nature' to take its course and leave the body alone to right itself: 'The judicious physician . . . confides in nature.'[18] At most, he should provide only minimal interference. The very best doctors did little more than watch over their patients attentively, calmed their nerves and anxieties, and buoyed their mood if they slumped. They might ply the sick with tonics and pills, but they were only ever intended to assist the body in its natural healing. This was true for mild, short-term ailments, such as the common cold, and for severe, chronic maladies, like gout. Doctors had to work with the body, not against it, and their remedies were often conservative.

These ideas about healthcare, emotions and the body informed Hofer's attitude towards nostalgia and the remedies he recommended. He was very clear about the malady's prognosis: it was potentially fatal, particularly if left untreated. To return order and balance to a stricken nostalgic, he prescribed an unspecific combination of dietary adjustment, warm baths and a change of circumstances. Only very rarely did he recommend more extreme treatments, such as bloodletting and purgatives. In such cases, patients should ingest mercury or arsenic, and leeches could be applied to veins. In line with pre-modern ideas about the importance of supportive, holistic remedies, he also included recreational therapies such as outdoor exercise and pleasant conversation, especially in nostalgia's early stages.[19] If these methods failed and the disease

advanced, then nostalgia could only be resolved by a return to the
victim's homeland. If this was not possible – for example, if the
patient was conscripted to an army or under employment as a
domestic servant – then the outlook was grim. In such cases, the
malady was incurable, if not deadly. Sometimes, the patient might
be so far gone that they refused the trip home. These circumstances
were particularly dire. But often patients could be much improved
by little more than hope. If doctors and friends could promise to
take the patient home, they might rally enough for the journey to
be undertaken safely. In these instances, the patient should be taken
away, however weak and feeble, without delay, 'by a travelling
carriage with four wheels, by a sedan chair, or by any other means'.[20]
The journey alone could prove restorative.

*

Hofer might well have been the first to name and diagnose nostalgia,
but he was certainly not the last. The disease spread through Europe,
preoccupying the minds of medical men and incapacitating the
continent's youth. As it travelled, it acquired new meanings, identities, treatments and emotional baggage. It became more closely
tied to ideas about national character and was mixed up in the new
tendency for early modern Europeans to take trips and move abroad.
We might think that the populations of the sixteenth, seventeenth
and eighteenth centuries tended to be stationary and remain in their
respective cities, towns, villages or hamlets for much, if not all, of
their lives. Travel, unaided by the steam or electricity of later centuries, was slow, arduous, hazardous and expensive. For the poor,
their universe mostly remained small. But, for anyone with sufficient
disposable income, the early modern world opened up, criss-crossed
by the paths of previous travellers who journeyed for fame, fortune
and curiosity.

The pursuits of people like the English adventurer and diplomat
Sir Robert Shirley and his Circassian wife Teresia, who travelled
from the court of King James I in England to that of the Persian
Shah in the early 1600s, were unusual, but not unheard of.
Idiosyncratic travellers such as Thomas Coryate populated the early

modern world. In the seventeenth century, he walked almost 2,000 miles across Europe, visiting forty-five cities and ending his journey in the Mughal court in India.[21] People like Shirley and Coryate were exceptionally well travelled, but, while they were adventuring, other humans, animals and goods were also journeying increasingly far and increasingly frequently. Merchants carried spices and silks across deserts; aristocrats travelled leisurely from archaeological sites to great cities; and kings and queens colonized distant lands.

In 1710, Hofer's dissertation was reprinted by a little-known Swiss doctor called Thomas Zwinger as part of a new medical compendium. While much the same as the original text, Zwinger added a story about a sweet Swiss melody which produced pathological homesickness in anyone who heard it. He even added the musical notes, so that readers could play this disease-inducing tune for themselves. 'Kühe-Reyen', a milking song played on the horn of an Alpine herdsman as he drove his animals, was thought to be such a trigger, and its impact so debilitating on the armed forces, that its playing among mercenaries was punishable by death: 'Instances are not wanting, that on the recruits for the Swiss regiments piping or singing the cow-brawl, a common tune among the Alpine boors, the old soldiers have been seized with such a passionate longing after their country . . . so that to prevent desertion, the singing or piping of this tune has been suppressed. In the Piedmontese service, every offence of this nature is punished with the *gantlope*.'[22]

The 'gantlope' later became known in English as the 'gauntlet'. Running the gantlope or gauntlet was a military punishment in which the culprit had to run, stripped to the waist, between two rows of men who struck at him with a stick or a knotted cord.[23] Jean-Jacques Rousseau included the 'Kühe-Reyen' in his *Dictionary of Music* (c. 1778), commenting on the tune's ability to make the listener 'burst into tears, desert, or die'.[24] This was not just a piece of music, but a dangerous aide-mémoire.

Nostalgia seemed peculiarly Swiss – it was first identified by Swiss doctors, and foreigners remarked on the disease's unusual prevalence in the mountainous country. One German doctor even blamed the famed Alpine air. He suggested that the Swiss were so acclimatized to their home atmosphere that it made them unable to breathe properly in other places. In a brief essay, published in 1705 and again in 1719, yet another Swiss physician, Johann Jakob Scheuchzer, took issue with these accusations, angered by any implication that Swiss lungs were in some way inferior. Instead, the patriotic Scheuchzer insisted that there was nothing inherent in the bodies of Swiss people that made them prone to nostalgia, but instead it was the result of sudden changes in altitude. He argued that, if anything, the problem was that Swiss air was *too* refined. When people accustomed to the superior mountain climate descended to the lowlands, the subsequent increase in atmospheric pressure forced an excess of blood into their brains and hearts, slowing down the circulation of bodily fluids.[25] In sensitive young people, these changes could bring about a serious case of nostalgia. Just as the passions could invoke physical illness, so bodily changes could prompt chronic or fatal emotional disturbances.

Another doctor from Bern, Albrecht von Haller, also thought that nostalgia was an unfortunate side effect of rapid changes in altitude. He recommended an unusual, if logical, cure. He suggested that sufferers from the sickness should be put in tall towers so that they might be elevated to almost Alpine heights. Haller also developed another explanation for nostalgia's strangely Swiss character – and, in doing so, delivered it to the world of literature and myth. Written on his return to Switzerland after medical studies in the Netherlands, his poem 'Die Alpen' ('The Alps') portrays the Old Swiss Confederacy as a new Utopia – an earthly paradise comprised of honest, simple and virtuous peasants shielded from the pressures of the increasingly chaotic and modern age by glorious, protective mountains.[26] He also identified a couple of things about nostalgia that have proved remarkably enduring. Much as we do today, Haller saw nostalgia as patriotism gone wrong. It was prompted by an intense love of your home nation and the pain caused by leaving your old way of life behind. There was clearly something about eighteenth-century Switzerland that made its inhabitants slightly sentimental. It was also a troubled response to a rapidly transforming world and a too-quick change of pace. When they left the cosseted enclaves of the Alpine slopes and encountered the increasingly busy world of eighteenth-century Europe, the Swiss wanted to retreat, alarmed by the hectic modernity they found abroad.

While nostalgia was first thought to affect only the Swiss, before long the diagnosis was also applied to Scottish and French soldiers serving overseas and to English students enrolled in foreign universities. Because nostalgia was increasingly associated with altitude, all highlanders, irrespective of their nationality, were potential victims. But nostalgia was not confined to those who lived in mountainous regions.

Nostalgia first appeared as a term and diagnosis in the English language in 1729. In his essay on medicine in the Bible, the English historian and doctor Jonathan Harle identified it as a pathological 'desire of being at home' which was frequently encountered by Swiss physicians. According to Harle, a range of different personal circumstances could get you out of conscription to the Swiss army and prevent outbreaks of nostalgia. Anyone who had recently 'marry'd wives', 'built a new house' or 'planted vineyards' was exempt, so that their 'minds not droop when they went out to battle, and hanker after what they left delightful at home'.[27]

Prolific German travel writer Johann Georg Keyssler journeyed through Bohemia, Hungary, Switzerland, Italy and France in the 1750s. In the hefty, four-volume tome he published in English on his return, Keyssler also described nostalgia as a kind of homesickness, something that especially afflicted people from Bern (but could be experienced by others elsewhere).[28] The British physician Thomas Arnold similarly described nostalgia in the 1780s as an 'vehement' desire to return to one's parents and to one's native land.[29] Unlike the Swiss doctors who identified the pleasures of their country's landscape as one of the causes of homesickness, Arnold criticized nostalgics as the 'offspring of an unpolished state of society' and argued that it mostly affected the inhabitants of 'dreary and inhospitable climates'.[30] The English have long made a habit of denigrating their European neighbours.

Also in the 1780s, Johann Georg Zimmermann's medical textbook

was translated into English from German. He called nostalgia an
'uneasiness' brought about by an extreme desire to revisit one's
native country. It presented itself with melancholy and trembling
limbs, and often proved fatal after only a short period of time. While
he admitted that the Swiss were particularly vulnerable, it was not
unique to Alpine dwellers. He described its appearance among
Burgundian soldiers who were forced into service, and in young
Austrians enlisted by force who 'despaired of ever seeing their home
and friends again'. These young soldiers were silent, languid, pensive,
emitted deep sighs, seemed exceedingly sorrowful and gradually
lost interest in the outside world. But by the end of the eighteenth
century, Austrian generals had begun to limit the number of years
served by those enlisting. After their term of service finished, they
were discharged to their homes. Nostalgia, which had been all too
frequently diagnosed in Austrian troops, became extremely rare.

As Zimmermann insisted, nostalgia occurred in 'men of every
nation', who, when in foreign countries, missed all the pleasures,
delights and ease of being among their friends at home.[31] John
Trusler, an Anglican priest and doctor, wrote an epic series of books
describing, in great and often tedious detail, the entire habitable
world. Published in 1788, it covered different countries' climates,
agriculture, animals both wild and domestic, customs, trade, reli-
gions and forms of government. In his account of the inhabitants of
Lapland, he described their 'dark-grey eyes', 'thin beards' and 'brown
hair'. Alongside a list of abrasive racial stereotypes, Trusler also said
that the people of Lapland were deeply proud of themselves and
their country. As a result, 'when removed from the place of their
nativity', they often died from nostalgia, or what he also called a
'longing to return'.[32]

In 1781, an Ipswich doctor called Robert Hamilton was working
in a barracks in the north of England. A soldier who had recently
joined the regiment was sent to see Hamilton by his captain. He had
only been a soldier for a few months, was young, handsome and
'well-made for the service'. But 'a melancholy hung over his coun-
tenance, and *wanness* preyed on his cheeks.' He complained of what
he called a universal weakness, a noise in his ears and a giddiness of

his head. He slept poorly and was off his food and drink. He sighed deeply and frequently, and something, it seemed, weighed heavy on his mind. Strangely, he did not seem to have many physical symptoms. Hamilton encouraged exercise, which the soldier did only occasionally and reluctantly, and recommended wine as a remedy. All proved ineffectual and he was admitted to hospital. He remained bed-bound for nearly three months, becoming gradually more emaciated. He was struck down with a fever and spent the nights bathed in sweat. Hamilton expected the worst and put him down as a lost cause.

One morning, the doctor happened to speak to the nurse. She mentioned that the soldier spoke, obsessively, of home and his friends. She had not thought to mentioned it before because it seemed to her to be just the 'common ravings of sickness and delirium', but the young man had kept up a running commentary on his desire to return home ever since his arrival at the hospital. When Hamilton went up to see the stricken man, he asked him about his native Wales. The soldier responded with real enthusiasm, became obsessive and would not stop talking about the glories of the Welsh valleys. He asked Hamilton, 'with earnestness', if he would let him go home. The doctor cautioned that he was still very weak – too unwell to undertake the journey back to Wales immediately – but he promised that, as soon as the soldier's physical condition had improved, he could return for a six-week break. The patient revived at the very thought. Despite making a promise that he was actually unable to fulfil (he did not have the authority required to grant recruits leave to return home), Hamilton managed to persuade the commanding officer – and the young soldier, now much recovered, set off to Wales with a spring in his step.[33]

As a pre-modern doctor, Hamilton knew that emotions played a huge part in a person's health and understood that medical men had to attend to their patients' feelings, not just their bodies. The physician's role was to soothe tempers, raise spirits and encourage what we would now call a positive mental attitude. In a world where the line between mind and body was faint or non-existent, the friendship and affection of your doctor could be life-saving, not just calming. Even Hippocrates had advised physicians to distract patients with jokes, play-acting and 'hilarious' skits. To ease their subjects' suffering, doctors should fine-tune their conversation skills and offer their patients affection, friendship and emotional support. They must be amiable, always on hand to deal with concerns, and understand the importance of a strong and compassionate bond between doctor and patient.[34] For the nostalgic Welshman, relief came from the nurse's conversation and Hamilton's compassionate ear.

*

It is tempting to diagnose all those poor people who died from nostalgia in early modern Europe with modern medical conditions. Did they succumb to a physical disease unknown to their doctors? Were the soldiers victims of scurvy, malnutrition or malaria? Or, perhaps more likely, did they die from depression? Did they suffer nervous breakdowns or experience bouts of psychosis? Or were they experiencing a kind of pre-modern eating disorder? So many nostalgics starved to death, perhaps they were anorexics instead? The answers to these questions are unknowable. We have no bodies to examine, and, even if we did, depression leaves no sign in bones or mummified flesh. The medical record for the seventeenth and eighteenth centuries is scant and efforts to identify what really happened to nostalgia's unfortunate victims won't prove that rewarding.

This is true for many past medical conditions. History is littered with forgotten diseases – maladies that no longer seem to threaten us. Some, like smallpox, have been eradicated or effectively managed by modern medicine; others have transformed, changed shape and reinvented themselves across the centuries. Melancholia, dropsy, consumption, onanism, neurasthenia and hysteria were all once diseases that threatened bodies and minds. They all have something in common with illnesses we still experience (even if we don't always still consider them diseases). Melancholia is much like modern-day depression, dropsy shares symptoms with heart disease, consumption is more or less equivalent to tuberculosis, and onanism means masturbation. Neurasthenia and hysteria are a bit trickier to pin down, but they roughly correlate with the dangerous psychology that supposedly accompanies being female or even just effeminate. But these definitions do not tell the whole story, because early modern people understood the world differently from how we do today. The diseases they experienced were specific to the social and cultural lives they lived, and they had alternative ideas about what their bodies could do and why they worked the way they did.

If today's writers re-categorize early modern nostalgia as depression, anorexia or psychosis, then we lose something in the process. We flatten the texture, richness and subtlety of our ancestors' illnesses and experiences if we try to shoehorn their world into ours. It also makes it almost impossible to track how things like nostalgia have changed since the eighteenth century. Back then, nostalgia was a disease. It was the preserve of doctors, even if doctors were different. In the nineteenth century, medicine began to change. It became increasingly familiar to us, and increasingly scientific. Physicians untangled body and mind, and identified new psychiatric disorders with recognizable (if now out-dated) names like 'manic depression'. Against this backdrop, nostalgia's medical identity hardened. It was investigated, analysed and treated with greater intensity, and in nineteenth-century France it rapidly became one of the nation's most studied clinical conditions.

It also became even more deadly. It continued to disturb the passions and created a roster of psychiatric symptoms, such as depression and disturbed sleep. But this mysterious disease also caused bodily symptoms, like heart palpitations and unexplained ruptures in the skin. Some doctors even went in search of a 'nostalgia bone', hidden somewhere in the body. It was particularly common in the United States, France and its North African colonies. During the American Civil War, more than 5,000 soldiers were stricken with nostalgia.[35] The pace of change that had troubled all those Swiss students in the eighteenth century only accelerated. Science, technology and industry transformed the way people worked and lived, wresting people from the comfort of their homes and hurtling them into an anxious new world. As the nineteenth century drew to a close, nostalgia's grip on the medical imagination slowly waned. But it took until the early twentieth century for the malady to claim its final victim. Indeed, the last person to be diagnosed with and die from nostalgia was an American soldier fighting on the Western Front in 1918.[36]

CHAPTER TWO

DYING FROM NOSTALGIA

In April 1877, Henry Williamson Howgate hatched a plan to colonize the North Pole. White men who set out to conquer new territory were not uncommon in the nineteenth century, but Howgate was particularly single-minded. Against the substantial odds of ice and isolation, he intended to establish a permanent American community in the Arctic. This 'thoroughly equipped, self-supporting, and self-reliant colony' would push, 'ever northward, the limits of discovery'. Undeniably ambitious and a veritable adventurer, Howgate was also a somewhat dubious character. Born the son of a British shopkeeper in 1835, he emigrated to America on his own at just twenty-one. He first worked as a journalist, before joining the US Signal Corps. In the 1860s, having had enough of the military and its constraints, he signed up to the international ice race, competing with representatives from rival countries who all sought to expand their existing landholdings into the frozen north. These attempts to be the first nation to reach the North Pole soon degenerated into an international sporting event, largely dominated by Americans (although an Italian expedition set a new record in 1900 for the furthest north travelled). Three expeditions in the early twentieth century claimed to have reached the pole (in 1908, 1909 and 1926), but the first undisputed success story was that of the Norwegian expedition leader Roald Amundsen, who overflew the area in an airship in

1926, with sixteen men on board. The first confirmed overland expedition wouldn't take place until 1968.

The late nineteenth century was the height of rapacious Western imperialism, when Europe's great powers redrew the global map according to ancient, arbitrary rules of sovereignty. Just two decades before Howgate set his sights on the North Pole, India had become a formal part of the British Empire, with European states like Germany and Belgium eagerly carving up the African continent. The first person to set foot and plant their flag controlled the resources, for as long as they could defend them. Howgate's personal target was the Arctic. Fascinated with the frozen north, he had built up a massive collection of literature on the region's inhabitants, natural history, climate and geology. He also embezzled over $133,000 from the US government, escaped custody while on trial and evaded the secret service and the Pinkerton Detective Agency for thirteen years, all the while working as a reporter and running a New York City bookstore.[1]

The 'Polar Colonization Plan', as Howgate called it, consisted of a party of at least fifty men, who were to be provided with provisions and other necessary supplies for three years. At the end of that period, they would be restocked and 'revictualled', and again left to their work. Howgate took inspiration from the towns in northern Asia that already lined the Arctic circle. The flourishing Russian city of Archangel was not far outside the frosty perimeter, while, in the eastern Siberian town of Yakutsk, the ground was frozen solid all year round and only thawed a few inches during the hottest of summers. Despite the inclement weather, this was a town occupied by a population of 'four thousand hardy, prosperous, and contented human beings'.[2] If the Russians could manage it, Howgate reasoned, surely the Americans could too. Of course, Howgate frequently skated over the fact that Indigenous people had been living and thriving in the Arctic for millennia.

Howgate was apprehensive about the physical demands that would be made of the intrepid fifty. But he was also cautiously optimistic. Six years earlier, the self-taught Arctic explorer Charles Francis Hall had set out on a similar American-funded expedition to reach the

North Pole, and, while Hall had died aboard ship under highly suspicious circumstances (probably poisoned with arsenic), Howgate insisted that he had evidently been well suited to the climate and possessed all the necessary survival skills. Howgate attributed Hall's acclimatization to the chilly temperatures to the eight years he had spent living with Inuit communities. Each year, Hall had found himself 'better fitted to withstand the severity of the Arctic circle', and Howgate believed that his colonizing party would become similarly adapted to the environment over time.[3]

But physical peril wasn't the only risk. Howgate was just as, if not more, concerned by the threat of emotional turmoil.[4] In florid, nineteenth-century prose, he described the dangers of nostalgia:

That dreaded foe of isolated men, found in the members of former exploring parties an easy prey through the long, sunless, Arctic night, and drove some to mutiny and others to suicide, while when the hour of deadly peril came – the supreme moment of despair – the stoutest heart was appalled by the knowledge that succour, if sent at all, must be guided by the merest chance, and that the rude cairn which covered his last resting-place or his frozen effigy upon some drifting ice floe might never meet the gaze of human eye.[5]

He need not have worried, for the things that actually disrupted his polar colony plan were far more mundane. Heavy gales, unseaworthy ships and financial difficulties prevented Howgate from ever launching a successful Arctic expedition. Not that that stopped him pocketing hundreds of thousands of dollars of cash invested by others in the adventure. He was indicted for embezzlement in 1882, but slipped away from authorities while on a court-supervised visit to his home. His daughter distracted the attending marshal by singing, while Howgate busied himself upstairs. Claiming he needed to change his underwear, he instead climbed out of a window, fled across the Potomac River and evaded the courts until 1894, when he was finally captured and sent to Albany Penitentiary in upstate New York.[6]

Despite his extraordinary life, in some ways Howgate was not all that unusual. He was, after all, not the only man preoccupied with the promise of the polar north in the 1800s. Throughout the nineteenth century, Arctic exploration dominated popular culture in Europe and North America, much as space exploration did in the twentieth. As the writer Kathryn Schulz put it, it is almost impossible to overstate just how 'deeply everyday citizens of the Victorian era were absorbed in Arctic arcana.'[7] This distant place became central to nineteenth-century life.[8] People hosted polar-themed dinner parties, sang frosty songs and attended vast convention halls to watch staged recreations of polar expeditions. Both the ice race and the space race involved competitive attempts to achieve major geographic prizes; both led to fame and honours for the returning explorers; and both had their fair share of death, disease and disaster.[9] But, more relevant to our story, Howgate was also not the only nineteenth-century traveller preoccupied with the threat of nostalgia.[10]

*

Against stiff competition (this was the era of cholera and tuberculosis, after all), nostalgia was one of the most studied medical conditions of the nineteenth century. As we have seen, nostalgia first entered the medical lexicon in the 1680s, and had been used as a diagnostic category throughout the ensuing century. But it was during the early decades of the 1800s that it first attracted considerable professional attention, discussion and intervention, and there was a dramatic increase in medical writings on the disease, its causes, consequences and potential cures.

In the early nineteenth century, French doctor Jean-Baptiste-Felix Descuret documented a series of troubling case studies.[11] For Descuret, nostalgia was a contagious, severe and potentially fatal disease that indicated something rotten at the core of the French spirit and psyche. According to Descuret, nostalgia affected the very young, the very old and everyone in between. The practice of sending babies away from their parents to rural wet nurses was common among middle- and upper-class French families, and at least 40 per cent of babies born in Paris in the mid 1800s were placed with women living in the city's surrounding countryside. In 1841, Descuret described the case of baby Eugene, sent to a wet nurse in the Amiens area and brought back to his family in the capital when he was two years old. He was a healthy little boy, who had evidently been well cared for. His nurse accompanied him home, to help ease the transition, and she stayed for around two weeks. As soon as she left, however, his health took a turn for the worse. He became pale, sad and morose. He was unresponsive to the caresses of his parents and refused his food. Struck by the sudden change, Eugene's mother and father summoned their doctor, Hippolyte Petit, who immediately diagnosed the baby with nostalgia.

Petit recommended the normal course of treatment: frequent walks and frivolous, distracting play. But the unhappy child remained despondent. He became weaker and weaker, prostrate with misery, his eyes turned towards the door through which he had seen departing the only mother he had ever known. The physician declared that the only way to save the child was to have his nurse return immediately and take Eugene back to the countryside. When she arrived, the little boy erupted with cries of joy, and from that moment he began to revive. He stayed away for about a year, thriving. During his second return to Paris, the doctor progressively separated the nurse from the child – first for a few hours, then for a whole day, then for a week – until he had acclimatized to being without her. Eugene was cured of his nostalgia, but it had been touch-and-go for a while.[12]

Cases like this suggested to some parents and physicians that perhaps wet-nursing wasn't such a good idea, after all. While the practice had been common for centuries, it was not uncontroversial. Since the Enlightenment, European women had increasingly been urged to breastfeed their own children.[13] It was supposed to confer benefits to the mother, protecting her from extreme physical dangers, like breast cancer. And it was also supposed to defend the child from moral or mental distresses, such as nostalgia.

Not many babies today are diagnosed with depression, but Eugene's symptoms had a lot in common with what nineteenth-century physicians called melancholy. He was morose, lethargic and off his food. While doctors spent plenty of time debating whether nostalgia and melancholy were quite the same thing, nostalgia was generally identified as distinct because it tended to be about something, someone or somewhere specific. Whereas melancholy was a general mood – misery in response to both everything and nothing – nostalgia was about a particular place, object or person left behind.[14] Nostalgia was also supposed to come on much more quickly, and patients could fade remarkably rapidly. Ignored, nostalgia would almost invariably prove fatal, whereas people could live long melancholic lives.

There were various theories about the causes of nostalgia and even some possible cures, and, by the time Eugene fell ill, a consensus had emerged about the disease's basic characteristics. The major symptom was, of course, an excessive attachment to some past place – usually, but not necessarily, one's native soil or home town. The disease did not discriminate according to age or gender. Indeed, doctors identified a vast litany of vague and contradictory aspects of a person's life and identity that could predispose them to nostalgia. Everything including too lenient an education, too strict a regime or no education at all might make a person more vulnerable. Unfamiliar food, masturbation, sadness, excessive study of philosophy, and womanizing were also all potential risk factors, particularly for young men.

Regardless of the cause, nostalgia made the patient sad and taciturn; they refused food, retired to weep alone and indulged in 'long reveries of home.' After this first stage, the patient would then suffer from headaches and sleeplessness, delirium, prostration and diarrhoea, eventually terminating in death.[15] This was very much a physical condition, one that left tangible marks on the body that were akin to those caused by 'accidents, fatigue, chill, partial starvation, and loss of bloods'. And it was not just humans who died from nostalgia, but animals too. And especially when living in captivity. Birds, dogs and even moles were examined by physicians after death and were found to have organs that had 'undergone the same kind of degeneration' as that caused by poison or the 'germs of infectious disease'.[16]

But perhaps the greatest danger to the potential nostalgic was travel. Eugene was, of course, far too young for any of the predisposing factors to have taken hold, but he had been wrested from home – or at least been forced to leave his wet nurse and abandon the only place he could remember as home. Trips taken by the traveller's own volition did not concern nineteenth-century physicians. For the pleasure seeker, fame hunter or money maker, nostalgia did not tend to be a problem. Instead, it occurred most often in the minds and bodies of displaced people who shared what historian Thomas Dodman calls a 'sense of isolation and estrangement in a foreign place'.[17] Nostalgics were often the forced, coerced and manipulated – the people who had been moved by the will of others, not by their own design. Indeed, at the time, physicians like Descuret were concerned that nostalgia was becoming more prevalent, and deadlier, precisely because travel and emigration were becoming a less negotiable part of both day-to-day life and the ambitions of nations and empires. People were travelling further for work, and imperial armies were becoming larger, more systematized, and were covering much greater distances in their efforts to bring far-flung populations under control.

Europeans first established trade contacts across the Atlantic in the fifteenth century, and the first enslaved Africans were taken to the South American colonies of the Portuguese and Spanish empires in 1525. Towards the end of the sixteenth century, the Portuguese began a regular trade in enslaved people to Brazil. The English, French and Dutch enslavers soon also brought captured West Africans to the Caribbean islands of Curaçao, Jamaica and Martinique, as they developed slave-dependent economies in the Americas. By the 1690s, the English were shipping more enslaved people from West Africa than any of their European neighbours. The transatlantic trade in enslaved people resulted in vast and unimaginable loss of African life. From the sixteenth to the nineteenth century, about twelve million people were forced to cross the Atlantic. Around one and a half million died on the journey alone – killed by the brutality of the traders and the appalling conditions on the slave ships. Unsurprisingly, these were often referred to as 'floating coffins', and the 'middle passage' as 'a voyage of death'.[18]

Of the many millions of enslaved people shipped across the Atlantic, a significant number died from nostalgia. In 1819, an illegal French slave ship sailed from the Bight of Biafra to Guadeloupe. A British newspaper reported that, on board the boat, the enslaved Africans took their own lives en masse. 'Locked in each other's arms,' they leapt overboard into the ocean. The ship's doctor claimed that they hoped, once their spirits had been released from their bodies, they could return home.[19] They had been driven to death by what the British abolitionist politician William Wilberforce called 'nostalgia'. A term, as he put it to Parliament, which meant, 'a passionate desire to revisit their native land.'[20]

To twenty-first-century readers, diagnosing people forced into bondage with nostalgia seems jarring, even flippant. But, in this world, nostalgia was a far more flexible and capacious thing than it is today. It had not yet acquired the association with kitsch self-indulgence that it has now, and homesickness was not yet something that just affected children. Instead, it still had the power to kill and disable. As a result, European abolitionists were acknowledging the collective tragedy of slavery. The instances of nostalgia they recorded, and even those diagnoses of the disease given by white doctors aboard these 'floating coffins', attest to enslaved people's grief, acts of resistance, righteous rage, and their desire for freedom and self-determination.

Nostalgia was first linked to enslaved people by the British naval physician Thomas Trotter in 1792. Sufferers became fatigued and their spirits flagged. They avoided work, brooded over their own feelings in solitude and indulged 'the most gloomy ideas'. Trotter initially became interested in the disease when working as a surgeon on the Liverpool slave ship *Brookes,* which left Britain for the Gold Coast and Antigua in 1783. As Trotter observed, 'It would be unjust to suppose that the African feels no parting pang when he takes the last farewell of his country, his liberty, his friends, and all that is to be valued in existence!'[21] These men and women, according to Trotter, spent their nights 'making very hideous kinds of moaning, something expressive of extreme affliction'. Upon enquiry, Trotter found that they were 'dreaming of being at home among their friends and relations'. When they awoke, they were gripped by 'mortifying disappointment' and 'utmost regret', and spent the rest of the day possessed with grief, groaning and weeping.[22]

Diagnoses and descriptions of nostalgia among enslaved people spread far and wide. In 1803, a British doctor who had been stationed in Sierra Leone wrote, 'Nostalgia . . . affects the natives of Africa as strongly as it does those of Switzerland; it is even more violent in its effects on the Africans, and often impels them to dreadful acts of suicide.'[23] In enslaved people, nostalgia induced hallucinations of home that were so all-consuming that victims took their own lives. Spanish physician Francisco Barrera y Domingo, who was living in Cuba at the end of the eighteenth century, defined 'nostalgia of the Negroes' as 'a melancholic sadness that attacks them suddenly without delirium, furor, or fever born out of a strong aversion to anything that could distract them from their fantasies, unless it is the return to their beloved *patria* (or fatherland).'[24] Barrera published lengthy medical texts devoted to the diseases experienced by enslaved Africans in the Caribbean. He was particularly concerned with nostalgia and saw it as the primary cause of the high suicide rate among enslaved people in Cuba. Africans newly arrived on the island often withdrew into themselves, overcome with inconsolable sorrow, refused all food and drink, showed almost no interest in living and soon died.[25] This was the so-called *banzo*, or slow suicide – a kind of terminal, melancholic nostalgia.[26]

While the transatlantic trade was the most deadly of the existing routes, and involved the forced movement of the largest numbers of people, captured West Africans were also taken to other parts of the European empires. When enslaved people were brought to Egypt from what was then called the Gold Coast, their passionate desire to return home produced a 'languishing malady, of which they die in frightful numbers.' Observers compared nostalgia in Egypt to the bubonic plague, which also swept away enslaved people in 'immense multitudes'. The two epidemics meant that the forced labourers in Egypt had to be continually replaced, as they seldom lived for long.[27]

For a few European observers, the prevalence of nostalgia among enslaved people suggested that slavery and other forms of coerced labour were morally wrong, and that the Black Africans captured, transported and tortured were capable of the same kind of emotional inner lives as Europeans were – irrespective of race. The tragic image of suicidal, nostalgic slaves and sailors appeared in a range of humanitarian and abolitionist poems, like Henry Wadsworth Longfellow's 'The Slave's Dream' (1842), James Montgomery's 'The Voyage of the Blind' (1810) and William Wordsworth's 'The Brothers' (1800):

> He was in slavery among the Moors
> Upon the Barbary coast—'Twas not a little
> That would bring down his spirit; and no doubt,
> Before it ended in his death, the Youth
> Was sadly crossed—Poor Leonard! when we parted,
> He took me by the hand and said to me,
> If e'er he should grow rich, he would return,
> To live in peace upon his father's land,
> And lay his bones among us.[28]

As strange a strategy as it might seem to us, these abolitionists were using nostalgia as evidence that enslaved people were people – men and women who could love, feel loyalty and experience other complex human emotions.

However, for every abolitionist who believed in the humanity of the enslaved, there were many more European doctors, natural philosophers and politicians asserting that Black men and women were incapable of higher thoughts or profound feelings. This diminishing of Black humanity was used to justify the transatlantic trade in enslaved people and absolve enslavers of their sins. In 1774, Edward Long (1734–1813) published a book titled *The History of Jamaica*. Reflecting a widely held view that lasted well into the nineteenth century, he asserted that 'the Negro' was 'void of genius' and 'incapable' of civilization; indeed, he was so inferior as to constitute a separate species of humankind.[29] This view was shared by many of the eighteenth- and nineteenth-century physicians who wrote about nostalgia. This was not only patently untrue, but it reveals one of the more disturbing truths about the history of medicine. Medical men of the past were as often agents of misery and coercion as they were people invested in the improvement of society's lot and the lessening of human suffering.

But, while enslavers clearly cared little about the feelings or well-being of their property, the health, strength and survival of enslaved people was an economic problem for the traders and plantation owners alike. This is why doctors were brought aboard slave ships or sent to colonies in the Americas to diagnose, treat and prevent sickness among the Africans. Medical care for enslaved people became something of a cottage industry and various physicians wrote lengthy textbooks on the subject. Unlike the abolitionists, however, these doctors and the people employing them were not preoccupied with the evils of the middle passage or with ending slavery. They were simply committed to producing a more efficient and effective workforce. Nostalgia was bad for colonial business.

*

The transatlantic trade in enslaved people peaked in the 1780s, when some 80,000 Africans were brought to the Americas each year. From then on, it gradually declined. In 1791, enslaved people revolted against French colonial rule in Saint-Domingue, now Haiti. The Haitian Revolution ended in 1804 with the former colony's independence and ex-slave Toussaint Louverture as the new nation's most prominent general. In 1792, Denmark became the first European country to ban the trade through legislation, and its close neighbours slowly and reluctantly followed suit. Britain and the United States both abolished the trade in enslaved people in 1807 (although not slavery itself). In 1810, an Anglo-Portuguese treaty was signed, and Portugal agreed to restrict its trade to its own colonies; in 1813, Sweden did the same. At the Treaty of Paris in 1814, France agreed with Britain that the trade was 'repugnant to the principles of natural justice' and committed to abolishing it within five years. The same year, the Dutch made similar promises. The last known slave ship to land on US soil was the *Clotilda*, which smuggled several captured Africans into the town of Mobile, Alabama, just five years before the country abolished slavery in 1865. Matilda McCrear was the last surviving enslaved person brought from Africa to the United States of America. She died in 1940.

The transatlantic trade in enslaved people was a singular horror, but its abolition did not end the forced movement of people for the sake of imperial nations' labour demands. Even as slavery was slowly outlawed (at different times, and in different places), indentured labour continued, and more and more people were forced to migrate vast distances for work and economic opportunities. Even as slavery declined, there were still plenty of coerced and manipulated people – people who had been moved by the will of others – who felt a sense of 'isolation and estrangement' while they lived and worked far from home.[30] It was among these people that nostalgia continued to thrive.

The nineteenth century saw the expansion and entrenchment of European empires. Britain especially extended its tendrils into more and more remote corners of the globe and interfered with greater rapacity in the lives and activities of other people. The British colonialists were enthusiastic in their dominion, and enthusiastic in their documentation of their dominion. If you are interested in the activities and opinions of the architects of the British Empire, then there is no shortage of printed material. They took notes and published pages and pages of text, claiming expertise about everywhere from India to Samoa, from South Africa to British Columbia. The evidence for Victorians' atrocities and mundane cruelty is easy to uncover.

Nostalgia is everywhere in these documents, following in the footsteps of European armies and bureaucrats. It was a condition of empire, something that thrived under the subjugation of people who had either been forcibly removed from their homes, or had their homelands colonized and co-opted. As empire flourished, so did nostalgia. It acts as a kind of thread that weaves together otherwise very different places and periods. And even this very potted history of nostalgia and empires offers a tiny glimpse into the experiences and emotions of colonized and indentured people – albeit always through the eyes of the colonizers.

The New Hebrides, now Vanuatu, was an archipelago in the South Pacific Ocean. Shortly after Captain James Cook first visited in 1774, it was occupied by both the British and the French. The two countries eventually signed an agreement that divided the islands into two separate communities, one anglophone and one francophone. It stayed that way until 1980, when the New Hebrides finally gained their independence as the Republic of Vanuatu. But, in the 1860s, the people of the islands were still subject to colonial rule. Plantation owners in neighbouring colonies – Australia, Fiji, New Caledonia and the Samoan islands – established a long-term indentured-labour trade called 'blackbirding'. At its height, more than half of the adult male population of Vanuatu's Indigenous community, the Ni-Vanuatu, worked abroad. The labourers faced terrible conditions and abuse, and they had little natural immunity to foreign diseases. As a result, the Indigenous population of Vanuatu declined dramatically over the course of the nineteenth century.[31]

The situation in the Pacific was not unique. All over the world, the subjects of the European empires died in staggering numbers. In the 1870s, for example, India endured famine after famine. Exacerbated by British cruelty, neglect and mismanagement, over five million people died. In 1869, one English anthropologist described how many Indigenous communities had already disappeared: 'The Tasmanian has perished; the Australian is dying out; the Carib has disappeared from the West Indies; the Maori race is diminishing; the Esquimaux is decreasing in numbers; the North American Indian dwindling away.'[32]

Much like sickness and suicide among the enslaved, these deaths were less a tragedy for the colonialists and more an inconvenience. Partly because they interfered with the labour market, and partly because they were concerned about the threat of contagion to white settlers, colonial governments sometimes paid more than a passing interest in the reasons for widespread disease and decline among their subjects. In 1894, Irish naval officer Boyle T. Somerville published an account of the New Hebrides in which he considered the declining population. He wrote about one of the archipelago's islands, Efate: 'About forty years ago this decimation began with kidnapping, followed by the "sandalwooders", who shot down the natives.' 'Sandalwooders' were traders in sandalwood, a valuable timber, who arrived on the islands with English missionaries in the early nineteenth century. Once the islands' wood reserves ran out, the sandalwooders trafficked many of the Ni-Vanuatu to Queensland, Australia, to continue logging. The indentured labourers died of diseases like consumption and alcoholism, but, according to Somerville, they also died of nostalgia.[33]

Nostalgia was a problem among workers in other parts of the British Empire too. In the late 1880s, J. M. Vermont described the challenges of the Straits Settlements, a group of British territories in Southeast Asia. Originally established in 1826 as part of the holdings of the East India Company, the Straits Settlements came under the control of the British Raj in 1858, and then under direct British rule as a Crown colony nine years later. The Straits Settlements originally consisted of Penang, Malacca and Dinding (all now in modern-day Malaysia), as well as Singapore. Christmas Island and the Cocos Islands were added in 1886.

In the late nineteenth century, Britain encouraged Indian immigration to the Straits in massive numbers. By 1901, there were almost 60,000 Indians living in the Straits, constituting around 10 per cent of the total population. Vermont was not, however, all that impressed by the people who arrived by their thousands aboard emigrant steamers. They were 'poor in physique and unused to field work'. This was not just a problem for the immigrants themselves, but was primarily framed as an issue for the colonialists. The men who arrived were 'only a source of loss to the employer, and tend to augment the death-rate materially.' A local physician, one Dr McClosky, described how so many 'succumbed from nostalgia'. The sorry souls 'lost heart, longed for home' and remained in hospital for weeks, even months. Their constitutions withered and, in spite of all treatment, they gradually 'sank from sheer general debility and exhaustion'.[34]

Rather than giving the colonialists pause that perhaps they were causing unimaginable suffering to the people they governed, the prevalence of pathological nostalgia among Indigenous populations was, for many, an indicator of fundamental biological inferiority. In 1867, the cleric and comparative philologist Frederic W. Farrar described the eradication of Indigenous communities as a 'process of extinction' – something that had already 'obliterated innumerable tribes'. Trading in the language of his time, he argued that 'savage and civilised life cannot co-exist side by side.' Even when so-called 'savages' attempted to adopt the trappings of civilization, they failed: 'they seem to wither away with a kind of weary nostalgia, a pining sickness, a deeply-seated despair, and an inevitable decay.'[35] For him, nostalgia was a marker of 'savage' inferiority, of inherent feebleness.

When writing about different races and the diseases they seemed particularly vulnerable to, Farrar was part of a busy and prolific community of writers and thinkers. These were the early days of social Darwinism, and the idea that human races were locked in a deadly contest, also known as the 'survival of the fittest', infiltrated the writings and practices of colonialists from Tasmania to the Caribbean. Farrar was himself a pall-bearer at Charles Darwin's funeral. After around 1860, British science, medicine and anthropology became increasingly committed to ideas about inherent Teutonic (Germanic) or 'Anglo-Saxon' superiority, and were invested in broader notions of biological racial determinism.[36] This kind of racialization of populations established rigid hierarchies between colonizers and colonized, and even between different white nations (the Italians and the Celts, for example, were at the bottom of the European pecking order). This period witnessed a hardening of racial distinctions and a heightened commitment to the importance of biology in dictating behaviours, tendencies and sicknesses. This coincided with, and was used to rationalize, an increasingly rapacious and fretful imperialism.

Indeed, writers in and about the European empires talked a lot about the bodies of their subjects, and were keen to justify their occupation and rule along biological lines. And the Ni-Vanuatu were not the only colonized community that were believed to be constitutionally inferior, or to suffer from particularly acute bouts of

nostalgia when forced far from home. In 1898, the botanist Frederick
Manson Bailey observed that the Indigenous people of what was
then called British New Guinea (now Papua New Guinea) had 'very
strong feelings with regard to relations and friends, and also great
fondness for the place where they were born.' European miners
elsewhere on the island would employ Indigenous Papuans as
'carriers'. But, after a while, 'the feeling of nostalgia' would become
so strong that they would abandon their employers and make a
journey of hundreds of miles along the coast, back to their home
villages.[37]

Just as prevalence of nostalgia was taken to indicate weakness
in non-white races, its absence was taken as proof of inherent
European superiority. Indeed, one of the many hypocrisies of
empire was that nostalgia among white people was understood as
an indicator of emotional sensitivity, even nascent nationalism,
whereas nostalgia felt by non-Europeans was a sign of inferiority.
In 1834, plague arrived in the port of Alexandria, in Egypt. An
infectious disease, now known to be caused by the bacterium
Yersinia pestis, plague was carried by the fleas on rats. It has been
humanity's constant, if episodic, companion since at least the sixth
century, when the plague of Justinian eradicated almost 40 per
cent of the population of Constantinople (now Istanbul) and almost
half of the population of Europe. After the second plague pandemic,
which reached Europe in 1348 and reduced the world's population
from c. 450 million to c. 350 million, the disease became endemic
and recurred regularly. A series of major plague epidemics flourished in the late 1600s and cropped up throughout the eighteenth
and nineteenth centuries.

Since 1805, Egypt had been ruled by the *Wali* (viceroy) Muhammed
Ali, who had been sent by the Sultan of the Ottoman Empire in
Istanbul to recover the country from Napoleon's occupation. In the
first few weeks of the epidemic, which raged from 1834 to 1836, Ali
immediately designated an isolated cemetery, just outside the city,
where bodies could be safely buried. He ordered the sick and their
families to quarantine in their own homes, under surveillance, and
instructed the government to provide the needy with daily rations.

Muhammed Ali was an ambitious, reforming leader. He established a dynasty that was to rule Egypt until its revolution of 1952. His primary focus was the military. He annexed Northern Sudan from 1820 to 1824, as well as parts of Arabia and Anatolia. He also attempted to modernize the country. He sent students to Europe and invited training missions to Egypt. He built a system of canals for irrigation and transport, and reformed the civil service. He introduced long-staple cotton in 1820 and transformed its agriculture into a lucrative monoculture before the end of the century. Trade flourished, and merchants and their ships became more and more crucial to Egypt's economic success.

When the plague arrived, Muhammed Ali worked hard to ensure that work at Alexandria's dockyards would continue uninterrupted. He placed the entire arsenal under quarantine, a decision that was quickly met with opposition. Poor Egyptians were routinely conscripted into the arsenal, navy or army, and this new rule that prevented them from leaving their place of work for home and their families was roundly resisted. In 1836, after the plague had been raging in Egypt for two years, the Englishman Arthur T. Holroyd arrived in Alexandria. Holroyd eventually ended up as an Australian lawyer and politician, but at this point he was just an average British busybody, interfering in the affairs of a foreign nation. On his travels up the Nile, he missed few opportunities to graffiti his surname and his year of travel into the ancient monuments he visited. This casual vandal also wrote a scathing letter to an MP back in England, John Cam Hobhouse, moralizing over the Egyptian government's handling of the plague epidemic. He criticized the 'system of sanitary regulations' and argued that they had been inflicted 'so arbitrarily, and imposed so unjustly'.[38] He was not really worried about the Egyptians, but more concerned by the sanctions levied at European merchants. Holroyd was part of a long lineage of British tourists who felt qualified to meddle in the governance of the places they visited. In 1882, this meddling turned into indirect rule, when Egypt became a British protectorate.

But Holroyd was probably right about the physical and emotional toll placed on conscripted soldiers by the quarantine rules introduced during the 1834–6 plague epidemic in Egypt. Anyone 'so unfortunate as to be taken for the arsenal, navy, or army' was already susceptible to pathological homesickness because he was 'an exile for ever from his home, his wife, and his family'. These feelings were exacerbated by a two-year-long quarantine, because now the men weren't even allowed home to visit their loved ones. Instead, they became sick with dread and melancholy: 'Those who had been impressed into the Pacha's service . . . suffered severely from nostalgia.'[39]

Holroyd did, however, add an essentialist twist to his analysis. He thought that Egyptians were especially vulnerable because 'among no people is the attachment to their soil so strong.' This was a tendency shared by their close neighbours in Sudan. Just a few years later, up to 18,000 Sudanese conscripts were believed to have died from nostalgia in the Egyptian army.[40] This North African trait contrasted with the adventuring spirit of British people, who, according to the graffiti artist Holroyd, thrived off travel and exploration, and made great merchants, traders and campaigning soldiers. Holroyd's interpretation of the nostalgia problem in Egypt was not just indebted to social Darwinism or biological essentialism; he was also writing in the context of another, relatively new, powerful set of social, cultural and political forces: nationalism and patriotism.

Nationalism developed in the late eighteenth century, in both the Americas and in Europe, but soon spread to the colonies and countries of the Global South. Nationalism means more than just living in a particular country; it is a kind of 'imagined community', a sense of communion or comradeship between people who might not know each other, who may never have met and might live very different lives at opposite ends of the country. Nevertheless, and despite these differences, they imagine belonging to the same community, sharing in a common history, traits, beliefs and attitudes. Nationalism replaced the traditional ties between family that had been the foundation of the state, and superseded other connections between members of a local community and to local lords or landholders.

Just because the nation was predicated on imagined connection did not, of course, mean that its political consequences were not profound or were unreal. On the contrary, this imagined community created something incredibly powerful – something for which countless people the world over have since willingly sacrificed themselves. It made conscription possible and has, since the nineteenth century, propelled millions of people to voluntarily participate in far-flung wars. It also made it possible for someone like Holroyd to make broad, sweeping statements about the adventuring spirit of the British, and to describe the Egyptians as deeply attached to their soil. Nationalism was, therefore, a precondition for the rise of nostalgia in the nineteenth century.[41] While people – most notably the Swiss – had been sad to leave their homeland in the seventeenth century, the nature of national identity in the nineteenth century meant that the home exerted a new and acute pull on people. More people might have left home than ever before, but they also felt more strongly about home than ever before – or at least they felt more strongly about an imagined, abstract, political home than ever before.

In some places, nationalism was underscored by the kind of racial determinism I've described. Fictions of inherent, biological superiority only made British nationalism, for example, more powerful. And yet, despite the predominance of what historians have since called 'racial anthropology', there was still plenty of debate over what precisely distinguished different societies or ethnicities from one another, and there were plenty of people who thought the 'problem' of the tropics (where nostalgia seemed to flourish) had less to do with the biology of the people who had long lived there, and more to do with its climate. Late-nineteenth-century writers disagreed over whether susceptibility to nostalgia was a consequence of something bodily, something inherent to certain races, or whether it was something to do with a mismatch between bodies and environments – because there were white men and women who succumbed to the disease, especially when they found themselves far from home, in hostile surroundings. After all, by the end of the nineteenth century, nostalgia had maintained its reputation as the 'Swiss disease' for almost two hundred years. Even the superior and self-obsessed Brits had to admit that the Swiss were, at the very least, white.

Nostalgia was evidently everywhere and could be found in all sorts of bodies. It seemed clear, to some people at least, that it must be more to do with circumstance than biology. In 1847, a plantation owner wrote to the *Jamaica Times* to complain about the quality of his immigrant workforce. He had imported several labourers from Madeira, who were probably either Guanches (the Indigenous people of the nearby Canary Islands), captured Berbers or West Africans, but, wherever they were from, they were not faring well. They were costly to transport, feed and pay (they received one shilling per day), but they did not seem to be worth the investment: 'The expense has been most serious; all sorts of food being so high. Had they physical strength and will to perform their engagement with me for the next eighteen months, it might pay, but I ask you, how can they do this?' He griped about their inability to acclimatize to the Caribbean weather (they were as useless as the 'Europeans' in this regard), and they suffered from fever, sores and lethargy. Most concerningly, they pined for their homeland – so much so, that many Madeirans died from nostalgia. This plantation owner had already lost two children to the disease, but, on a neighbouring estate, seventeen workers had died, including the interpreter.[42]

This letter was used to evidence an inquiry into the consequences of emancipation and post-1807 immigration to the Caribbean. The author of the eventual report had a very different take to the writer of the original letter. While the plantation owner was complaining about the inherent weaknesses and lack of 'physical strength' of his Madeiran workers, the investigator was much more sympathetic to the immigrants' plight. He noted that the letter constituted a 'plain admission' that the Madeirans' wages were too low, and 'insufficient for the due support of life'. Nostalgia, he implied, might be prevented by better working and living conditions. There clearly was not anything constitutionally wrong with the Madeirans, they were simply suffering under impossible circumstances.

Challenging the idea that nostalgia was a flaw inherent to Black and Brown bodies, there were also numerous examples of nostalgia among British people who had failed, in some way, to acclimatize to the hot and humid corners of their empire. In his 1872 essay on the island of Zanzibar, off the coast of Tanzania, Sir Richard Francis Burton painted a bleak picture of white frailty and his fellow citizens' inability to adapt to equatorial climes: 'European women here . . . rarely resist the melancholy isolation, the want of society, and the Nostalgia – Heimweh or Homesickness – so common, yet so little regarded in tropical countries.' In most cases, equatorial Africa was 'certain death' for English visitors. Burton was alarmingly sardonic about the risks posed by this place, suggesting that men who murdered their wives via more conventional means – poison, for example – were foolish. Instead, those men who were 'anxious to be widowers' could much more easily, 'neatly and quietly' achieve their desires by spending a few months in 'African air'.[43]

Indeed, homesickness was a ubiquitous and highly symbolic part of the colonial experience. At the opening ceremony of the Colonial and Indian Exhibition in London, in May 1886, the popular Victorian song 'Home, Sweet Home' was performed between renditions of Handel's 'Hallelujah' chorus and the jingoistic jingle, 'Rule, Britannia!'[44] The author J. E. Dawson cited this performance as evidence that nostalgia was a national and imperial condition: 'When we find on a great occasion that a picked elite of ten thousand of our countrymen and women are moved to tears at the sympathetic rendering by one woman's voice of the popular little song "Home, Sweet Home", we must feel convinced that both the sentiment and the music appealed to one of the strongest and most deep rooted of our national passions.'[45]

In India, the *Calcutta Review* claimed that Britons in India were often nostalgic for a distant home: 'The saddest, yet inevitable result of Indian life, is the loosening of the sacred family bond.' Directly contradicting claims that nostalgia was a condition of inferior races or incivility, the writer argued, 'It is said, and said truly, that the Englishman is pre-eminent among the nations of the earth for his love of home!'[46] Because of this inherent tendency

towards homesickness, the exhibition tried to represent the empire
as a destination, a place where plucky adventurers might also be
able to set up future, British homes. As the Prince of Wales insisted,
'We must remember that, as regards the Colonies, they are the
legitimate and natural homes, in future, of the more adventurous
and energetic portion of the population of these Islands.'[47] Indeed,
longing for home, and attempting to recreate the rituals and comforts
of home, was characteristic of European colonists abroad. As
mentioned, this was just one of the many hypocrisies of empire.
When Europeans experienced nostalgia, it was a sign of good
breeding and heroic patriotism. When non-Europeans experienced
the same, it was a sign of weakness.

The fact that nostalgia was a problem for white people too was
made all too clear by its prevalence among soldiers during the
American Civil War. Soldiers were particularly vulnerable to the
disease because they were absent from their home, in new and
strange surroundings. The risk was highest in moments of military
weakness, when the fighting had to be done in retreat, when they
were exposed to cold and hunger, had to sleep on damp soil, had
been taken prisoner or were suffering 'frightful thirst'. Under these
conditions, 'the remembrance of the country he has left behind him,
of the mother, the wife, or the home, awakens and brings a tear
into the eyes of the bravest.' In the first two years of the conflict,
2,588 men were diagnosed with nostalgia and thirteen died. While
nostalgia might have been the sole cause of death in just thirteen
men, it exerted its 'depressing influence' in many more cases of
death, which might otherwise 'have terminated favourably'.[48] Indeed,
as the doctor Roberts Bartholow put it, 'these numbers scarcely
express the full extent to which nostalgia influenced the sickness
and mortality of the army.'[49] Bartholow believed that nostalgia eroded
the stamina of the soldier, making him more susceptible to other
diseases and more likely to die once unwell. Other estimates attributed 'no less than 10,000' deaths among Civil War soldiers to
nostalgia.[50]

But some men were more likely to be struck down than others.
Bartholow noticed that 'young men of feeble will, highly developed

imaginative faculties, and strong sexual desires,' along with 'married men, for the first time absent from their families,' were frequent among his patients. He was concerned about the 'monotony of winter camps,' because active campaigning helped divert the soldiers' attention and prevent them from succumbing to nostalgia. Men with no 'physical nor mental occupation' turned their attentions homeward: 'They fell into reverie, and allowed their imaginations to run riot amid the images of home conjured up.' Their eventual symptoms included hallucinations, constipation, indigestion, disturbed sleep and melancholia. Much like the French doctors who cared for baby Eugene much earlier in the century, Bartholow and colleagues thought that nostalgia was a relative, version or 'species' of melancholia.[51]

The epidemic of nostalgia that swept through the soldiers of the European empires, and through the volunteer armies of the American Civil War, demonstrated that it was not just an affliction of non-white races. However, the kind of men supposedly susceptible to the disease were, nonetheless, defective. Or, at least, defective in the eyes of nineteenth-century doctors. Those particularly prone to nostalgia were unmanly somehow, not quite up to the standards expected of virile and stoical soldiers. Bartholow thought that the biggest risk factor when it came to nostalgia was 'deranged social functions' and, more specifically, masturbation, which 'produced a mental state more favourable to nostalgia than any other cause'.[52]

That nostalgia became implicated in anxieties about men and masculinity in the nineteenth century is clear from the suggested remedies. The popular magazine *Scientific American* published an article in 1864 which argued that 'any influence that will tend to render the patient more manly will exercise a curative power.' Like historians of the twenty-first century, the author acknowledged that nostalgia seemed more prevalent in oppressive institutions. Nostalgia was as common in boys' boarding schools as it was in army camps. In both, ridicule was an effective treatment. Banter and mockery would shake the nostalgia loose from the man, berating him into good humour. The nostalgic patient could often be 'laughed out of it by his comrades, or reasoned out of it by appeals to his manhood'. The best cure, though, was war itself: 'An active campaign, with its attendant marches, and more particularly its battles, is the best curative.'[53] In general, idleness was a key cause of nostalgia. Patients should be made to work hard all day. Labour would make him sleep soundly at night, relish his rations and prevent him from thinking of home. Work would keep him sane.

*

People living under oppressive regimes and those who had been forced to move elsewhere were the ones most vulnerable to nostalgia in the nineteenth century. Whether that was slavery or indentured labour, and whether it was adults conscripted into armies or babies sent away from home, the nineteenth century was full of coercion. It was under these circumstances, then, that nostalgia seemed to thrive. And this was a feature of the disease recognized by both contemporaries and historians since.[54]

But something else was also going on. Lots of people were nostalgic, and dying as a result, but lots of people were also worrying about nostalgia. They were concerned about what the seeming prevalence of this disease might reveal about the world in which they were living. Early modern diagnoses of nostalgia reflected apprehensions about the pace of social change in places like Switzerland. People had similar concerns in the nineteenth century. Since the end of the Middle Ages, society has repeatedly registered the pain caused by cultural and technological change overreaching, insisting that excessive transformation makes you ill or inept. Victorians worried about the impact of railways, steamships and telegraph cables on their collective health and well-being, and attributed widespread degeneration to a departure from nature and so-called natural ways of living. Even today, think pieces panic over the negative consequences of mobile-phone masts and social-media use.

Like so many other things, nostalgia was seen as a symptom of the nineteenth century – a peculiar, pathological response to the accelerating pace of modern and 'civilized' life. But it was also tied up with other anxieties. Anxieties that had certainly existed before, but became more acute and more fractious with the expansion and intensification of empire. While some people invoked nostalgia as a sickness associated with certain races, or a consequence of supposedly biological or inherent differences between societies and cultures, others were much more concerned with what it seemed to indicate about the frailty of white people. Especially those who went to live along the equator. If empire was so great, and if European colonizers were so superior, then why did they seem to struggle so much and succumb to nostalgia when living in hostile climates, whether frozen or tropical?

This idea that epidemics of disease might indicate some kind of constitutional degeneration among supposedly 'advanced' nations and races was very common in the late nineteenth century. All sorts of physical and psychological disorders – like neurasthenia, hysteria and cancer – were taken as symptoms of a declining West and over-stretched empires. Nostalgia among Europeans, and particularly among their soldiers, was one of many signs that perhaps the seemingly 'natural' hierarchy of races was due an upset. The fact that armies appeared to be especially vulnerable was worrying, not just because it threatened imperial and military strength, but because it also seemed to undermine Victorian assumptions about male superiority and strength.

Returning to the Arctic, the remedies suggested for nostalgia among American soldiers were mirrored by advice given by Howgate and other explorers of the ice. They, too, participated in busy schedules of studying, reading, cleaning and socializing to avert the profound emotional and physical consequences of lengthy isolation and distance from home. Business and productivity were a key part of how nineteenth-century Europeans and white Americans were supposed to survive Arctic expeditions. This was a very nineteenth-century solution to a very nineteenth-century problem. And it shows how diseases, both then and now, become magnets for things that are really nothing to do with medicine at all. For all of their claims to the contrary, science and medicine are just as susceptible to the strange biases, proclivities and ethical pretensions of a society as anything else. This is true today (think Covid-19, HIV, cancer) and it was certainly true of the Victorian age.

The number of nostalgics may well have increased with the growth of slavery and empire, but the nineteenth century also witnessed an increase in nostalgia anxiety, its own kind of moral panic. Much like other moral panics, the growth in literature about nostalgia, reflecting on its apparent increase, was also about other things, other concerns like racial superiority, imperial overreach and white fragility. This was to be the first of many 'nostalgia waves' that rolled over the West, although both Britain and America would have to wait until the 1970s for the second.

CHAPTER THREE

HOMESICKNESS

Arnold Ambler was born in September 1899 in Halifax, Yorkshire. In the nineteenth century, Halifax was a busy and expanding industrial town. Textile factories jostled with back-to-back slums, and terraces clung precariously to steep hillsides. At first, the booming town paid little attention to basic public amenities, and in 1843 it was described as a 'mass of little, miserable, ill-looking streets, jumbled together in chaotic confusion'.[1] But, with the slow influx of industrial wealth and a reforming, Victorian zeal, the infrastructure of the town was slowly developed. Schools and mechanics' institutes were opened, and hospitals, alms houses, workhouses, parks, public baths, cemeteries, gas works, a public library and a museum were all established. A railway station was built in 1844, horse omnibuses introduced in the 1850s, and trams first rattled the streets in 1898. Despite these improvements, Arnold's young life was difficult. He was one of thirteen children, all born at the poor end of town. He left school at eleven to help his mother in the home, and then, while still in his teens, he took odd jobs like selling hot cross buns and picking coal at the mine. His father had three jobs of his own and worked seven days a week, selling the papers on Sundays. Arnold was just fifteen when the First World War broke out. Underage, he signed up anyway. When the army realized quite how young he was, he was thrown out, but he enlisted a second and then a third time, before finally being sent to fight on the Western Front aged just seventeen.

In his very first battle, Arnold was shot in the right arm. The bullet passed directly through a can of bully beef he carried in his pack. Telling the story, seventy years later, he laughed: 'I've always had a kind of a soft feeling for corned beef.' Arnold was sent back to England to recuperate in Brighton. But, despite making a full recovery, he never returned to the front line. Just after Armistice Day, in November 1918, he met a girl at the theatre. They courted and Arnold spent much of his time in 1919 visiting his sweetheart in the affluent London suburb of Richmond. After a year of working hard and pooling their savings, they married in a small ceremony one Monday morning. Just two days later, they set sail for America. After over a week spent in steerage, the cheapest passenger accommodation on the ship, Arnold and Doris went out on the deck to watch the Statue of Liberty loom into view.

Theirs was a pretty typical story. An estimated 3.5 million English people emigrated to the US after the revolutionary wars of 1776.[2] Throughout the nineteenth century, English settlers were a steady and substantial influx. The first wave began in the late 1820s and was sustained by social and political unrest in the United Kingdom until it peaked in 1842. Most of those who made the journey were small landholders and tenant farmers from depressed rural areas of southern and western England, or urban labourers fleeing from the industrial turmoil of expanding towns and cities like Halifax. Some were drawn by visions of utopian futures and others were attracted by the more tangible allure of new lands, factories, railroads and mines. From the 1860s to the 1890s, annual English immigration grew from 60,000 to an average of 82,000.[3] The building of America's transcontinental railroads, the settlement of the great plains and industrialization attracted even more skilled and professional immigrants from England and elsewhere. Cheaper steamship fares also enabled unskilled English urban workers, like Arnold, to come to America, and these labourers, miners and hawkers soon made up the majority. The pace slowed in the early twentieth century, but picked up again after the two world wars. In the 1940s, over 100,000 English people moved permanently to the United States. By the 1950s, average English immigration had increased to over 150,000 per year.[4]

As we know, the nineteenth century witnessed a massive expansion in the movement and migration of people. Emigration became easier and increasingly common as railways and steamships got better at travelling further, faster and for a lot less money. Refugees and migrants travelled far, looking for more enriching and comfortable lives, and escaping poverty and deprivation. Europe's late nineteenth century, with its rising political instability, economic distress and religious persecution, fuelled the largest mass human migration in world history. Between 1855 and 1890, approximately eight million immigrants arrived in Manhattan alone. But there was a trauma associated with migration, a trauma that has not always made its way into the history books. Because, with travel, came homesickness.

Arnold loved his new country. But Doris was desperately homesick. Sure, 'every once in a while' Arnold would get depressed, and 'wish to hell [he] was back over there'. But not for long. '[America] has been good to me. Let's face it.' Doris, on the other hand, was miserable. They went back to England five times in their first five years in America, and each time Doris stayed with her sister, refusing to leave her childhood home. Despite her protestations, the couple repeatedly returned to New York, and stayed there for the rest of their lives, although Doris never became an American citizen, refusing to renounce her country of birth.[5]

*

It was in the early decades of the twentieth century, when Arnold and Doris uprooted themselves, that nostalgia and homesickness began to part ways. In the eighteenth and nineteenth centuries, homesickness and nostalgia sat on the same spectrum, one deadly and one relatively benign, but both a desperate longing for a place departed. Homesickness existed alongside nostalgia, and for every white British wife who died of the latter while living in the tropics, there were countless other Europeans who survived their journey abroad, but still keenly felt the pangs of homesickness. The two feelings were similar, but crucially not the same. However, to understand nostalgia and its strange trajectory, we need to spend some time with homesickness and follow its journey from elevated sentiment to

immature sentimentality – a route nostalgia also followed at approximately the same time, albeit ending up in a slightly different place.
As nostalgia and homesickness parted ways, they were both slowly
denigrated. One became an infantile attachment to home and family,
the other an ill-informed bond with the past.

At first, the feeling of homesickness was a noble condition because
it demonstrated a commitment to your family and your deep
emotional roots. It was a virtue, a sign of sensitivity and patriotism.
Then, as the nineteenth century progressed and as the Enlightenment
ideal of the free-moving individual took hold, along with the growing
forces of capitalism and colonialism, homesickness became increasingly infantilized and trivialized.[6] As the historian Susan J. Matt has
argued, an emotion that tied people to the place they were born
no longer worked in an increasingly global world, one with porous
borders, which relied on a mobile workforce.[7] This way of thinking
about homesickness has, in turn, shaped the way we think and write
about migration, both past and present. Most tales of international
travel focus on the social, economic and political causes and consequences of migration. Rarely do these histories focus on feelings.[8]
But not only did homesickness occupy a prominent role in the
personal and medical writings of the nineteenth century, as a fundamental part of ordinary life, it was also an agent of change. It pushed
people abroad and then pulled them back again. It shaped social
relationships and carved out new trajectories for people who thought
they had concrete plans in place.

While adventuring souls like Henry Williamson Howgate were
propelled to journey abroad in search of fame and fortune, the love
of home still held sway, both personally and politically. You can see
these tensions playing out in the early decades of the nineteenth
century. In 1834, an anonymous Scottish gentleman published what
could best be described as an advice manual for emigrants.[9] It proved
so popular that it went through three editions, lapped up by eager
Scots keen to leave their homes. The guide laid out the possible
destinations – Canada, the United States, Australia or New South
Wales, Van Diemen's Land (now Tasmania), Nova Scotia (not yet
part of Canada) and the Cape of Good Hope – and tellingly described

moving to these places, already occupied by multiple Indigenous communities, as akin to 'colonizing a desert'.

Such a move was not for the faint-hearted. It would require leaving behind 'easy chairs' and 'many domestic comforts', encountering potentially 'fatal climates', 'misery, suffering, or death'. Echoing anxieties about nostalgia's threat to well-travelled white people, the Scottish gentleman warned that many places were 'too hot for European constitutions' and hosted hordes of 'natives, wild beasts, and noxious reptiles'.[10] As a result, he recommended either the United States of America or British Canada – although any traveller to the US must learn to 'gulp down in silence' any of his many criticisms of the relatively new republic, otherwise he risked engaging in 'continual quarrels'. The Americans were, after all, 'a people proud of their country'.[11]

Evoking Enlightenment ideas suggesting that 'civilized' humankind – especially men – were inherently predisposed to travel and adventure, and echoing colonial assumptions about British superiority, the author part-explained the rise of emigration from Britain to North America by saying, 'It seems never to have been intended that man should remain stationary in the place which gave him birth. He is an active and an energetic being; and we find him in all ages and countries moving from place to place, and from country to country, impelled by necessity or induced by the sense of utility to make the wide world his home and the men of all nations his brethren.'[12]

And, while many might balk at the idea of emigrating, America was like an 'immense field, calling for reapers, who have skill and ability to labour.' Again ignoring the rights and existence of Native Americans, the author described an 'abundance of unoccupied land in that country', land that only required 'the hand of man to convert it into the means of human subsistence'.

Despite the guide's gung-ho attitude towards the opportunities America had to offer, the author recognized that many Scots might still be constitutionally predisposed to staying at home. While there were plenty of robust adventurers in the early nineteenth century, they were still going against the tendencies of the age by leaving home for good. Another anonymous Scottish gentleman moved from

Aberdeen to Michigan in September 1832. While America was a 'country of *hope*' and Scotland a place of 'fear', he acknowledged that a 'good many emigrants get homesick.'[13] These poor souls suffer under the pressures of 'everything being new to them', and they sooner age and decay. Their emotional turmoil limited the scope of their travels, restricted the abundance available to them and, for many, it sent them back to where they came from.

And it wasn't only Scots who took time to acclimatize to the brave new world of international travel. The immigrant writer Frederick Gustorf observed the lives of middle-class German families in nineteenth-century Illinois and Missouri. He, too, identified misery, suffering and homesickness among his fellow travellers. 'Their experiences are beyond imagination,' he lamented, 'their despair can be read in the deep, dark lines of their faces.'[14] Even for those relatively well established in the new world, reminders of home could shatter the emotional facade they had built and worked to maintain. In 1853, American writer and political activist Jessie Benton Fremont travelled to Missouri as part of one of her many tours of the Western frontier. When she checked into a hotel, her German hostess immediately became overwhelmed with grief and longing for her homeland. She took one look at Jessie's gloves and exclaimed, 'Ah, dear God! You are a lady from my country.' The hostess lamented that it had been twenty-four years since she had left her homeland, but still she 'loved it best'. She broke off her exclamations, weeping.[15]

Nicolaus Hesse had settled with his wife and six daughters on the banks of the Maries River in what is now Osage County, an isolated location he had 'discovered' on one of his explorations into the interior of Missouri from the city of St Louis. Hesse had been a wealthy and influential man back in Warburg, Westphalia, but he had fallen victim to the 'emigration fever' sweeping Germany, inspired by published accounts of American life. But, in April 1837, he decided to return to Germany, less than two years after settling in Missouri. Hesse had had ambitious plans for his new life in America, but his wife suffered 'disabling homesickness' and was unable to stay. When he returned to Germany, he wrote about his life on the frontier: 'The memory of relatives, friends, and old acquaintances causes a longing which in many, especially tender-hearted women, creates a homesickness that often degenerates into real melancholy that cannot be cured by any medicine.'[16] His wife had not been driven by reason, but by emotion. While he framed it as a particularly acute female complaint, he also acknowledged that homesickness was still natural, something experienced by everyone: 'The cause is not in a faulty judgment of the conditions of the old and new home, but rather the love of the original home, which is common to all people of the earth.'[17]

Indeed, it was not just 'tender-hearted' women who were afflicted. Before the Hesses left Missouri, they had been joined by another German family, recently emigrated. Henrietta Bruns, known as Jette by all her family and friends, was a young woman who had arrived in America with her husband and children, along with a few of her siblings. In September 1836, she wrote a letter home about her brother Bernhard, who suffered very badly from homesickness and who had become 'very melancholy and strange'. Like Nicolaus and his wife, Bernhard eventually decided to return to Europe. Jette herself also regularly succumbed to bouts of homesickness that she tried to hide from her husband and children. Fifty years later, in 1882, she wrote another letter home: 'It is a harsh homesickness which I have to fight against,' she wrote. 'I wonder whether I can regain a joy for living on?' Eleven years later, in a letter sent just after her eightieth birthday, Jette described how she still suffered from homesickness, her longing to return unabated by the more than sixty years she had spent in America.[18]

Before 1890, individual US states, rather than the Federal government, regulated immigration into America. But it soon became apparent that this system was ill equipped to handle the sheer numbers of people wanting to make their home in the United States. In response, the Federal government constructed a new immigration station on an island in New York harbour. On 1 January 1892, Ellis Island received its first immigrants: Annie Moore, a teenager from Ireland, accompanied by her two younger brothers. Over the next sixty-two years, more than twelve million immigrants would arrive at Ellis Island hoping to settle in the United States, including Arnold and Doris Ambler.

But, as the scale of immigration expanded, homesickness declined in significance. While in 1837 the 'love of the original home' was a natural impulse 'common to all people of the earth', by the time the new century had got underway, homesickness held a less revered position in the American psyche. Paradoxes remained; patriotism continued to be an important part of American life and, if anything, national feeling and protectionism only intensified. Homesickness began to carry some social stigma, but that did not mean people stopped feeling it.[19] Indeed, homesickness left its trace all over the historical record of immigration, cropping up again and again in interviews with those who entered the US through Ellis Island. For American citizens, Ellis Island embodied everything the American dream had to offer.[20] The country's emerging national identity was that of a place that appealed to and welcomed newcomers, a nation built on immigrants. Encapsulating these themes, the bronze plaque placed at the base of the Statue of Liberty famously includes a poem by Emma Lazarus, written in 1883:

> Give me your tired, your poor,
> Your huddled masses yearning to breathe free,
> The wretched refuse of your teeming shore.
> Send these, the homeless, tempest-tost to me,
> I lift my lamp beside the golden door![21]

While powerful and resonant, these words do not, however, capture everything immigrants felt, nor how they perceived Ellis Island — nor, indeed, America as a whole.

For many aspiring citizens, the US was an alluring land of opportunity, but immigration was a complex experience. Ellis Island itself was as much a place of fear as it was of prospect, and even those who were allowed through America's borders and passed the immigration centre's eugenics-inflected medical assessments were in for a long and bumpy ride of acclimatization and acceptance. For example, in 1985, Emmerich Gorozdos was interviewed about his experience of arriving there from Austria in 1921. Emmerich was born in 1903 in Vienna, where his father was a streetcar motorman. After graduating from high school, Emmerich joined a large bank as an apprentice, working there throughout the First World War. But Austria struggled after the war, and Emmerich described how he and his sister would eat bark off the trees to stave off hunger. In 1921, the siblings travelled by old army trucks to Rotterdam, before catching a ship to New York.[22]

The pair moved with relative ease through Ellis Island, and then set off on a sixteen-hour train ride to meet their aunt and uncle in Chicago. About a week after they arrived, Emmerich got his first job as a private secretary to a German-speaking businessman. Though he would work for that company for twenty years, the early days were tough. 'I was homesick. I was homesick. Very much.' The interviewer asked if he missed his family. 'Yeah. And, you know, in those days, it took a month to get an answer to a letter.' Emmerich kept writing home. Every day, he wrote a letter home to his girl-friend. In 1923, she finally joined him in America and, two months after she arrived, they married.[23]

In a very similar vein, Bridget McGeohegan left her home in Ireland for New York in 1923. In Donegal, her family were poor. They had a little farm, a cow, potatoes, vegetables, milk and butter, 'things like that', but there was nothing to do, no work. She didn't want to be poor all her life. She could have married an old farmer if she'd wanted to, and stayed in rural Ireland for the rest of her life. But America appealed instead. There was 'always an opportunity there', it was a 'great country'. And so she set sail from Moville, near Derry, aged twenty-two. But, when she arrived, the gloss tarnished. 'I was gonna go back. Oh, I was homesick. It was terrible.' At Ellis Island, they made her change her name so it would be easier for Americans to pronounce. She became Bertha McGaffighan and left her old life behind.[24]

One of the most acute pains of homesickness was the under-standing that a return − however much desired − might prove impossible. Which is not to say that people like Bertha were neces-sarily prevented from going back to Ireland, but that the Ireland she left would not stay the same. Places, even childhood homes, change, however much we might not want them to do so.

*

In the nineteenth century, hundreds of thousands of people left their homes in search of a new life abroad. In the twentieth century, millions were forced to do the same. In a 1948 essay, the philosopher Hannah Arendt wrote, 'Contemporary history has created a new kind of human being – the kind that are put in concentration camps by their foes and internment camps by their friends.'[25] The twentieth century had created the refugee. The pogroms – violent attempts to massacre or expel Jews from towns, cities and regions – that repeatedly swept Eastern Europe in the late nineteenth and early twentieth centuries prompted mass migration. More than two million Russian Jews fled in the period between 1881 and 1920. The Balkan Wars of 1912–13 caused 800,000 people to abandon their homes. One and a half million people fled the Russian Revolution of 1917 and the subsequent civil war, which did not end until 1921. In that year, around 800,000 Russian refugees became stateless when Lenin revoked citizenship for all Russian expatriates. In 1923, more than a million Armenians left Turkish Asia Minor following the Armenian genocide. It was then that refugees became a legal category, mandated by the League of Nations. The rise of Nazism in Germany and the Second World War provoked another, cataclysmic wave of escapees.

It was in this context that a more problematic version of homesickness took shape. Less deadly than nineteenth-century nostalgia, but still difficult, even impossible, to cure. Immigrants, refugees and the displaced might have yearned for the homes they had left behind – but those homes had gone. They longed for somewhere, but that somewhere was a place preserved in a particular moment in history. For some, their homes had been quite literally destroyed – through war, genocide or natural disasters – and, for others, the time elapsed between leaving and the potential for return meant home was unrecognizable. The Ireland left by those who had emigrated to America, for example, changed – as did the rest of the world. These people were homesick for places to which they could never fully return. As the researcher Dieu Hack-Polay put it, reflecting on twenty-first-century refugees, 'the fact they cannot go home increases the level of stress. The difference is the choice.'[26] While students, for example, might choose to move away from home, danger strips refugees of that agency.

Europe, then, was a complex and dangerous place in the early twentieth century. And some unlucky people became refugees many times over. One such person was Julia Israel Schueler, who was born in Moscow to Russian parents on 6 April 1923. Her father, Jiffim Israel, was a journalist and a Menshevik, or Social Democrat, activist. He was an excellent, expressive orator – and handsome. He liked the ladies and the ladies liked him. According to Julia, her mother Ida was born in the wrong century. The first woman to graduate from medical school in Moscow, Ida believed that women ought to have the same rights as men. She should perhaps have been born in time for the era of women's liberation in the late 1960s or 1970s. When the Bolsheviks took over in 1917, Jiffim was jailed for his political leanings and, in 1922, given a choice – leave Russia and go into exile, or be executed. He opted to leave. Ida, who was pregnant, remained, but, when Julia was just three months old, she followed her husband to Berlin.

The family lived well. As a little girl, Julia led a 'very sheltered life'. She had a maid and a room of her own. Unusually for the time, Julia's mother was a doctor at the nearby hospital. She'd come home and complain about the dreadful language that the surgeons used in the operating room. They lived just across from the zoo, and Julia spent every morning sitting on a bench with her maid, watching the chimpanzees. This was where she learnt table manners. A big chimp was trained to give theatrical performances. He sat at a table and had a napkin tied around his neck. Julia had a hard time holding a spoon, so she watched him very carefully to learn the best technique. Her 'greatest joy', though, was to visit her father in his library, where she'd scoot around the hardwood floors on his wheeled typewriter chair.

Despite her family's affluence, their existence was precarious: 'I just had the feeling that my parents' world was not very secure because we were exiles. This was not our country.' She remembered as a child being asked, 'Who are you?' and 'What are you?' and she would just say, 'Nothing.' And people would say, 'Well, what do you mean? Don't you have a country?' Young Julia would respond, 'No . . . I literally grew up not having a country.' She had left Russia at just three months old and she had no memory of her supposed homeland. And, while her father thrived in the intellectual Russian circles of interwar Berlin, he never learnt to speak German with any real proficiency, and her mother missed her family and her home back in Moscow desperately. Neither Russian nor German, Julia had no home of her own.

But she liked Berlin, thinking it a beautiful city. They had a happy life there – until, that is, everything changed. In 1932, when she was just nine, Julia started amusing herself by counting the Nazi flags hung up in the street outside her family's apartment. Each day, there were more. Boys started turning up at school in their youth-group uniforms. The Nazification of Berlin started slowly, creeping across the summertime city. But, by the autumn, things began changing rapidly – or at least that's how it seemed to Julia. Day by day, the flags multiplied. 'I kept count of the flags.' All the other little girls had to wear swastika pins, but Julia was exempt because she wasn't German. Instead of standing up in class every morning and saying, 'Guten Tag,' the children started greeting their teacher with, 'Heil, Hitler.' One day, on the way to school, she walked past a group of Nazi youths beating up an old man. He was lying on the pavement, covered in blood. As soon as she got to class, she rushed up to her teacher's desk to tell her what she had seen. Her teacher just looked at her and said, 'Julia, you did not see anything. Nothing happened. Now, go sit down and shut up.' As she later recalled, 'For me, that was the beginning of the Holocaust.' People started disappearing. Her music teacher vanished, as did her art teacher.

One morning, at 5 a.m., her mother woke her up: 'Julia, we are not going to school today. We are going to take the train. What would you like to take with you, your teddy bear or your doll?' She chose her teddy bear, selected one single book in German, and the family moved to Paris. The transition was painful. Julia struggled with the language, her parents were very poor and her mother wasn't allowed to practise medicine in France. They were, by this point, 'professional exiles and refugees.' But, beset by homesickness, they still yearned to return to Russia. They thought, or perhaps hoped, that the Communist regime would slacken and they'd be able to go home. Her mother in particular was acutely homesick. She had only left Russia because of her husband, and just wanted to return home. In Paris, Julia's parents received countless refugees from Czechoslovakia and Poland, Yugoslavia and Hungary, and people who had escaped from concentration camps in Austria and Germany. One man had walked to Paris all the way from Siberia.

In 1938, the political situation in Europe deteriorated. Following Germany's Anschluss with Austria, Julia's aunt, who had left Russia in 1929 to marry an Austrian and live in Vienna, crossed the Alps on foot with her young son to escape to Switzerland. They arrived in Paris, unannounced, in the middle of the night. In 1939, France declared war on Germany following the German invasion of Poland. Julia's brother was enlisted into the French army, and Julia and her mother fled first to Angers, a city in western France, then to Bordeaux, then to Toulouse, where they waited for three months for an American visa and were eventually joined by Julia's father and injured brother.

Together, the family travelled to Marseilles and on through decimated Spanish villages – 'Every time we stopped [on the train] there was a sign of the name of the village and nothing but rubble' – to Barcelona, and then finally to Lisbon. From Lisbon, they boarded a ship and sailed across the Atlantic to America. Julia and her family were in third class, sleeping in crowded bunks. But the trip was 'marvellous': 'There were all these groups from every part of Europe . . . Each group was trying to learn as much English as they could, and each group was dancing and playing music and talking.'

After almost a month at sea, the ship arrived in New York. Julia's father was 'absolutely enthralled. He was the happiest person alive to come to America.' But her mother found it hard. She wasn't able to work as a doctor, or even as a nurse, so she took a job as an orderly in the emergency room of a hospital in Harlem. She saw terrible things and despised taking orders from people she considered both cruel and ignorant. Julia found it tough, too. She was incredibly homesick for Paris and Berlin – for New York was nothing like Berlin.[27] She might not have been German, but it was the place she knew best, it was the closest she had to a home. Indeed, Germany occupied a central role in the consciousness of American Jews after the Second World War. But, for those who had fled the country to settle in the United States, their feelings about their former home were complicated.[28] After the war, West Germany was America's close ally, but, for many who escaped the Holocaust, it was also the ultimate villain. Refugees experienced a mixture of homesickness, regret and anger at what had been destroyed by the Nazis. But, while they might miss the life they had had to leave behind, there was nothing to return to. The dead could not be brought back to life.

The exodus from Nazi Germany precipitated a wave of homesickness that spread across mainland Europe, the Atlantic and the Channel. In April 1940, a young woman called Kathe Kupferberg sat down to write an account of her arrival in London as a refugee. Kathe was one of about 20,000 Jewish women who travelled to Britain from Nazi-occupied territories in the late 1930s on domestic-service visas. Like most of these refugees, Kathe was a single woman in her early twenties. It quickly became apparent that she and many others were ill equipped for what was required of a housemaid in a wealthy British home. She arrived from Leipzig with only a small suitcase. In her diary, she lamented having 'to go to a strange land and start all over again . . . all seemed lost and forlorn to me.'[29]

On her days off, Sundays, she walked about outdoors. But even the fresh air failed to make her any happier: 'I walked down strange streets and heard the voices of strangers and thought about my loved ones and dear friends back home, feeling . . . desperately alone here, so that suddenly a terrible wave of homesickness constricted my heart and I burst out in tears. I felt ashamed to be crying there out in the open, but I had nobody I could pour my heart out to.'[30]

Refugee domestics were the largest single group admitted into the UK in the interwar period. Many were mothers whose children came on the Kindertransport, though domestic service meant they could not live together. Others were suspected of being enemy informants, or endured sexual harassment and abuse, suffering physical and emotional harm. Intense homesickness so often accompanies forced migration, and Julia and Kathe were neither the first nor the last to experience it.

*

Julia was only a baby when she left Russia, and still only a child when she fled first Germany and then France. At the beginning of the twentieth century, children were expected to miss their parents when they went away from home – it was a relatively common and appropriate emotional response to radical change. A writer in the magazine *The Youth's Companion*, for example, was sympathetic to the plight of homesick children: 'The person who has not, as a child, suffered the pangs of homesickness, has been fortunate in missing a real and great grief.' She also acknowledged the near-universality of the emotion: 'Many a little one knows what it is to start out, in holiday array, to pay a joyfully anticipated visit, only to find the days long and the nights terrible.'[31] As the century progressed, the expectation that children would feel homesick remained and strengthened, but the emotion also became increasingly associated with infancy and immaturity. In much of the public and academic discussion of homesickness, children became the *only* members of society for whom the feeling was acceptable, and, even among the young, homesickness was increasingly derided. These ideas emerged in children's literature and in the work of psychologists and doctors, who conducted research studies on homesickness and not only concluded that young people, and especially children, were peculiarly susceptible to the emotion, but that those who displayed a tendency to homesickness were also likely to be maladjusted in some way.

In 1902, a magazine ran a competition to find the 'best short juvenile story suited to children between eight and twelve'. The winning entry was 'When Nancy was Homesick', by Miss Lucie D.

Welsh of Hudson, Massachusetts. In the story, five-year-old Nancy leaves her family to join another as a 'bound girl', a custom whereby a wealthy couple took in the child of a poor household to help them around the house until she turned eighteen. Nancy was considered 'very fortunate' to have been offered such an opportunity, but, as she rode away with her new foster father, the stern and elderly Deacon Stowe, she felt forlorn. 'You are very small to leave your mother,' he said; 'do you think you'll be homesick?' Even in 1902, homesickness was already acquiring infantile associations. As a result, Nancy thought it best to avoid indulging in 'any such feeling', so she replied quietly, 'No, sir.' Living with the Stowes made for a very different life from the one Nancy was used to. She collected eggs, helped with housework, sewed patchwork and stockings, and braided straw. 'And with it all, Nancy carried a heavy heart, for she did so long to see her mother once more.' Finally, it got too much and she burst into tears. She sobbed to Mrs Stowe, telling her all about her homesickness and her desperate desire to see her mother again. Nancy was treated with kindness and taken back to visit home the very same day.[32]

Homesickness among children was seen as especially understandable under extreme and unusual circumstances. During the Second World War, thousands of British children were sent to Canada to escape German bombing. Articles about the evacuees in the Canadian press included advice for foster parents in case they encountered a homesick child. They were warned that 'a homesick child is not necessarily an endearing child.' Rather than looking 'wistful and far away' or 'huddling into a corner like a sick puppy' – which would naturally elicit sympathy and comfort – they usually displayed their sorrow with 'singularly unlovable behaviour'. The homesick child might 'jump off the porch into the petunias although he has been told a hundred times to be careful', he may 'bully the baby and tease the cat' and he may 'say no to all the things to which he should say yes'. But this bad behaviour should be treated with care and affection: 'He is protesting against the unhappiness that has crept upon him, and he is all the lonelier and more miserable because he is in the wrong with the entire household.'[33] The context of war and the extreme distances travelled by these unaccompanied children made homesickness something to be expected for these diminutive delinquents.

Compassion was especially important because homesickness, even among children, could have devastating, tragic consequences if not taken seriously. In 1938, Edward Praeger, a fifteen-year-old German Jewish refugee who had been sent to a boys' camp in upstate New York, died by suicide. The 'homesick youth', who had been barred from the games of other children by his inability to speak English, had quietly disappeared from the camp after the evening meal. He had, according to newspaper reports, been 'intensely unhappy' since his arrival. Despite the realities of life for Jewish people in 1930s Germany, he had written several letters to his parents begging them to come and collect him. But his father urged him to adapt himself to the new life as quickly as possible. As the days passed, Edward felt more and more like an outcast and he kept himself as much as possible to his room. The camp alerted the police the morning after his disappearance, and his body was found at dusk, in a thickly wooded hillside, less than a mile away. Edward's parents were too grief-stricken to speak to the reporters.[34]

By the 1940s and 1950s, homesickness had come to be understood as a typical part of the childhood and adolescent experience. In a 1943 essay by a North-Dakota-based professor of civil engineering and summer-camp counsellor, the author described a conversation he had had with a young boy. The professor asked if the boy had ever been sent away to summer camp. Without hesitation, the kid blurted, 'Ted has all the luck. I wanted to go there, but Mom said that I would get homesick the first night; that I had to grow up first.' Ted, his older brother, was a senior in high school and so deemed mature enough to cope with the distance. The professor acknowledged that most parents believe that seven- and eight-year-olds, like the little boy in question, are too young to be sent away to camp, because children are 'prone to homesickness'.[35] In 1955, the *British Medical Journal* reported, 'Adolescents are usually the victims, but it is common in children.'[36]

But, as homesickness became an increasingly common subject of children's literature, it was newly associated with younger, more pitiable and more feeble children, and the importance of stoicism, even in the very young, was, as the twentieth century continued, emphasized more and more. This was true in both America and Britain. Enid Blyton was an English children's writer whose books have been worldwide bestsellers since the 1930s. She is mostly remembered today for her Noddy, Famous Five, Secret Seven and Malory Towers series, and more recently for accusations of racism, xenophobia and sexism in her novels.[37] But her books also cemented a vision of homesickness that has proven remarkably enduring. Both the Malory Towers and the St Clare's series are set in all-girls' boarding schools and feature recurring storylines about homesickness. Invariably, the girls who cry from homesickness on the first night of term are bullied, dismissed, or marked out as wet and pathetic.

Psychological studies from the first half of the twentieth century increasingly made similar arguments to those implied by Blyton's fiction. From the 1920s onwards, psychologists began to think that fears and anxieties could be overcome by education and changes to behaviour. Children must learn to manage their emotions, including homesickness, and maturity was marked by the new-found ability to master their feelings.[38] Many psychologists, such as the American Edmund S. Conklin, started to advise parents to teach their children to overcome homesickness. Conklin argued that, while young people frequently became homesick, they should not be allowed to return home. Giving in to the pangs of homesickness not only would undermine the good work done by their ambitious adventuring, but subject them to shame and embarrassment. Echoing late-nineteenth-century advice on how to overcome nostalgia, he suggested that they should instead work hard, which would distract them from their feelings. Conklin advised parents to prepare children for their future departure, 'Through an early training in independence and self-reliance . . . through occasional absences from home at summer camps . . . [and] through a careful avoidance of that excess of petting and coddling which develops parental fixations.'[39]

In 1943, Willis H. McCann, a psychologist at the state hospital in St Joseph, Missouri, conducted a study of homesickness among college students.[40] He interviewed two hundred students: one hundred who were, or had recently been, homesick, and one hundred who had never been homesick while away from home. McCann defined homesickness as 'a longing for home of sufficient intensity to cause unhappiness', and provided a long list of symptoms: 'a strange hollow feeling in the pit of the stomach', 'a lump in the throat', 'a strange tightening inside', feeling 'blue' and lonely, feeling that everything has gone wrong and feeling that something terrible is about to happen back home.[41] McCann's study was pretty critical of the homesick cohort. They were much more likely to show signs of emotional instability, were much less self-sufficient, were more likely to be introverts, were more likely to 'substitute daydreaming for action' and they were more likely to feel insecure and inferior.

Even the North Dakotan civil-engineering professor and camp counsellor conducted his own mini-study on homesickness among the youth he encountered. While working at one junior camp for children aged six to twelve, he investigated the backgrounds of the homesick kids. Of the fifteen to twenty case histories he compiled, he failed to find a single one that did not show signs of 'serious maladjustments'. One little homesick boy, John, had a twin brother who had died of pneumonia at age four, and his mother had lavished all her grief and attention onto her remaining son, supposedly leaving him spoilt and overindulged.[42] In her 1927 master's dissertation in sociology, American Maria M. Tewater concluded that the teenager, Daisy, was homesick because she had been bottle-fed and subsequently neglected by her mother, who favoured her sister Mildred.[43] Another young boy, Denny, was prone to homesickness for quite the opposite reason: he was his mother's favourite, and she had failed to see him as 'a person with his own desires'.[44]

Views on homesickness have softened since, and the emotion is no longer understood in quite such deviant terms. But the feeling is still associated with young people: children, teenagers and university students. One study from 2010, published in the British Journal of Psychology, found that in the UK as many as 80 per cent of students missed friends and family, and found it difficult to adjust to university life.[45] Homesickness in this context has something in common with loneliness, isolation and alienation. It might mean feeling disconnected not only from the people you left behind, but from the people who now surround you. Sufferers might not feel as though they belong in their new environment, their new – albeit temporary – home. This psychological study claimed that homesickness was a kind of 'mini grief', a loss or bereavement. But it wasn't just a feeling about people, but about places too. Students yearn not just for their parents, siblings and friends, but for their house, their school, their neighbourhood and the city they left behind.

The treatment for homesickness, according to McCann in the 1940s, was quite simple: 'return home.'[46] And, for most of these children and young people, that was possible, at least temporarily. Little Nancy was eventually able to visit her mother, and she had not actually moved that far away. Children sent away to school and students at university came home for the holidays, and even evacuees eventually returned to bombed-out British cities. For the children who longed to return home from school, summer camps or domestic service, their emotions were relatively straightforward and relatively straightforward to resolve. Homesickness in these circumstances could be managed, even cured. But, for some people who left home – adults and children alike – a return would prove impossible, rendering their homesickness into something new, strange and much more intractable.

*

Homesickness was and remains a fundamental part of the immigrant and refugee experience. And it takes on a different inflection from the feeling that is supposed to be felt by children at summer camp or sequestered at boarding school. While the latter is still mostly seen as a restrictive emotion, a hallmark of childhood and immaturity, migrants' homesickness is an enormously powerful feeling. When interviewed by a journalist in 2020, psychotherapist Sarah Temple-Smith, who works for the UK's Refugee Council, called the loss of home for refugees an 'existential loss . . . if you've lost your home, you've lost *everything*.'[47] Homesickness can be acutely destabilizing and acutely motivating. One of the characteristics of diasporic communities now, according to one researcher, is a kind of nostalgic 'homing desire'. For some, this desire is unquenchable – the only solution is to return to whence they came. Today, the majority of immigrants to the United States of America return voluntarily. Even the undocumented do not wait to be deported; they leave of their own accord.[48] Many of them mention feeling homesick and missing their families as explicit reasons for not staying abroad for longer stretches of time, or not making their move more permanent.

But, rather than always just sending them back, homesickness among migrants can also propel them strangely forward. For the cultural theorist Stuart Hall, this longing transforms itself into a powerful creative force, 'a renewable source of desire, memory, myth, search, [and] discovery'. In other words, homesickness prompts migrants to fashion a new home.[49] While they might not be able to source mementos from their actual places of origin, they find things they associate with a romantic or sentimental image of home to populate their new lives. For American soldiers fighting in the Second World War, the humble Coca-Cola became an elixir that provided relief for the physical and emotional consequences of conflict abroad. The drink connected servicemen unconsciously with home. In soldiers' letters, Coke became a potent symbol of past civilian lives. 'The ole "Coke" sign', a serviceman wrote from Sicily, 'brings every soldier back to moments in his favourite drug store, where he sat and conversed with his friends'; while another soldier wrote that 'the shape of the bottle, the memory of the refreshing taste, brought to mind many happy memories.'[50]

Homesickness, then, like nostalgia, is a bittersweet feeling. But there are researchers today who insist that homesickness shares something else with nostalgia, or at least with the nostalgia of centuries past. There is evidence to suggest that homesickness is not merely an emotion, but an illness, one detrimental to both psychological and social well-being.[51] One study from 2012 found that homesickness had a powerfully negative effect on migrant workers, ranging from 'psychological disruptions' to 'physical manifestations' that impact work performance and affect the health and welfare of individuals. While in much of the literature on expatriate populations homesickness is linked to culture shock, some argue that the feeling has tangible physical, cognitive and behavioural symptoms. Sufferers complain of gastric and intestinal pains, lack of sleep, headache, exhaustion and disordered eating.[52]

Using language that might be familiar to an eighteenth- or nineteenth-century doctor, the displaced person develops 'obsessive thoughts about home and sometimes simultaneously negative thoughts about the new place'.[53] One psychologist identified a state of absent-mindedness among homesick people, as well as a tendency to idealize home rather than reckon with the problems they left behind. Behavioural symptoms include 'apathy, listlessness, lack of initiative and little interest in the new environment'.[54] The Mental Health Foundation reports that refugees in the UK are five times more likely to have mental-health needs than the general population.[55] Another study, in America, found Mexican immigrants had depression and anxiety levels 40 per cent higher than non-immigrants.[56] One researcher believes the explanation for these statistics lies in homesickness: 'From my perspective, you can't treat migrant stress without referring to home,' he explains.[57]

Today, in Britain, there is little empathy reserved for the home-sick migrant or refugee. Refugees are expected to want to return home. Leaving for a new life in new countries is supposed to be a last resort; if they suggest that perhaps safe countries in the West are preferable to their war-torn homes, then they are considered suspect, with this perhaps indicating that their reasons for leaving were not genuine. And yet, paradoxically, any sign of homesickness is seen as a suggestion of ingratitude, an indication that they do not fully appreciate the safe haven they have been offered. In his consideration of whether Britain should accept more Syrian refugees in 2014, a *Telegraph* journalist looked to Sweden, suggesting that a number of 'race riots' in the cities of Stockholm and Malmö were the result of migrants rejecting the Scandinavian nation's 'generosity' in allowing them entry.[58] Many refugees to Europe and North America have described the pressure they feel to perform gratitude to their host nation.[59] In some cases, the homesick migrant is seen as a failure – someone unable to adjust to new cultures and new customs.

The condition also remains a topic on the margins of psychology. As Hack-Polay says, 'People think homesickness is a normal thing. Therefore it's been relegated to a second-class condition.' Making homesickness sound like a pre-modern nostalgia repackaged for the twenty-first century, he explained, 'some people develop homesickness that goes into acute stress or depression, and some people have even taken their own lives.'[60] Hack-Polay argues that a better understanding of homesickness might help us better treat, and even prevent, refugee and migrant ill health. There is a tendency to treat other conditions – like PTSD, stress or depression – that have their origins in homesickness, rather than looking at the root cause. Homesickness is itself a condition, he insists, and it needs to be more recognizable and better managed.

1. Swiss physician Johannes Hofer coined the term 'nostalgia' in his 1688 dissertation.

2. Twentieth-century diagram of the four qualities, elements, humours and temperaments.

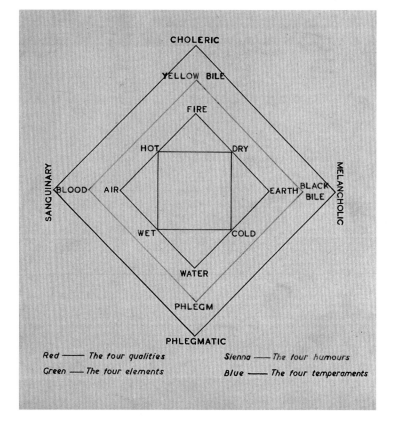

THE SOLDIERS DREAM OF HOME.

Stretched on the ground the war worn soldier sleeps.
Beside the lurid watch fire's fitful glare,
And dreams that on the field of Fame he reaps,
Renown and honors, which to battle's to share.

With those beloved ones who gathering come,
To bid their own dear husband, father welcome home
Fond dreamer, may thy blissful vision be
A true fore shadowing of the fates to thee.

5. This drawing of an Inuit village near Frobisher Bay, by an unknown artist, is based on sketches by the American explorer Charles Francis Hall and was published in 1865.

6. Engraving of a British soldier writing letters home from a foreign battlefield, circa 1880.

7. Boy 'putter' drawing a coal truck along a 24-inch-high seam in Halifax, Yorkshire, 1848. The northern English industrial town of Halifax was the birthplace of Arnold Ambler, who emigrated to the United States of America in 1920.

8. Entrance to the Berlin Zoo in 1930, where Julia Israel Schueler learnt her table manners from a resident chimpanzee.

9. Nandor Fodor, from *An Encyclopaedia of Psychic Science*, 1935.

12. An image plate from Charles Darwin's 1872 book,
The Expression of the Emotions in Man and Animals.

13. Brimfield Antique Flea Market in Massachusetts.

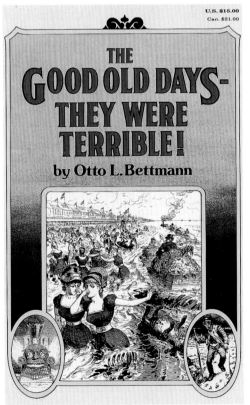

U.S. $15.00
Can. $21.00

THE
GOOD OLD DAYS—
THEY WERE
TERRIBLE!
by Otto L. Bettmann

14. In his book *The Good Old Days: They Were Terrible!*, Otto L. Bettmann rejected the nostalgia wave of the 1970s.

CHAPTER FOUR

THE PSYCHOLOGY OF NOSTALGIA

On 13 September 1848, twenty-five-year-old Phineas P. Gage was supervising a team blasting rock to make way for a new railway, just south of the village of Cavendish, Vermont. The russets and golds of early autumn foliage were beginning to spread their tendrils across the canopies of the dense forests and mountain foothills of the surrounding countryside. This was a newly thriving area of a relatively new republic. The first permanent European settlers arrived in Cavendish in 1769, naming the town after William Cavendish, the fourth Duke of Devonshire. Cavendish was a small, sleepy town and, for the first half of the nineteenth century, most of the events of note involved a minor rivalry between the settlement's two warring families, a conflict only resolved by the marriage of Redfield Proctor and Emily Dutton in 1858. Home to pretty gabled houses, a main street and a handsome, if unassuming, post office, this was a town where mostly nothing happened. When the Soviet dissident and Nobel laureate in literature Aleksandr Solzhenitsyn made Cavendish his home in 1976, he said, 'It didn't happen by chance. I chose this place. I dislike very much large cities with their empty and fussy lives. I like very much the simple way of life and the population here . . . I like the countryside, and I like the climate with the long winter and the snow, which reminds me of Russia.'[1]

On this ordinary September day in this quiet rural town, Phineas P. Gage was doing as he had always done, working on a railway line.

Gage was the oldest of five children born to Jesse Eaton Gage and Hannah Trussell in the neighbouring New England state of New Hampshire. While little is known about his upbringing or background, the events of that September day were to make him a minor celebrity and something of a scientific marvel. Blasting rock required workers to bore a hole deep into an outcrop, adding blasting powder and a fuse, and then using a tamping iron to pack, or 'tamp', sand, clay or another inert material into the hole to contain the blast's energy and direct it into the surrounding rock. At around 4.30 p.m., one of the tamping irons – a metal rod, around a metre long and three centimetres in diameter – sparked against a rock, ricocheted, and fired itself into the left side of Gage's face. The iron travelled upwards, fracturing his cheekbone, passing behind his left eye and through the left side of his brain, before exiting the top of his skull and landing point-first twenty-five metres away, 'smeared with blood and brain'.[2]

Gage was thrown backwards by the force of impact, but, despite a few convulsions, he remained conscious and spoke just a few moments later. He walked with only minimal assistance and sat upright in an ox cart for the ride back to his lodgings in town. About half an hour after the accident, local physician Edward H. Williams found Gage sitting in a chair outside the hotel, regaling passers-by with tales of his ordeal. He turned to the oncoming doctor and uttered one of the great understatements of medical history: 'Here is business enough for you.' Williams inspected the wound and observed the 'pulsations' of the exposed brain. When Gage went to stand, he doubled over, vomiting. The effort of the evacuation 'pressed out about half a teacupful of the brain . . . which fell upon the floor.'[3]

Despite a protracted and uneven convalescence, Gage miraculously survived. His defiance of medical odds, and the strange effects of his injury, made him into a fixture on the curricula of neurology, psychology and neuroscience, one of 'the great medical curiosities of all time',[4] and 'a living part of the medical folklore'.[5] Gage's survival alone would have ensured anyone a measure of local celebrity, but his lasting fame was due to the observations of John Martyn

Harlow, the doctor who treated him for a few months after the accident. Gage's friends noticed stark differences in the man's personality and his ability to communicate and understand emotions. The balance between his 'intellectual faculties and animal propensities' seemed altered: he could no longer stick to plans, uttered 'the grossest profanity' and showed 'little deference for his fellows'.[6] Today, frontal-lobe injuries can result in a range of behavioural changes, compromised decision-making, diminished self-control, unregulated emotions, a lack of inhibition, and compulsive or risky behaviour. Gage was supposedly so altered that he was 'no longer Gage', the man his friends and colleagues had known for some time, and, while he had been a model foreman, the railroad construction company that had employed him refused to take him back.

In November of 1849, Henry Jacob Bigelow, the professor of surgery at Harvard Medical School, brought Gage to Boston for several weeks and presented him to a meeting of the Boston Society for Medical Improvement. Otherwise unemployed, Gage became a living exhibit at Barnum's American Museum in New York City. Barnum's was part of a whole cohort of new museums of miscellany that popped up across Europe and the Americas in the nineteenth century. These cabinets of curiosity showcased sensational examples of science alongside quasi-mythic oddities. Rising showman P. T. Barnum had received the mysterious 'Feejee Mermaid' in 1842, making his museum one of the busiest commercial spaces in the nation's largest city.[7] Gage lived the rest of his short life as something of a medical oddity. To escape the scrutiny of the American public and the medical profession, he travelled to Chile, where he drove coaches, before joining his relatives in San Francisco. He died there in May 1860, aged just thirty-six, after a series of seizures.[8]

Gage's story is strange, but in its own way provides a perfect snapshot of nineteenth-century science and society. His life experiences and profession made him very much a man of his time. Gage was a railway worker, part of a whole army of labourers who eased the passage of the new steam engines and, along with the men who laid telegraph cables across the ocean floor of the Atlantic, contracted Victorian time and space. And his miraculous survival and his doctors' fascination with his altered mental and emotional state represented a new scientific interest in the workings of the human brain, personality and feelings. Indeed, his accident occurred at just the moment doctors were gaining in self-confidence and expanding their knowledge of the human body, its functions and dysfunctions. Science as a method for better understanding the world was also becoming increasingly robust, and more and more people were believing in its ability not just to explain things, but to change society for the better. New and altered professionals – scientists, physicians, industrialists – were transforming anatomical understandings and revolutionizing the technologies of manufacturing, travel and communication. By 1848, the year of Gage's accident, steam-powered passenger ships had been setting sail (they still carried sails) for just ten years, and the use of chloroform as an anaesthetic during surgery was only a year old.

Even the term 'scientist' was new to the English language. The Lancashire polymath William Whewell coined the term in 1834. He pondered what collective noun should be used to 'designate the students of the knowledge of the material world'. 'Philosopher' was too wide and 'too lofty', and 'savant' far too assuming. Instead, by analogy to 'artist', he proposed 'scientist': 'We might say, that as an Artist is a Musician, Painter, or Poet, a Scientist is a Mathematician, Physicist, or Naturalist.'[9] Soon, developments in microscopes would allow these new 'scientists' access to a world invisible to the naked eye, and this world was teeming with previously unseen bacteria and parasites. There were new theories of evolution, a new periodic table of the elements, new medications were invented and even new vaccines. As more people were convinced by the potential and promises of science, scientists became increasingly self-confident and expanded their repertoire. This intellectual land-grab transformed all sorts of things that had previously been the preserve of philosophers and religious thinkers into objects of scientific study. One of these things was emotion.

Gage's accident, his survival and his altered personality provided evidence for a new set of theories about the human mind and the functioning of personality. Since the mid seventeenth century, anatomists had conceptualized the brain as a machine — something that could be investigated by breaking it down to its constituent parts and seeing what they do. In the late eighteenth century, electricity had arrived on the social and scientific scene, and natural philosophers thought that perhaps the brain was full of 'electric fluid' and ran much like one of those new-fangled batteries.[10] By the mid nineteenth century, when Gage ejected half a teacupful of brain matter from the top of his head, nerves were being compared to telegraph wires, and the brain to a complex electrical communication system.[11]

Around the same time, the now-discredited science of phrenology produced detailed maps of how certain mental capacities and attributes could be found in different parts of the brain. Phrenologists were particularly captivated by Gage's case and his altered personality, as it seemed to evidence their idea that specific brain regions were important for specific functions. As the century progressed, an increasing number of scientists, anatomists, philosophers and physiologists entertained a variety of new theories about the brain. Many of these studies focused on the brain's material structure; its anatomy, chemistry and physiology. In the 1860s, physician Paul Broca (also an anthropologist and proponent of scientific racism) showed that certain parts of the brain were responsible for different components of speech. And, in the early 1900s, Spanish neuroscientist Santiago Ramón y Cajal discovered the precise physical structure of brain cells.

However, right from the very beginning of the nineteenth century — and running parallel to the investigations of phrenologists, Broca, and Cajal — physicians and philosophers were also interested in another aspect of the human mind and the way we think and feel. Originally defined as a kind of agitation, an excited mental state, it was only in the early 1800s that 'emotion' acquired today's meaning of a strong mental or instinctive feeling such as pleasure, grief, hope or fear.

The first expression of this new definition was in the work of poet, physician and philosopher Thomas Brown. Brown was the youngest in a family of thirteen children born to a clergyman and his wife.[12] He was earnest, endearing and something of an eccentric. He never married or had any children, but instead devoted his life to hard intellectual labour, including a decade as professor of moral philosophy at the University of Edinburgh, from 1810 to 1820. Brown's work on human feelings was published in the 1830s, but it took some time for the term 'emotion' to become widely accepted. Even as late as 1862, Whewell preferred to use the compound phrase, 'the desires and affections', despite acknowledging that 'emotional' had been adopted by some recent writers.[13] Words are both 'mirrors and motors' of historical change, and the invention of a new term signalled a new way of thinking about feelings.[14] Brown drew a sharp distinction between ideas and emotions. Emotions, or 'vivid feelings', might arise from mental 'consideration' of people and things, but they were not thoughts.[15] Instead, the expression and experience of emotion required a combination of both body and mind, and they sat somewhere between the senses and the intellect.

At around the same time that Brown was lecturing at the University of Edinburgh, the surgeon Charles Bell was conducting his own experiments with human feelings. Born in 1774, Bell was something of a marvel. A surgeon, anatomist, physiologist, neurologist, artist and philosopher, Bell identified new sicknesses, established new hospitals and spent time attending to and painting the wounded of Waterloo. His troubling and traumatic experiences of the war dead, combined with his understanding of the body, made him an expert in the emotions. He believed that mental changes or observations – such as grief, joy or astonishment – could become visible through 'outward signs' on the face or figure.[16] He placed great importance on bodily movements, especially of the heart and lungs, not only as observable evidence, but as the things that made feelings into emotions.

Bell's focus on the biological and physiological aspects of emotions was hugely influential on another early-nineteenth-century inhabitant of Scotland. Charles Darwin, who studied medicine at Edinburgh before becoming a naturalist, arrived at a similar view of the indispensable role of the body in emotions. Once he felt confident enough in his theories of evolution by natural selection to publish them in

1859, Darwin turned his attention to the emotions. He corresponded with the French doctor Guillaume-Benjamin-Amand Duchenne, who believed that human faces expressed at least sixty discrete emotions, each depending on their own dedicated group of facial muscles. Duchenne studied emotions by applying electrical currents to the heads of his subjects, sending their features into a state of continual contraction. By stimulating the right combination of facial muscles, Duchenne mimicked genuine emotional expression. He produced almost a hundred photographic plates of his subjects demonstrating what he believed were distinct emotions. In 1872, Darwin published one of his less famous books, *The Expression of the Emotions in Man and Animals*, in which he argued that all humans, and even all other animals, show emotion through remarkably similar behaviours.[17] For Darwin, emotions – like human beings – had an evolutionary history that could be traced across cultures and species.

Darwin, Charles Bell and William Whewell had a profound effect on another thinker about feelings. In 1884, the American philosopher William James wrote an article for the magazine *Mind* entitled, 'What is an Emotion?'[18] James was captivated by the emotions, but, despite the labours of his predecessors, he still wasn't quite sure what they were. Why do we run from a bear? Do we run because we are afraid, or are we afraid because we run? Were emotions a bodily thing? Elevated blood pressure in response to external stressors, for example? Were they something intellectual – a process of mind? And what was the relationship between the two? Did a physiological event make us think and then feel certain things? Or was it the other way around? Did anxious thoughts, for example, speed up our hearts and make our palms sweat? Or did a rush of hormones trigger feelings of love and affection? And did we all feel the same thing? Was one person's jealousy, boredom, apprehension, vexation, frustration, joy or fear the same as another's?

These men all thought about emotions in a similar way. They all thought that they were normal, natural things we all felt. Even if they hadn't quite settled on the precise mechanism or process by which external stimuli prompted feelings of fear, joy or apprehension, they agreed that they were physiological – something automatic, unconscious, that took place in our bodies. Emotions were, especially after Darwin, an evolutionary phenomenon. They helped us survive, thrive and communicate, and we had developed increasingly complex ways to feel in response to our increasingly complex lives.

Quite soon after James wrote his article for *Mind*, a new brand of scientist – the psychologist – started to apply this way of thinking about emotions to nostalgia. In 1898, a little-known American, Linus Ward Kline, received his Ph.D. from Clark University in Massachusetts. His doctoral thesis was entitled 'The Migratory Impulse vs. Love of Home'. [19] While thoughts about feelings had changed over the course of the nineteenth century, nostalgia was still very much akin to homesickness, and, as a result, Kline labelled the feelings of longing, regret and 'love of home' that he encountered in his study, 'nostalgia'. He took a quantitative, statistical approach, exploring the feeling as a function of age, gender and context, and his thesis contains lengthy, and sometimes moving, descriptions of the people he studied.

Kline presented some 'typical cases of nostalgia', taken from observations and interviews with 176 people. One boy went to stay overnight with a friendly family, just a few roads away from where he lived with his parents. He became so nostalgic that he had to be carried home in the middle of the night. An eighteen-year-old woman reflected on her first few weeks spent at boarding school: 'I felt dazed and for a long time I could not realize why I was where I was.' Another adolescent girl detailed her feelings of nostalgia as 'an indescribable longing. I seemed sick all inside myself and all choked up.' A thirty-year-old woman described experiencing a 'smothering sensation': 'everything seems closing in on me.' [20]

Kline concluded from these cases that young people, and especially children, were peculiarly susceptible to the emotion. He thought that nostalgia was a reaction to a loss of the familiar, the presence of the new or strange, or a response to a significant lifestyle change. Most of the people he studied reported feeling nostalgic, or homesick, when they first left home to go to school or college, or entered the army or navy. Kline likened nostalgia to seasickness, with the nostalgic having 'lost his psychical orientation', much as someone suffering from seasickness loses the sense of balance they have on dry land. He was sympathetic, to an extent, but also criticized people with nostalgic tendencies, or who took the feeling to the extreme. While most of his cases were 'sociable' and 'affectionate', they were also 'nervous', disliked crowds, were 'difficult to entertain' and had 'odd or provincial' interests.

However, of the 176 people Kline studied, just 6 per cent claimed never to have experienced nostalgia. He concluded, therefore, that the emotion was a standard, almost universal feeling, and not an aberration or sickness. He believed that nostalgia – like other emotions – was inherited and instinctual, a normal and universal pattern of thought and behaviour. While a few people might feel it acutely, pretty much everyone had experienced the sensations of longing, homesickness and bittersweet recollection that character-ized his version of nostalgia. Kline was inspired by Darwin, and argued that 'psychical evolution' ran parallel to 'the evolution of organic life'. Just like sexual attraction, fear and anxiety, nostalgia had evolved to serve certain functions. For Kline, everyone felt nostalgic at some point or another.

Just because nostalgia was normal – ubiquitous, even – did not mean it could no longer cause harm, and it did not mean that all manifestations of the feeling were equally benign. In the late nine-teenth century, German-American philosopher Paul Carus wrote an article for the journal he edited, *The Monist*. He described the blurred boundary between healthy and unhealthy feelings, between interest and obsession. He drew comparisons between religious fanaticism and the preoccupied nostalgic who could think only of 'his country and home'. He argued that 'disorder' was caused by the 'undue prominence of one emotion which thus dominates the whole economy of a man's psychic life'.[21] In other words, too much of any emotion, however common or seemingly benign, could prove psychologically problematic.

As we know, nostalgia had long had something of a bad reputation. In earlier periods, it was a deadly disease and, while it might have lost some of its killing capacity, in excess it could still cause psycho-logical (if not physical) harm. As Kline pointed out, people with nostalgic inclinations tended to have some pretty serious character flaws. As the new century dawned, this reputation hardened. People – and particularly a new brand of psychologists, the psychoanalysts – looked at nostalgia through a new lens and understood it according to a new set of anxieties and cultural identities.

Psychoanalysis was established in the early 1890s as a means of treating mental disorders. Its proponents suggest that a person's development is determined by often forgotten events in early child-hood, that human behaviours are determined by instinctual drives that are rooted in the unconscious, and that conflicts between conscious and unconscious thought can result in mental disturbances such as neurosis, anxiety and depression. Over the course of the past hundred years or so, some of the discipline's notions have been translated into pop psychology. Many people have at least a vague grasp of penis envy and the Oedipus complex, even if they don't necessarily subscribe to psychoanalytic theories or undergo psycho-analytic therapy. Many of us are probably also familiar with repression – the idea that people block out or bury distressing memories, thoughts or feelings, leaving them to fester somewhere in their unconscious, resulting in misery, isolation and, ultimately, a crisis.

Just two decades after psychoanalysis emerged onto the scene, the First World War started. The mass destruction destabilized the nineteenth century's optimism and self-satisfaction. The war upended people's assumptions about the inevitability of progress, and, in the aftermath, some responded by looking ahead to utopian futures, while others attempted to find shelter in the fairy stories and folk-tales of their youth. The interwar years thus cleaved into factions. There were those obsessed with the past, both ancient and recent, who sought to resurrect ghosts and ghost beliefs. Others, including the psychoanalysts, dismissed these people as foolish and deluded.

Somehow, in the minds of these psychoanalysts, nostalgics became tangled up with the ghost hunters and believers in fairies. Those susceptible to the emotion came to represent exactly the sort of people the scientifically minded analysts disliked. And this animosity only increased after the Second World War, when fascism and forced migration gave a new edge to the way people felt about their homelands and the recent past. Nostalgics were now particularly suspect, and tendencies towards the emotion became a troubling sign of the person's intellectual capacity, their position on the political spectrum, their place in the social hierarchy and their inability to keep pace with an ever-changing world.

*

In the autumn of 1938, Nandor Fodor sent his wife Amarya to the Hampstead home of the exiled psychoanalyst Sigmund Freud. Brandishing a bunch of tiger lilies, she charmed her way into the house and, over tea, proceeded to tell Freud all about her husband and his theories of psychology and the paranormal.[22] Freud had only very recently arrived in north London, having fled Vienna after the Nazis annexed Austria earlier that year. In the centre of his study, where Amarya was invited to sit, stood Freud's famous psychoanalytic couch, where his patients reclined before divulging their thoughts and feelings. Originally a gift from a patient, Madame Benvenisti, in around 1890, Freud covered the plain wooden frame with embroidered cushions and a richly detailed Qashqa'i carpet. When he left Vienna, the couch came too, and its luxuriant presence helped recreate the atmosphere of the city he had left behind. One of Freud's patients, Sergei Pankejeff, initially given the case name Wolfman to (unsuccessfully) protect his identity, described the house in Hampstead as a place of 'sacred peace and quiet'. The rooms were nothing like a doctor's office, but gave the feeling of an 'archaeologist's study', and everything contributed to the feeling of 'leaving the haste of modern life behind, of being sheltered from one's daily cares'.[23]

An almost-fanatical fan of Freud, Fodor was an author, journalist, ghost hunter and a fellow psychoanalyst. He was also a Jewish émigré, although he came from Hungary rather than Austria. Born in the late nineteenth century, Fodor studied law in Budapest before moving, in 1921, to New York to work as a writer.[24] In 1929, he arrived in Britain and threw himself into the 1930s supernatural scene. He joined the Ghost Club and the London Spiritualist Alliance, befriended members of the Faery Investigation Society and contributed articles to the spiritualist weekly, *Light*. These various organizations were mainly preoccupied with researching and, to some extent, proving the existence of ghosts and other paranormal beings. They investigated sightings and hauntings, counted some of the day's finest minds as their members, and a few of them still exist today. Fodor eventually returned to New York and became a United States citizen. With Amarya – who became a sculptor – and their daughter, he lived on the Upper East Side of Manhattan, next to Central Park.[25]

Indulging the first of his two main preoccupations, and while his wife was busy ambushing Freud, Fodor travelled to the Isle of Man to investigate a poltergeist named Gef.[26] Also known as the Dalby Spook, he lived in Doarlish Cashen, a bleak Manx farmstead, 'as isolated and promising as any spook hunter could wish for'.[27] Doarlish Cashen was also home to the Irving family – James, his wife Margaret and their thirteen-year-old daughter Voirrey. In September 1931, all three members of the family heard rustling and scratching from behind the farmhouse's wooden walls. The noises gradually became increasingly comprehensible and, before long, something that looked a bit like a ferret, or perhaps a small dog, announced himself as Gef, a mongoose born in New Delhi, India, almost a century ago, in 1852. Gef had yellowish fur and a large, luxuriant tail. Gef was not just any mongoose. He had not only far outlived the average mongoose lifespan, but was also a self-described 'extra extra clever mongoose', an 'Earthbound spirit', a ghost.[28] According to the Irvings, this spectral visitor made himself useful. He guarded their home and informed them of approaching strangers or guests. If any of the farm's human inhabitants left the fire unattended overnight, Gef would ensure the stove was snuffed out. He was a reliable alarm clock, and regularly assumed the role of the cat, keeping the house pest-free. Gef had expensive tastes. He enjoyed biscuits, chocolates and bananas – a rare luxury, at the time. He was talkative, sometimes incessantly so, but generally remained a benign member of the family.

The story of Gef enraptured the British tabloid press, and journalists flocked to the Isle of Man to try and catch a glimpse of this home-grown example of crypto-zoology. His fame spread far and wide, and the Irvings' elusive housemate appeared in newspapers and magazines from Toronto to Hong Kong.[29] In July 1935, Richard S. Lambert, who was the editor of *The Listener*, and his friend, the famous paranormal investigator Harry Price, visited the Isle of Man to appraise the case.[30] Price had gained public prominence for his investigations into psychical phenomena, his debunking of supposed hauntings, and for exposing fraudulent spiritualist mediums. Fodor arrived hot on Harry Price's heels and spent a week at Doarlish Cashen, hoping to catch sight of the spectre. Ghost hunting had recently become a popular pursuit of bored aristocrats, opportunistic journalists and serious psychical researchers alike, and the interwar years teemed with soothsayers, mediums and people who really, truly believed in fairies. Following the trauma and desolation of the First World War, the dead acquired new significance, and both spirit-ualism and the study of the paranormal exploded in popularity. More than 2,000 people attended Stella Hughes's séance in the Queen's Hall, off Oxford Street, in March 1938.[31] The dead were now a form of mass entertainment, and the medium Helen Duncan became famous and then infamous for producing ectoplasm and conjuring spectral assistants. In 1944, she would be the last and only person charged and convicted under the 1735 Witchcraft Act.[32]

Of course, some of these spirits weren't all that they seemed and there were plenty of inauthentic mediums, fraudulent soothsayers and suspect ghost-sightings. The most famous example of trickery was the case of the Cottingley Fairies. In 1917, Elsie Wright and Frances Griffiths, two young cousins living in Bradford, Yorkshire, took a series of five photographs that claimed to show images of garden fairies. Three years later, the pictures came to the attention of Sir Arthur Conan Doyle (of Sherlock Holmes fame), who used them to illustrate an article on fairies he had been commissioned to write.[33] The girls maintained that the photographs were real, and it was not until the 1980s that Elsie and Frances admitted that they were staged using cardboard cut-outs of fairies clipped from the illustrations of a popular children's book of the time.

With ghosts, goblins and sprites came enthusiasts, true believers and sceptics. Nandor Fodor did not believe in ghosts. Instead, he was interested in the intersection between the paranormal and the disturbed mind, and thought that poltergeists were embodiments of emotional disorders.[34] Drawing on his experiences with Gef, Fodor pioneered the now-popular theory that poltergeists are not disembodied spirits, but manifestations of conflicts within the subconscious. The workings of the human body and brain were as mysterious as the afterlife or spirit world, if not more so, and many researchers thought that things like ghosts and telepathy could be explained by some as yet unknown psychological or biological function.

Like other psychoanalysts, Fodor placed great stock in memories, childhood and adolescence. He thought it important that it was Voirrey, the Irvings' teenage daughter, who had first heard Gef speak. The mongoose was, he believed, the imaginings of a troubled adolescent girl. 'In some as yet unknown manner, a part of you may refuse to be confined within your body,' he explained in a later magazine article; 'it may perform your unconscious desires even though you think you have nothing to do with it. When this happens, you have a Poltergeist.' He diagnosed Gef as a symptom of a kind of mental illness: 'Usually it occurs in adolescence, but sometimes it takes place in mentally disturbed adults as well.'[35] By applying the tools of psychoanalysis to the problem of the paranormal, Fodor diagnosed the gullible with emotional disorders: 'You can be sure that where Poltergeists are on the rampage, somebody is sick.'[36]

Psychoanalysts developed a set of theories around emotions that are perhaps less well known than their other theories. Feelings, according to psychoanalysis, served a crucial social function; they held groups, families and communities together. But they could tear them apart, too. In Freud's earlier writings, emotions were generally seen as a cause of mental disorders, and they were what happened when an automatic or instinctual response was blocked or impeded. He called ineffective emotional discharges 'abreactions', and he thought they resulted from traumatic events in a person's life. Echoing the much earlier writings of Paul Carus, Freud suggested that emotions happened when an individual failed to cope with some troublesome encounter or experience – they were problems, deviances, things to resolve, and they could be the cause of hysterical or obsessional symptoms. And any kind of chronic or extended emotional state was particularly suspect.

In the ten or so years following his encounter with Gef, and his wife's meeting with Freud, Fodor clarified his own ideas about psychoanalysis, the paranormal and the emotions. He shared Freud's ideas about feelings and, partly because of his own life experiences, developed a particular interest in nostalgia. He thought that the emotion and poltergeists had much in common. Both were most frequently found in or identified by children and adolescents, both were responses to abrupt changes in lifestyle or place, and both were a kind of mental disturbance. When left untreated, too much nostalgia could develop into a monomaniacal, compulsive mental state that would cause the sufferer intense misery and prolonged distress.

Fodor eventually compiled his thinking about nostalgia into a book, *The Search for the Beloved*, published in 1949, and later into an essay entitled 'Varieties of Nostalgia', published in January 1950.[37] The ideas he put forward were eclectic and sometimes baffling; they were grounded not only in Freudian psychoanalysis, but in his experiences as a Jewish émigré writing in the years immediately following the Second World War. At a time of deep collective despair mixed with cautious optimism, Fodor reflected on the failed Utopias of the recent past. From Atarashiki Mura in Japan to Dartington Hall in England, early-twentieth-century people had left their jobs, homes, friends and families to reimagine what society could look like.[38] For Fodor, the genocides of the Second World War, and the mass destruction wrought by the great powers, rendered these efforts not just futile, but foolish. He was sceptical of these efforts and accused their proponents of languishing in a fictitious fairyland, one where all strife ceases and life rolls by smoothly in a state of perpetual perfection and bliss. Fodor fundamentally mistrusted any attempt to escape reality. And he saw utopianism and nostalgia as two points on the same spectrum. He compared collective nostalgia to classic literary Utopias, including Butler's Erewhon and James Hilton's Shangri La. Like the advocates for these speculative societies, nostalgia transformed homes and 'mother countries' into make-believe lands, where people could retreat from the uncomfortable reality of their day-to-day lives.

Both utopians and nostalgics believed in perfect places, or so Fodor thought. But, while utopians were trying to build something ideal for the future, nostalgics were attempting to return to something that already existed. This something, or somewhere, might be an actual, real place – like a person's childhood home, their place of birth or their nation of origin – but it also, according to Fodor, could be somewhere a bit harder to re-enter. While Kline explained nostalgia as a relatively straightforward response to a change in circumstance, or change in location, Fodor thought the feeling was the manifestation of a latent desire to return to the womb. Fodor put a lot of things down to this supposed urge and he was an influential thinker in the nascent field of prenatal psychology.[39] He believed that a pregnant mother could communicate telepathically with the mind and body of her unborn child. The mother, he thought, could impact the physical and psychological development of the foetus, depending on her state of mind. Anyone's emotional well-being, security and satisfaction was, therefore, profoundly influenced by their uterine experience, and Fodor believed that people, provided they underwent sufficient psychoanalysis, could recall that experience and use therapy to resolve any lasting negative consequences.

Nostalgia was one such negative consequence. But Fodor also believed that a whole range of personality quirks or behavioural oddities could be explained by these latent memories of life before birth. In fact, pretty much anything could be rationalized with his theories of prenatal psychology. Fodor suggested that those who curled up in bed and slept with their arms folded across their chests were unconsciously mimicking the position of the foetus within the womb. Anyone with 'water fantasies' had been similarly seduced by embryonic illusions. If you spend too much time in the bath, or are happy to while away many hours a day swimming under the water in warm seas, watching the wonders of marine life or the sunshine above, then you too dream of a life before birth.[40] These prenatal impressions were also to blame for those with a 'morbid love' of hothouses and an obsessive interest in 'things growing in flower pots'.[41] Babies in utero are, according to Fodor, tropical creatures, and the coldness of the postnatal world so shocks some of us that we spend the rest of our lives dreaming of damp warmth. Who would have thought that a predilection for house plants, sea swimming and hot holidays was a sign of profound mental disturbance?

Fodor even put the appeal and success of Edgar Rice Burroughs' hugely successful Tarzan novels down to a latent desire to return to the uterus.[42] The jungle, or so he thought, was a place of darkness and mystery, and had, strangely, much in common with the womb. His theory could explain everything from a liking for spy novels and cheap mysteries to submarine research, to the lure of faraway lands, to a passion for solitude or far-Right politics, to an interest in the Ten Commandments and even to Thomas Mann's *The Magic Mountain*.[43] Memories of a time and place before birth (and, by extension, nostalgia) were behind it all. Even the experience of déjà vu – that strange familiarity which unexpected landscapes sometimes inspire – could be explained by memories of our mother's womb. Anyone who fantasized about leaving behind the trials and tribulations of modern life was under the spell that prenatal security and happiness had cast over their unconscious imagination.

Echoing the infantilization of homesickness that was taking place in parallel, nostalgia was increasingly seen as a form of regression. It was, for Fodor, a deep-seated, almost primal desire to return to a person's place of origin (the womb was, after all, the original 'home'). He thus had little patience for the immature nostalgics he interviewed on his therapist's couch, thinking them self-centred people who disliked 'making efforts' for others. He accused chronic nostalgics of being neurotic – people who retreated to bed at any sign of stress or conflict. And, while he conceded that home and the nuclear family were the fundamental units of society, he also thought that they were a medium of escape for those unwilling or unable to face reality. All too often, nostalgics 'closet themselves in their home and deny admittance to others'.[44] Like that of the foetus, their happiness depended on complete isolation.

This damning representation of nostalgia and the people susceptible to it spread across the post-war psychoanalytic community, with theorists from Beirut to Boston obsessing over the emotion and its implications for modern society. Irish analyst Alexander R. Martin thought that nostalgia was the instinct we humans have in common with homing pigeons. He called it a surrender to a 'biological and rhythmic tendency' to return to the past, to childhood, to sleep and to the unconscious.[45] Nostalgia alone could be managed, provided it was moderate. But there was a more extreme, and troubling, version. 'Nostomania' and its counterpart 'nostophobia' were characterized by 'compulsive movements toward and against the home and whatever home means, literally and figuratively'.[46]

In an article published in 1950, Martin described one of his nostalgic cases. The woman had suffered from very severe homesickness during her late teens – so much so that she had been taken out of her boarding school by her concerned parents. In her late twenties, she became more and more withdrawn, refused to leave the family and had severe depression. She underwent shock therapy and intensive psychotherapy for years. By the time she had come to see Martin, she was in her early forties, 'a very passive person, self-effacing . . . dull, lethargic'. She started analysis and, talking about clothes one day, she said, 'I can't part with those dresses. They have a nostalgic feeling. What am I holding onto? I should get rid of the debris that is holding me back.'

When asked more about the nostalgic feeling, she replied, 'In a sense, it is an inability to look facts in the eye – wishful ideas – some day I'll be slim enough to wear it again, yet I know it is ridiculous. I bought that dress in my early twenties. I could not bear to part with it.'[47] Martin identified her problem – she had never effectively broken away from her mother: 'the relationship between her mother and herself remained unchanged, that she was still a little girl.'[48] This woman confirmed Fodor's theories. According to him and other psychoanalysts, nostalgics were regressive – unable to grow up and face the world. Lebanese theorist Dominique Geahchan interpreted nostalgia specifically as a person's subconscious obsession with their mother and an idealized vision of their childhood. According to his analysis, if nostalgics were obsessed with their own gestation and growth, then they were by extension obsessed with themselves. This fanaticism could prompt a kind of self-involved, narcissistic madness.

The way psychoanalysts thought about nostalgia reflected widespread cultural anxieties. Fodor was concerned the emotion was an affliction that could infect entire countries. He worried that, if this form of neurosis spread through nations, then the womb and the home might be replaced by the 'mother country', and political nostalgics would fight tenaciously to keep themselves away from the rest of the world, politically and culturally isolated, in a kind of fraught seclusion. This concern had obvious connections to his identity and personal background. Fodor had left Hungary, his place of birth, in his early twenties and showed little desire to return. He lived in Britain and the United States for his entire adult life, married an Englishwoman and had a daughter in Manhattan. He was, he wrote, prompted to investigate nostalgia by a nagging question, one he was personally unable to answer: 'Why does an old country, often of wretched and beggarly existence, become a fairy land to victims of nostalgia?'[49] It does not take a huge leap of imagination to think that perhaps Hungary was one of the old countries in question.

Indeed, Fodor, a man who had travelled widely and made his home far from his place of birth, was not inclined to look fondly on excessive patriotism or political isolationism. Like many of those who lived through the Second World War, he had witnessed the horrifying consequences of overly myopic nationalism – a sentiment he partially blamed on nostalgic tendencies among people who had never quite managed to wrest themselves from the fantasies of youth and the family. Fascism, for him, was an unintended consequence of societies that were resistant to change. Such societies were more preoccupied with the supposed sanctity of the domestic dwelling, the allure of the unchanging homeland and the potentially damaging effects of modern life, whereas Fodor celebrated places and people that were excited about the possibilities of the future (as long as it was a realistic one) and international cooperation. His assessment of nostalgia was as much driven by a dislike of provincial backwaters (as he saw it) as it was by a commitment to an imagined ideal of cosmopolitanism.

That Fodor and his fellow psychoanalysts rejected people predisposed to nostalgia isn't all that surprising. They were all part of roughly the same social milieu and were mostly self-consciously progress-focused, urban dwelling, well educated and mistrustful of individual and national isolationism. They also often held quite disparaging views about ordinary or working-class people, particularly those who lived in the countryside or in small towns. In 1965, psychoanalysts Mike M. Nawas and Jeremy J. Platt argued that the middle classes, whose education supposedly emphasized the importance of technology and progress, were less likely than 'lower-class' or 'tradition-bound' people to become nostalgic.[50] For Nawas and Platt, nostalgics were unable to adapt to modern times and new trends, forcing them into an unnatural and harmful psychological state. Having avoided becoming victims of nostalgia themselves, many psychoanalysts thought that those more susceptible were not just unlucky, but somehow defective, mentally regressive, compulsive and neurotic.

Nandor Fodor died of a heart attack in 1964. A Masonic funeral service was held in his honour and an obituary was published in *The New York Times*.[51] His death marked the beginning of the end of an era in nostalgia thinking. The idea that we all carry unconscious memories of our time in utero and that these memories prompt an eclectic range of cultural preferences, behaviours and feelings is almost as unfathomable to the twenty-first-century mind as the early modern notion that nostalgia was a disease that could kill. While admittedly bizarre, Fodor's theories nonetheless reflected a very particular, and very anxious, wartime and then immediate post-war moment. These theories did not, however, last very long. Nostalgia is a malleable emotion, one that is incredibly susceptible to the changing world it inhabits. While all emotions have changed over time, bending to the cultural norms, social mores and language of different ages and places, since the 1960s, nostalgia has undergone a particularly dramatic transformation. With Fodor's passing, a much more moderate way of thinking about the emotion re-emerged into the limelight and captured the imagination of the seventies and eighties.

*

In 1977, David S. Werman published an article that deftly summa-rized the last decade of theory and research regarding nostalgia.[52] He titled his article 'Normal and Pathological Nostalgia', and he discussed all the different shades of the emotion: the good, the bad and the ugly. Werman was born in Queens, New York, in 1922. He stayed in the city for high school and his first degree, before moving to Lausanne in Switzerland for his M.D. He learnt to speak French fluently and, during the war, he served as part of the European air offensive. He trained as an obstetrician and gynaecologist, practising in Manhattan until 1964, when he began studying psychiatry. He moved to North Carolina in 1967, completing his training at the Psychoanalytic Institute in Chapel Hill, before transferring to Duke University medical school in 1975, where he taught and practised psychoanalysis until his retirement in 1992.

Werman may have been a psychoanalyst, and in many ways profes-sionally akin to Nandor Fodor and his ilk, but his description of nostalgia resurrected an older version of the emotion – one first described by Kline in the late nineteenth century and one that is much more similar to the feeling we know and love today. He said that there was scarcely a person on earth who had never experienced nostalgia. It was both ancient and widespread, and had been a major theme in literature for millennia. He called it a 'human phenomenon' – part of the condition of being a person. It was a kind of mourning, a deeply felt desire to return to a place, a time past or to a beloved person. Unlike his psychoanalytic predecessors, and much like earlier psychiatrists, Werman thought that nostalgia was essentially normal, unless it dominated the 'psychic economy'. Compared with Fodor, Werman's vision of the emotion was far more benign.

This watering down of the harm it could cause also made it possible for nostalgia to become something of a fad. In the 1970s, writers and intellectuals from across Europe and North America worried about what the writer, futurist and businessman Alvin Toffler called a 'wave of nostalgia'.[53] The emotion seemed to grip the United States, and more and more widely read publications started reporting on the phenomenon. Panicked headlines and hand-wringing articles appeared throughout the seventies and eighties, and the nostalgia wave showed little signs of receding. Nor was it confined to America. In 1973, the German magazine *Der Spiegel* ran a cover story in entitled, 'Nostalgia: The commercialization of yearning', which detected a 'rampant passion for the passé'.[54] It presented nostalgia as the latest American fashion eagerly emulated by Europeans. While there was no mention of a 'nostalgia wave' in France, French intellectuals detected a widespread tendency to look back to the past, but they spoke of '*la mode retro*' rather than '*la nostalgie*'. In Britain, complaints about nostalgia became common in the late sixties, culminating in journalist and historian Michael Wood's exasperated 1974 article about the 'rampant, ubiquitous, unashamed nostalgia which leers at us these days whichever way we turn'.[55]

But why did the seventies see so much nostalgia? More on that later, but, briefly, the psychoanalysts who had come of age in the first few decades of the twentieth century – and who had almost invariably been forced to flee their homes, escaping isolationist, retrograde and ethno-nationalist regimes – had an understandable suspicion for a feeling that seemed to glorify these same impulses. For Fodor and Freud, backward-looking navel-gazing meant returning to a time and place of intense misery and oppression.

But things had changed. The psychologists and journalists of the seventies, as well as the people they wrote about, had grown up in a very different world, with a very different set of reflections about the recent past. Young adults participating in the 'nostalgia wave' might dimly remember the end of the Second World War, but their immediate collective histories made for more comfortable reflection. As a result, journalists might have been exasperated about their contemporaries' nostalgia, but they weren't worried about their health and safety. This was no epidemic disease, like the one that had lain waste to Switzerland in the seventeenth century. Instead, nostalgia was a normal feeling that had simply got a touch out of hand. It was a cultural problem, rather than a clinical one.

CHAPTER FIVE

THE NOSTALGIA WAVE

In the 1970s, nostalgia was everywhere. No longer a threat to body and mind, the feeling became something of a fad. Throughout that decade and into the 1980s, nostalgia began to plague the West again. It was the first time, too, that journalists started to report on and analyse nostalgia. Writers from across North America worried about what the writer and businessman Alvin Toffler called, in his immensely popular 1970 book, *Future Shock*, a 'wave of nostalgia.'[1] In 1974, *The New York Times* reported on the 'massive wave of nostalgia' which had engulfed America over the past few years, 'with millions basking in the fascination of the "good old days."' A year later, a journalist lamented in *Variety*, 'It seems that everyone has climbed on the "nostalgia" bandwagon.' He complained about the 'Gatsby clothing styles', the 'films about the "olden days"' and the 'books and articles with nostalgic plots'.[2] But, just because nostalgia was no longer deadly, it did not mean that it was no longer complicated, nor that it no longer carried plenty of emotional baggage.

It all started in the late 1950s, when *The New York Times* reported on an emerging phenomenon. At the department store Bloomingdales, located in Manhattan, nostalgia had swept over the book department on the sixth floor. This was one shop doing its utmost to bring back the 'good old days' – in this case, by selling nineteenth-century children's books. But this was only the beginning of a new trend. In 1966, the Italian director Michelangelo Antonioni released his cult film *Blow-Up*. In one scene, the protagonist, a London fashion photographer played by actor David Hemmings, goes into a junk shop and walks out with an old wooden aircraft propeller, which he takes home to his studio. As the *Guardian* journalist Ian Jack put it forty years later, his character was a 'new kind of man who bought old objects simply for the interest and charm of them, because he could afford it.'[3]

By 1966, people had already been selling antiques for quite some time. The Second World War had prompted an increase in second-hand buying and selling due to rationing and scarcity, especially in America. In 1943, Harold Reed, owner of Reed's White Elephant Shop in Milford, New Hampshire, reported the unprecedented growth of his nationwide mail-order business, as rationing and delays to production forced families to look to second-hand stores for household basics like cookware, bedsprings and stoves. But, in the post-war decades of relative abundance, at least in the United States, such pressures decreased and the appeal of second-hand stuff shifted. Antiques and 'retro' things became increasingly popular, and even objects produced relatively recently were swept up in what historian Tara H. Saunders calls the 'ever-expanding nostalgia boom' of the mid twentieth century.[4] In 1959, Gordon Reid convened sixty-seven dealers in Americana in the field behind his house, in what became known as the Brimfield Antique Show. By 1979, the show had transformed into a town-wide, 2,000-dealer event, known today as the Brimfield Flea Market. Eighteenth- and nineteenth-century objects were still around, but shoppers were now also looking for Roy Rogers lunch boxes, Nazi memorabilia, and baseball cards – things that might more accurately be termed 'collectibles' than 'antiques'.

By 1979, the prices of both antiques and collectibles had sky-rocketed. A pair of Queen Anne chairs, made in Philadelphia circa 1750, sold at Christie's auction house in New York for $176,000 – fifteen times what they would have fetched at the beginning of the decade.[5] But, as in Brimfield, it wasn't just 'quality' antiques (things made before 1830) that were appealing to buyers. According to a *Newsweek* article, Americans were 'snapping up anything faintly covered with dust'.[6] Even swizzle sticks from Philadelphia's defunct

Bellevue Stratford Hotel (site of a famous outbreak of Legionnaires' disease) were selling like hot cakes. 'People are grasping for something that their parents had or that their grandparents had,' said George Lamb, owner of Unique Antiques in Galena, Illinois. This move was not just a 'sudden burst of nostalgia', but an attempt on behalf of dealers to rid their business of its elitist image. Some, however, felt the fad had gone a bit too far. Kathryn Oestrich, another antique-shop owner, said, 'A lot of what people are buying is just plain crap.' Regardless, the antiques business was now a $5 billion industry and the time frame for what constituted 'collectible' was rapidly growing. Even modernist Scandinavian furniture – an aesthetic all about the future – was being caught up in the 'nostalgia wave', and journalists wryly commented that things produced as recently as the fifties were being revived as early as the late seventies. As one writer reflected in 1979, 'It may not be long before collectors start bidding up the price of the original Hula-Hoop', which sold in 1958 for just $1.98.[7]

Nostalgia did not just shape the buying and selling of antiques and collectibles. 'These days', *Newsweek* reported in 1970, 'nostalgia is big business.'[8] Even in its very first year, the *Chicago Tribune* had already dubbed the decade the 'Second-hand '70s'.[9] The bookstores were loaded with tomes that 'look back lovingly on the virtues of a golden age long past,' and, by implication, 'contrast them with the evils of the present.' And this nostalgia trend wasn't confined to collectible objects, but extended to every realm of life, from what people ate to education, from film to theatre. Take, for example, the lost, supposedly wholesome food of yesteryear. The diets of this vague 'golden age' were regularly contrasted with the 'adulterated, artificial foods' of the present. The pollution of the 1970s was compared negatively to the 'fresh air and closeness to nature of the good old days'. School in this elusive 'golden age' was the 'good old one-room school house', and, like society at large, was 'free of the problems of bureaucracy, credentials and . . . unions.' These were the places where the 'Abe Lincolns' of the day were taught by 'uniquely versatile, dedicated teachers'.[10]

The decade also witnessed a seventies revival of the work of

F. Scott Fitzgerald and the 1920s world he captured.[11] The 'giant wave of nostalgia' was 'awash with the flotsam and jetsam of the period.'[12] People were obsessed with memories of short skirts, long earrings, high heels, shingled heads, cloche hats, the Charleston, roadsters, racoon coats, hip flasks and speakeasies. This was the 'glittering jazz age', as *The New York Times* put it in 1979, full of 'beautiful girls, music, champagne'.[13]

The press was quick to capitalize, putting out a flood of articles that analysed, critiqued and exploited the rose-tinted spectacles that seemed to have become glued to the face of America. The second-hand seventies did not just witness a surge in nostalgic sentiment, but a surge in theorizing about that sentiment. In 1972, *Variety* magazine published a 'Nostalgia Quiz'. The journalist started by admitting that he, too, had been 'drawn into the Vortex of Yore'. He waxed lyrical about the 'artifacts, fads and foibles' of his youth and luxuriated in memories of hula hoops, the twist and sleeping on tenement-house fire escapes during big-city heatwaves. He spent so much time out on the metal that, until he turned eighteen, he 'suffered from rust'. The quiz itself was mostly about 1930s celebrities, scandalous news stories and entertainment, like the 1934 death of America's public enemy number one, John Dillinger, and the 1939 film classic *The Wizard of Oz*.[14]

Other magazines followed suit, producing their own nostalgia quizzes for readers to assess their ability to recall the good old days. In 1974, *Billboard* published a 'Nostalgia I.Q. Test' which tested people on how many songs they could remember out of a list of more than a hundred.[15] The songs listed were released from 1920 right up to 1966, just eight years before the test was published. Indeed, music was not immune to the nostalgia bug. While they might not have been releasing many new tunes in the seventies, the Beach Boys were 'more popular than ever'. Their song 'Good Vibrations' had been a landmark of sixties pop, and, with the 'paucity of exciting new acts' and a 'nationwide hunger for simple-good-times music', people were listening to it again – so much so that they became bigger stars in the 1970s than they ever had been before. The band had come to represent not just a much-loved musical style, but an epoch in recent history that seemed better than what the present had to offer. 'There is a demonstrable desire,' wrote *The New York Times,* 'for what the group had to say in the past.'[16]

Theatre, too, was vulnerable to the infectious charms of nostalgia. And, like fiction and fashion, it recalled the Jazz Age of the 1920s. For example, 'No, No, Nanette' – the musical comedy with lyrics by Irving Caesar and Otto Harbach – was something of a flop when it was first staged in 1925, but, when it reappeared on Broadway in 1971, it was a real hit: 'This year New Yorkers have been in the mood for a spot of melodious daftness.' While 'serious plays about homosexuality' had been produced all over the city, 'all the serious homosexuals are at "No, No, Nanette."' The 'wave of nostalgia' washed over the cinema screen as well, with a reawakening of interest in everyone from the 1920s canine star Rin-Tin-Tin to George 'Spanky' MacFarland, the actor famous for his appearances as a child in the *Our Gang* comedy series from the 1930s and 1940s.

Fashion also harked back in the 1970s, and not only to the Roaring Twenties. At his 1971 autumn show in New York, the designer Halston revived the twin sweater set. This classic paired garment had delighted the suburbanites and college girls of the previous generation. Other revivals also made an appearance, like coats with a silver-fox collar that were supposed to spark the thrill of recognition in older women, who could remember its previous incarnation, and enable younger fashion fans to indulge in nostalgia for yesteryear. This bit of nostalgia centred on the 1940s, but Halston had updated the classics, giving them a new lease of life. Nostalgia also reigned at the 1974 Valentino show in Rome, which was 'full of nostalgia for the 1930s and the grand days of the couture'.[17] Songs like 'Lullaby of Broadway', first released in 1935, accompanied the models down the catwalk.

The nostalgics of the 1970s were scattergun in their approach to past decades, and almost any point in history could stand in for the 'good old days' if required. The period of time that people seemed to miss was not at all consistent. In 1975, the magazine *America* reported that, while nostalgia for the 1920s might have passed, a 'new ripple [had] appeared on the horizon.' It was now the 1870s that were capturing

audiences. This passion for the 'gilded age' first took the form of a
Sherlock Holmes binge via a Broadway play, then a glut of new novels
set in the nineteenth century. The target for nostalgia had become so
specific and seemingly arbitrary that there were even reports of a man
from Iowa who was both miserable and lonely because he was nostalgic
only for the sixteen-year stretch between 1752 and 1768. His frustration was that he could not find a single other person who shared his
yearning for this particular period of time.[18]

As one writer put it, nostalgia was so much in vogue in the
seventies that people had begun to move beyond simply indulging
in it, to 'musing openly on what the vogue is about'.[19] Indeed, a lot
of the journalistic commentary on the subject struck a note of
petulance, complaining that the media was itself fanning the flames
of the trend. In 1973, *The New York Times* featured a page of satirical
letters. While they weren't, of course, genuine complaints from
readers, they did capture the mood of the press at the time. Everyone
was either complaining about nostalgia or complaining about the
obsession with nostalgia. One wrote, 'Doesn't the press have anything
to write about but nostalgia? The people are sick of this constant
harping on nostalgia, nostalgia, nostalgia . . . Get back to writing
about the important things about America the way the media did
in the good old days.' Another fictional writer complained, 'Take
me back to the good old USA, where the worst thing they've got
is a little nostalgia.' One of the faux letters even suggested (in
nostalgic tones) that this current focus on nostalgia was a distraction
from all the other, real problems facing American society: 'It is not
nostalgia that is wrecking the dollar. It is not nostalgia that is to
blame for the rising incidence of illiteracy, malnutrition, bribery,
air pollution, heat waves, shark scares, pornography, country music
and $4 wheat. No, it is not nostalgia that has done these things to
us, but the media's insistence on dwelling constantly on nostalgia.
Once you media people let America forget that it is up to its ears
in nostalgia, things will straighten themselves out again, and life will
once again be what it was back in 1946.'[20]

There was also plenty of real pushback against nostalgic narratives
of American history. People were not just angry about the all-

consuming nature of the phenomenon but were also cross that the current obsession with the past obscured its grubby and often painful reality. Books, articles and radio programmes had largely been presenting rose-tinted visions of the 1870s, 1920s and 1950s, but, for the most part, the 'golden age' they portrayed 'never existed for the masses of people'.[21] In 1974, Otto L. Bettmann published a book called *The Good Old Days: They Were Terrible!* 'The good old days', wrote Bettmann, 'were good for but the privileged few.' For the average farmer or labourer, though, 'life was an unremitting hardship.' Bettmann was unsparing in his account of what the 'golden age' was really like for most people: 'what we have forgotten are the hunger of the unemployed, crime, corruption, the despair of the aged, the insane and the crippled.'[22]

Bettmann's book was crammed with nostophobia, rather than nostalgia, and full of lengthy accounts of just how much worse the past was than the present. Children living in poverty roamed the streets of New York in the 1880s, forced to adopt the wily instincts of stray cats to survive. They slept in boxes and barrels, scrapped and begged, and were forced to resort to sex work and crime. This was supposed to be a 'gilded age', a golden era of rapid economic growth and industrialization, gorgeous frocks and fabulous parties. But, for Bettmann, it was a period that offered a haunting reminder of how much progress had been made, and how much better life had become. Especially for workers. Bettmann had been expelled by the Nazis from his post as curator of rare books at the Prussian State Art Library in Berlin, and came to America in 1935. He founded the famed Bettmann Archive in New York, a picture library with over three million prints and photographs. Like his fellow émigrés, some of whom became the psychoanalysts of the previous chapter, Bettmann's own history no doubt predisposed him to a certain degree of scepticism about rose-tinted visions of the recent past. Indeed, the 1970s might be a decade of depression, unemployment and budget cutbacks, but Bettmann's account offered some solace. As bad as things might be now, they were infinitely worse in the 'good old days'.

*

While much of the nostalgia wave felt very American, about American moments in history and delivered in very American ways, it nevertheless soon travelled across the Atlantic, flooding Britain, France and Germany with old-fashioned films, 1950s music, and journalists wringing their hands over the decrepit state of society. One British journalist expressed his concern about the overseas threat: 'I grow worried about the new nostalgia wave that seems to have built into tidal proportions in America.'[23] And, in 1971, the British *New Statesman* magazine reported that nostalgia was being 'peddled everywhere today'. This nostalgia, whether on stage, screen or in print, 'seems to be for the past simply because it is past'. The writer identified 1942 as the year when everything seemed have changed, when 'the golden years . . . appear to turn tarnished.'[24]

As in America, nothing was safe from contagion. The left-wing magazine *Tribune* reported that 'reliable sources are suggesting a growing nostalgia market for the dance bands of the thirties.' The success of films like *The Way We Were*, *Gatsby*, *The Sting* and *American Graffiti* also signalled that the nostalgia wave was lapping at European shores. Analysis of this trend was not always complimentary. One journalist was particularly unimpressed. He rejected a British film culture that wallowed in sentimental visions of the past and turned his nose up at the industry's self-indulgence. Unsurprisingly for someone writing for a left-wing publication, the journalist treated any trace of conservativism with grave suspicion: 'It is part of the "camp" sensibility to prise its objects out of time, out of history, out of social processes and then to hypostasize and venerate them – a politically conservative act.' He was uncompromising in his critique: 'This intellectually flaccid surrender to nostalgia and masturbatory fantasy must be resisted at all costs by the Left.'[25]

But his lamentations were largely in vain. On television, *The Waltons* (BBC2) and *Doc Elliot* (BBC1) became incredibly popular with the British public, despite being set in the United States. Both relied on their nostalgic appeal. One portrayed a huge rural family of the 1930s, stricken by the Depression. The other was the tale of a contemporary doctor, gone to the rural West, where culture clashes revealed the strong homely virtues of backwoods America. While reviewers were slightly baffled at British people's apparent interest in the American past, they recognized the yearning embedded in these programmes. 'Nostalgia, is, of course, a hankering after a Golden Age of innocence and joy which never existed. These programmes and their ilk are idealised – Norman Rockwell paintings become flesh.'[26] But not everyone was that impressed: 'Anyone who hankers after the Depression has to be out of his mind – but that yearning seems to be the basis for this soppy programme's popularity.'[27]

As in America, art and fashion were quickly gripped by nostalgia. A 1972 exhibition of 1940s art at the Whitechapel Gallery in London was praised for the emotion it evoked: 'This show is not great by international standards. But I wallowed in it. It is unflashy, honest, rather gentle . . . unexpectedly sombre in colour . . . A visible recognition of something about my own country which I value.'[28] This assessment tapped into the idea that people were drawn to the relatively recent past because it offered something simpler, something that appealed to ordinary people with plenty of common sense. Rather than being drawn to the flashy, progressive promises of the future, these were humbler folk, who longed instead for more quotidian luxuries, commodities and experiences.

In Britain, there was a new trend for Victorian styles of dress, particularly in children's clothes: 'Once upon a time there was a little girl who was seen and not heard . . . The wave of nostalgia that parents feel for this vanished dream expresses itself in the new Victorian Look for children.'[29] Like in America, antique and flea markets boomed. *The Guardian* reported in 1976, 'Since the one-day markets began three years ago their popularity has grown steadily. Now at least three or four public halls in the North of England are crammed every weekend by collectors of faded memories.' Carried on a wave of nostalgia, these markets were 'colourful proof that everything has its price and a buyer'.[30]

The nostalgia wave also travelled across the Channel, hitting France at almost the same time as it arrived in Britain. The record business celebrated the return of the golden age of artists like Damia and Vincent Scotto, and songs such as 'Rue de la Joie', which by the mid seventies had already been around for at least thirty years. Popular with both parents and their teenage children, these tracks were generally out of copyright and the artists were mostly dead. Record company executives were delighted: 'The operation is very profitable.' [31] In West Germany, historic spas – '[bubbling] along merrily on a wave of nostalgia' – and traditional baking were now viewed through rose-tinted lenses. [32] Every morning, Lorenz Zavelberg of Muffendorf woke up at 4 a.m., although 'sometimes 4.30 is close enough', to light an ancient coal-fired baking oven, mix about fifty pounds of fragrant wheat-flour dough and bake 500 '*brochten*' biscuits to satisfy the nostalgic tastes of the local population. 'By mid-morning, housewives or small children on missions from home will have come to buy up the entire stock.' 'Real bakers' like Zavelberg were not the 'last representatives of a dying breed', but part of a booming industry. [33]

This description of so-called 'real bakers' appeared in *The New York Times* and was another manifestation of American nostalgia for an imagined past – one that they believed still existed in old Europe, even if it had since been extinguished in the United States. The article complimented the relatively narrow portion of the market occupied by the baker's 'more mechanized "industrial" competitors, who make bread for supermarkets.' While bleached flour might have been common in American factory-made bread, in West Germany it was banned. Baking traditions dated back to the Middle Ages, when 'every village had a community oven' to which housewives took their home-mixed dough. The very nostalgic writer identified a wistfulness for these ancient customs, which had led to a revival of these practices. In Banse, a small town in Wittgenstein, for example, twenty-five families contributed thirty dollars apiece for a new, collectively owned oven.

As in America, the nostalgia wave was not just a real, tangible increase in the commercial viability of the old, but a subject of feverish cultural commentary. A 'curious atavism' had afflicted nations on both sides of the Atlantic. *The Times Higher Education*

Supplement reported on what it saw as its apogee – a piece of graffiti on the walls of the men's toilets next to the refectory of the
Middlesex Polytechnic's Hendon campus in north London: 'Nostalgia
isn't what it used to be.'[34]

*

The European nostalgia wave was not entirely benign, however, and
not confined to bread-baking, spa-going or movie releases. In 1978,
The Guardian reported on a 'booming trade with political overtones'
that was developing in the field of Nazi militaria and other memorabilia of the Third Reich.[35] While war nostalgia had long been a
thriving industry in Britain, the Germans had been reluctant to
partake until recently, according to a journalist in the *New Statesman*.[36]
In the 1970s, this changed. 'We Germans are the best soldiers in
the world', declared an advertising poster for *Zweite Weltkrieg* magazine in which a gruff, helmeted soldier looks out to readers, with
the caption 'Blitz-Kreig against Poland'. 'The Second World War,
never more dramatic and never more authentic', would-be readers
were promised. A Berlin court even had to forbid an advertising
stunt by its publishers, John Jahr Verlag, which would have involved
the flying of thousands of swastika-emblazoned flags on the city's
newspaper kiosks. According to a British writer, any German station
bookstall could now provide a profusion of 'adrenalin-arousing
nostalgia'.[37]

Books, magazines and newspaper articles about military para-
phernalia and weaponry were everywhere. Even philately, according
to *Der Spiegel*, was in on the trend: 'Hitler is in. The value of Third
Reich stamps has boomed lately.'[38] Third Reich records were also
inescapable in 1970s Germany. Two LPs of Hitler's speeches reached
the charts in 1977 and there was an entire array to choose from:
Marching Music of the Third Reich (including 'Bomben auf England'),
'The Hitler Youth' or perhaps 'Not Guilty' – about the Nuremburg
Trials.[39] At around the same time, *Gong*, a mass-circulation television guide, featured a double-page advertisement headlined 'The
Second World War'. In the background, a line of soldier silhouettes,
wielding rifles, were making a dawn attack. The advert was

promoting a series of fifty silver medals that featured various scenes from the conflict, including the British invasion attempt at Dieppe, the siege of Tobruk and the 'Atlantic Wall', an extensive system of coastal defences and fortifications built by Nazi Germany between 1942 and 1944 along the coast of continental Europe. The medals were emblazoned with portraits of Field Marshal Gerd von Runstedt, Luftwaffe leader Albert Kesselring (who was convicted of war crimes), the Admiral Karl Dönitz (who succeeded Hitler as head of state in May 1945, days before the German surrender) and Hans-Ulrich Rudel (a Second World War flying ace and a prominent post-war neo-Nazi).[40]

Some of this memorabilia made its way to Britain. Gestapo badges, SS daggers and prison-camp officers' armbands were sold by mail order and across the counters of antique and militaria dealers throughout the UK.[41] One mail-order company called Vikings Documentary Recordings advertised widely in the trade press. Their catalogues offer cassette recordings including *Hitler in Words and Music* ('joyous quality'), *Germany Calling* ('His famous broadcast on Poland'), *Stuka Pilot* ('narrated by an American Nazi'), *Benito Mussolini* ('the speeches that inspired the Italian people') and *Non-stop Songs of the Brownshirts* ('ideal for the car').[42] In 1977, the Central Association of Jews in West Germany warned of a possible 'Hitler nostalgia wave' following the surprising success of a documentary about the man himself. The historian Joachim Fest had written a bestselling biography, *Hitler: A Career*, which was then made into a film. While criticized by contemporaries, the documentary's positive influence on Hitler's reputation was unintended. Werner Nachman, board chairman of the Central Association of Jews in West Germany, warned that the younger generation of Germans was being presented a picture of Hitler that was far from accurate.[43]

None of this memorabilia, whether sold in Britain or in Germany, mentioned the death camps. The impression it conveyed was that war was just a bunch of rip-roaring fun, full of schoolboy japes and no unethical action. As *The Guardian* put it, 'It's all a calculated exercise in self-glorification and celebration of war for profit.'[44] And much of it was packed with neo-Nazi talking points and Holocaust denial. In the UK, some of the dealers blatantly pandered to right-wing extremists and, in at least one instance, Nazi militaria and memorabilia was being sold with white supremacist and anti-Semitic reading material to raise funds for a British neo-fascist organization.[45] Many of the people behind these publications and the recordings of speeches or wartime music had neo-Nazi ties. Dr Gerhard Frey, the publisher of *National Zeitung*, was in the news in the early 1970s for planning a memorial to the SS war criminal Joachim Peiper at the Dachau concentration camp. The magazine included articles which promised to explain which criminals had actually caused the war, and ran headlines like 'No gassing of Jews in concentration camps' and 'What Hitler was really like – anti-German lies unmasked'. Readers were informed about 'How pictures of Jews in concentration camps were falsified' and 'How the death of six million Jews was a concocted swindle'. There was also a calendar for 1977 featuring the SS old boys' organization, and jigsaw puzzles of East Prussia and Pomerania: 'Piece by piece the child can compose a picture of the Fatherland, and patriotism becomes fun.'[46]

The boom in Nazi nostalgia in the 1970s was accompanied by a growth in the militancy of neo-Nazi groups in West Germany and a rise in terrorist activities. Between 1976 and 1977, the number of criminal investigations into right-wing extremist groups grew from eighty to over three hundred. The nostalgia for the Nazi era was echoed in increased harassment of Jewish people and violent incidents in the armed forces. The popularity of war memorabilia and publications dedicated to celebrating the war meant that the neo-Nazi groups were able not only to recruit veterans of the 1930s and 1940s, but also young people with no memory of the period. Concerned, in 1978, the former chancellor Willy Brandt appealed for 'heightened vigilance' against the activities of neo-Nazis and right-wing extremists. As a result, a bill was drafted to strengthen government control over the dissemination of materials glorifying the Nazi era.[47] The German penal code now prohibits publicly denying the Holocaust and disseminating Nazi propaganda and imagery.[48]

*

What was it about the seventies that prompted some to look back with rose-tinted spectacles, and many others to contemplate the meaning of this fond and ferocious reminiscence? There was no shortage of nostalgia in the 1970s, there was no shortage of commentary on nostalgia, and there was no shortage of analysis of what this memory boom might say about the state of society, culture, politics and even modernity itself. The British left-wing magazine *Tribune* reflected, as early as 1974, that the nostalgia wave was partly just a product of ageing: 'To some extent the nostalgia bath is just a result of the fact that we are all ten years older. Some are mourning their late, departed youth.' But the magazine also pointed out that the youth experienced by the adults of the 1970s was much sweeter than life lived today.

In Britain especially, the analysis of the 'nostalgia wave' took on a certain inflection, mired in the pervasive sense that the 1970s was a decade of particular decline. The previous ten years had witnessed 'practically everything bloody and painful and heavy in our current collective political memory'. This was a time of deep bitterness between the 'classes, the races, the generations'.[49] The world had been made much less good, and this journalist primarily blamed the impact of the war and its 'endless physical and social destruction'.[50] This idea, that the 1970s was a decade of social, political and economic collapse, was everywhere then, and it's everywhere now. In 1977, the *British Medical Journal* called the 1970s the 'decade of the decline' of the NHS.[51] It crops up in epithets like 'the winter of discontent' – a season of unprecedented strike action that brought Britain to a halt between 1978 and 1979 – and it's there in politicized comparisons between the former Labour leader Jeremy Corbyn and the economic doldrums of the 1970s. Journalists and academics alike tend to characterize the 1970s as a truly dismal decade. One historian said that, while the seventies might have 'started well', they soon 'ended in disarray'. Another wrote, 'When it comes to 1970s Britain . . . [historians] depict a shallow, supine, and ultimately moribund social democracy.'[52]

The *Tribune* journalist agreed, lamenting a pervasive lack of creativity and innovation in film, theatre and fashion, and outlining what he described as a 'disturbing thesis', that 'false dreams of the past' had replaced enthusiasm for social and cultural progress.[53] Four years later, another writer in the same magazine similarly blamed the process of ageing, arguing that elderly people were too often oriented towards the past, 'the time of their vigour and power', resisting the future as a threat. He made an analogy to Britain, an entire culture in an 'advanced state of loss of relative power and disintegration', lamenting its long-gone golden age and a life lived sluggishly in the present. Historian R. S. Lynd agreed, diagnosing the 1970s as a period of acute stagnation.[54]

This malaise was specific to Britain and reflected a widespread discontent over the waning of the nation's imperial powers. All those films and television shows that had recently become popular not only harked back to 'happier' and 'more settled' times, but they also recalled periods in history when the British Empire had reached its zenith – the Victorian and Edwardian eras – or when the facade of the nation's robust capitalism last appeared most convincing – the early Georgian period – or so the *Tribune* journalist insisted. He was deeply dismissive of the nostalgia wave, believing that it was getting in the way of radical social change.[55] Nostalgia was an ideological intervention, not just a set of trends and fads.

Previously the preserve of physicians, psychologists and psycho-analysts, by the end of the seventies, nostalgia had drifted into the realm of cultural commentary. It also became a topic of interest for sociologists. Fred Davis was one of them. An American, Davis diag-nosed the United States as suffering from a similar kind of emotional turmoil to that experienced in Britain. Unlike the United Kingdom, however, the nostalgia wave in the US was not so much about faded imperialism, but more a crisis of confidence in the nation's institu-tions. Born in Brooklyn in 1925, Davis received his Ph.D. from the University of Chicago in 1958. He started his career as a sociologist of medicine and disability, before moving on to study occupations like driving a taxi (inspired by his own experience as a cab driver). In 1975, he joined the Department of Sociology at the University of California, San Diego, before publishing his most famous and influential book, *Yearning for Yesterday: A Sociology of Nostalgia*, in 1979.

Davis was one of the first social scientists to theorize nostalgia. He argued that nostalgia made false use of the past. It is a reconstruction of events that can never offer a perfect facsimile. As a result, nostalgia tells us more about the present, its moods and anxieties, than about past realities. To draw his conclusions, Davis conducted multiple lengthy interviews with study participants. These testimonials persuaded him (although other social scientists disagreed) that the past which is the object of nostalgia must, at least in some way, be a personally experienced one, rather than an account drawn from chronicles, history books, memorials or legend. However, nostalgia being based on personal experience does not mean, according to Davis, that the past either causes or explains nostalgia. In other words, what the past was actually like makes no difference to whether or not, or how intensely, the people of the present feel nostalgic. Instead, current circumstances prompt people to find nostalgic echoes in the experiences of their youth. It is the present that is the trigger. What was it, then, about the 1970s that encouraged people not only to look back, but to look back on so many different eras, too?

Davis dismissed the tendency of some contemporaries to explain the current nostalgia wave by focusing on particular features of the period in question. He believed that such explanations were themselves nostalgic reflections. The power of past time periods, fashions and events lay in the way they could be made to contrast with the present. He also argued that, while remembrance, recollection, reminiscence, revivification and recall are all English words which mean the 'mental state of looking back in time', none of them quite evokes exactly the same feeling as does 'nostalgia'. He explained that several of his interviewees claimed to feel nostalgic for the future. Clearly, for Davis, nostalgia had to involve more than simply the past. It had to be imbued with special emotional qualities or opportunities for comparison. Only present-day fears, discontents, anxieties or uncertainties could create nostalgia out of the past.

For Davis and other social scientists, like Alvin Toffler, nostalgia was essentially a normal psychological reaction triggered by fear of actual or impending change. For Toffler, whose book *Future Shock* has sold over six million copies worldwide, nostalgia was a response to 'too much change in too short a period of time'. The seventies' nostalgia wave was a kind of psychological lust for an imagined, simpler, less turbulent past. And it didn't matter whether that past was actually better than the present day. Nostalgia is used, albeit unconsciously, as a comfort, to avoid the threat of what Davis called the 'wolf of insignificance'. Nostalgia is one of the many psychological resources that we deploy to defend ourselves against the threat of change.

While Davis insisted that nostalgia was more about the present than the past, he himself drew on the radical energy – or 'massive identity dislocations' – of the 1960s to help explain the nostalgia wave of the 1970s. But this wasn't because there was something appealing about the sixties that made people want to return to that era, it was because the decade so fundamentally upset the conventional order of things that it had left people feeling adrift, in need of a psychological salve in the form of nostalgia. Davis offered up a long list of things that had happened in the sixties in America, including the Vietnam War, the assassination of Martin Luther King and the brothers Kennedy, the race riots, student protests, civil rights marches and the Kent State massacre (which actually took place in 1970). In the 1960s, millions of Americans experienced a fast-paced, sustained and profound assault on what most of them had considered the natural order of things. Rarely in modern history, he argued, had the common man had his fundamental convictions about 'man, woman, habits, manners, laws, society and God' so challenged, disrupted or shaken. This onslaught was only made more intense by television and mass media.

The sixties in America seemed to produce a '*collective* identity crisis', something profoundly troubling to people's sense of who and what they were. It genuinely seemed that the centre would no longer hold, that any trace of certainty had vanished. For many, it was as if a 'rash of moral madness' had swept away the world as they knew it. The nostalgia wave offered them a 'retreat, a haven, an oasis' from radical change. For Davis, the speed of that wave, and the profusion and variety it manifested, was a measure of how deep, comprehensive – and catastrophic – the 'identity disturbances' of the sixties had been. People had been badly psychologically bruised by the turmoil of the preceding decade, and nostalgia became one way in which they could retain and reaffirm a sense of self: 'Nostalgia's gaze looks backwards rather than forwards, for the familiar rather than the novel, for certainty rather than discovery.'[56]

Fred Davis was a sociologist, and so for him nostalgia was not a medical or psychiatric diagnosis, nor a mark of inherent or individual deviancy, nor was it a tendency that necessarily emerged from the biographical details of a person's life or experiences. Instead, it was a social, cultural and political feeling. It might be an emotion felt by individuals, but it was really about how one related to the surrounding world. On the one hand, nostalgia was 'deeply impli- cated in our sense of who we are, what we are about, and . . . whither we go.' It was one of the many means at our disposal for the 'never-ending work of constructing, maintaining and recon- structing our identities', an attempt to salvage a self from the 'chaos of raw, unmediated experience'.[57]

On the other hand, what Davis called the 'nostalgia orgy'[58] of the 1970s was a collective experience, something that had to be under- stood in terms of its close relationship to the social upheaval that characterized the 1960s.[59] Nostalgia was a 'crepuscular' emotion, something that takes hold when the 'dark of impending change is seen to be encroaching.' It was, for Davis, a kind of inversion of Harold Lasswell's famous definition of politics as 'the displacement of private affect onto public objects'. Nostalgia did precisely the opposite. It drained moments of transformation in the public sphere of their pain, anxiety and discontent, and rechannelled them into a more private world of shared memories, consumer habits and indul- gent sentiment over the way things were.[60]

In the way he worked, his life experiences, the research methods he deployed and the arguments he crafted, Davis was very different from the psychoanalysts who had turned their attention to nostalgia. But his characterization of those with nostalgic tendencies was not actually all that dissimilar. The 1960s was and remains, at least for many people, a decade of progressive social change. It was the

'Swinging Sixties' after all – the era of feminism, civil rights, sexual liberation, Woodstock, the pill and youth culture. And, while people have since acknowledged that the radical transformations might not have been as radical as has been claimed, Davis at least bought into this vision of the sixties. As a result, his nostalgics were tradition-alists, conventional, suspicious of revolution and reform. They were possibly religious, politically conservative and maybe even Luddites. They were unconscious consumers of media, driven to devour things of yore by an imprecise feeling of present-day discontent.

This narrative should be familiar to us because Davis was not the first to deploy it. It appeared in the writings of Nandor Fodor and other psychologists in the first half of the twentieth century. It appeared in accounts of acute homesickness, identifying it as an infantile and immature condition. And, while they were quite different in the way they conceptualized the emotion (or disease), late-nineteenth-century writers lamented their own 'nostalgia wave'. Davis would not be the last to think of nostalgia in these terms, nor to identify nostalgics with such tendencies. Each new decade sees concerns that perhaps this generation is the most nostalgic of all. But something new *had* happened in the 1970s. Not only was Davis part of a wave of his own – a torrent of academics in the humani-ties and social sciences who turned their attentions to nostalgia – but he also identified a genuinely new phenomenon.

Unlike the nostalgia of the previous decades, the nostalgia of the seventies was big business. This was the beginning of a moneymaking machine that swallowed up the United States, Europe and ultimately the world, in what Davis called the 'American nostalgia industry'. There was cash to be made from nostalgia, and so the cycle of nostalgia spun more rapidly, and the media had to 'devour their past creations at an ever-increasing rate'.' The lapse between something's original appearance and its nostalgic recycling shrank in the 1970s. By the end of the decade, barely a few years would pass before a reinvention, rediscovery or remake emerged. Davis was sceptical about the effects of this industry, concerned about the supposed corruption of the private and intimate parts of our nostalgic memory – sunsets, birthdays, family gatherings, friends and lovers – and the exploitation of our emotions for commercial gain.[61] But, regardless of whether it was good or bad, the nostalgia industry was here to stay. More and more companies and cultural creators cottoned on to its commercial power and became increasingly adept at exploiting the feeling's seductive qualities.

CHAPTER SIX

HOW TO TURN AN EMOTION INTO REVENUE

In 1973, the British bakery firm Hovis released an iconic television advert. 'The Bike', set to a soundtrack of Dvorak's Ninth Symphony and filmed in Dorset, in the south-west of England, was directed by Ridley Scott, who went on to make Hollywood blockbusters like *Alien*, *Blade Runner* and *Thelma & Louise*. In the advert, a small boy pushes a bike with a basket full of bread up a steep hill, before freewheeling his way back down. A year later, Hovis released a follow-up called 'Our Dad', in which an elderly man narrates his childhood in a thick Yorkshire accent over footage of a little boy in Edwardian garb. The slogan intones, 'As good for you today as it's always been.'[1] The explicitly nostalgic advert was designed to pull on the heartstrings of viewers to sell not just bread, but a portal to a bygone era – a time when loaves were home baked and deliveries were conducted on bicycles. A world that, even in 1973, had already more or less disappeared in Britain. As a result, the advert quickly became a much-loved classic of the genre, and in 1978 the Two Ronnies comedy duo satirized the clip in a skit of their own.[2]

But the advert, nostalgic by design, also became an object of nostalgia itself, prompting people who saw it the first time round, often as children, to reflect with rose-tinted spectacles on the viewing habits, styles of life and commercial culture of their youth. Comments under digital versions of the advert, relatively recently uploaded to sites like YouTube, are full of nostalgic reverence. One viewer wrote,

'I do remember these ads with very fond memories. I got misty eyed watching these.' Another top-rated comment was, 'This advert is magical. It transports me back to my childhood and invokes in me a warm feeling of nostalgia and comfort.' Another: 'So nostalgic, so beautiful, so peaceful . . . Now 53 and would love to step back in time for just one day.' At fifty-three, this commenter was likely born in the late 1960s, fifty years after the Edwardian setting of the original advert. They are, therefore, expressing nostalgia not about the time period captured by Ridley Scott, but for the 1970s of their childhood. They can't remember the 1930s setting, but they might remember watching the advert for the very first time on their family television set. YouTube user Jcw-Is1kg was even more explicit about what and when they yearned for: 'Remember watching that advert when I was a child with mum and dad . . . Great memories . . .'[3]

According to the *Daily Mail*, 'The Bike' rapidly became a national treasure, representing a 'slice of British history'.[4] People who watched it felt a combination of both nostalgia and patriotism. One YouTube user wrote, 'Everything it means to be British, neatly summed up in one advert. A great part of our social history.' Another simply put, 'It makes you proud to be English.'[5] In 2013, Carl Barlow, the child actor who pushed his bicycle up the hill in the advert, was invited back to the location where it was shot, to turn on the Christmas lights in the town of Shaftesbury, in Dorset. In 2019, a survey of 1,200 consumers voted the advert the UK's most 'heart-warming and iconic advert'. To celebrate this popular success, the commercial underwent a 4K digital restoration, its score was rerecorded by a new generation of the original Ashington Colliery brass band and it returned to TV screens for a brief run.[6]

While these Hovis adverts were voted the best of the genre, and remain instantly recognizable to people who grew up in Britain in the later decades of the twentieth century, this was not the only company that used nostalgia to sell things and make people money. The 1970s had seen the birth of the nostalgia industry, which developed alongside another relatively new invention: the TV commercial. The television had been invented in the late 1920s and it did not take very long for advertising executives to see the potential of this new technology. At first, agencies' television departments were small and understaffed, but that situation changed quickly. In May 1941, the United States Federal Communications Commission issued commercial licences to ten American TV stations. On 1 July, the first ever television commercial aired. It was for the Bulova watch company, and it cost them just nine dollars.[7] Rosser Reeves, a pre-eminent advertising executive, noted, 'We discovered that this was no tame kitten; we had a ferocious man-eating tiger. We could take the same advertising campaign from print or radio and put it on TV, and even when there were very few sets, sales would go through the roof.'[8] As TV technology evolved, with colour pictures, more channels and increased distribution, the advertising industry quickly grew into a creative moneymaking behemoth. By 1951, TV advertisement spending in the US had reached $128 million, up from $12.3 million in 1949. And, in 1955, US TV commercial spending crossed the $1 billion threshold.[9] This growth was also taking place against a backdrop of relatively low TV ownership. In 1950, just 9 per cent of American homes owned a set. By the decade's end, TVs were present in 87 per cent of US households.[10]

In Britain, the television advert was born in the 1950s. With the launch of ITV in 1955, commercials — or 'natural breaks', as they were originally known — began appearing on the nation's TV screens. The very first British television commercial, for Gibbs SR toothpaste, was broadcast on 22 September 1955, at 8.12 p.m. A tube of toothpaste embedded in a block of ice appeared on screen (real ice had had to be abandoned in favour of plastic), and viewers watched as an actress by the name of Meg Smith brushed her teeth, 'up and down and round the gums'. In a voiceover, Alex Mackintosh declared (with the immaculate diction he was famous for in his role as a BBC continuity announcer), 'It's tingling fresh. It's fresh as ice. It's Gibbs SR toothpaste.' The running water in the advert, all 400 gallons of it, had to be siphoned off into the gentlemen's lavatory at the Pathé Studios in Wardour Street, London, where the advert was filmed.[11]

By the late 1950s, television had become the leading advertising medium on both sides of the Atlantic. Catchy slogans and jingles were part of everyday conversation and had infiltrated the minds of ordinary people. In the US, sponsors were spending between $10,000 and $20,000 for one-minute slots, ten times more than for radio adverts. And, by the sixties, TV commercials could reach 90 per cent of all US households, the only medium with that capability.[12] As a result, advertising became increasingly creative, an art form in itself. This, as well as the business's cut-throat and financially lucrative nature, was brilliantly captured by Matthew Weiner's TV drama *Mad Men*, which ran for seven seasons and ninety-two episodes from July 2007 to May 2015. Its fictional time frame ran from March 1960 to November 1970, and it followed the dramas of an advertising agency in Manhattan's Madison Avenue. The series' main character was the charismatic advertising executive Don Draper, played by Jon Hamm, whose erratic behaviour is counterbalanced by his creative genius.

It was in the period dramatized by the programme that companies began using nostalgia as a tool to shore up their customer base and sell products. The best example of this comes not from the 1960s itself, but from *Mad Men*. In an early episode, 'The Wheel', Don Draper talks at length about the power of nostalgia to cultivate emotions on behalf of viewers and sell goods. He admits that technology might be a 'glittering lure', but that the only way to engage with the public is to make them develop a 'sentimental bond' with the product. At Draper's first job, he was doing in-house advertising for a fur company. One of his colleagues, an 'old pro copywriter', said that, while the most important idea in advertising might be 'new', something that creates an 'itch', 'nostalgia' creates a 'deeper bond with the product'. This colleague told Draper that, in Greek, his native language, 'nostalgia' literally means, "the pain from an old wound". It's a twinge in your heart, far more powerful than memory alone.' What advertising men needed, then, was not so much a spaceship, but a time machine: 'It goes backwards, forwards. It takes us to a place where we ache to go again.' Not a wheel, but a carousel: 'it lets us travel the way a child travels. Around and around, and back home again . . . to a place where we know we are loved.'[13]

Don Draper might have been a fictional character, but his belief in the selling power of nostalgia was grounded in fact. From the late 1960s onwards, nostalgia was an ever-present feature of advertising and it exerted its strange emotional power over viewers with remarkable frequency. This was true in Manhattan, but it was also true in Britain. Hovis was not the only company to exploit fond feelings for yesteryear. In 1966, British confectioners Cadbury made a thirty-one-second advert for television to promote their new cake range. 'The Years to Remember' started with three simple questions: 'Do you remember when bakers still baked their own bread, and cheeses still came from the farmhouse? And good cooks would only bake with butter?' The voice-over was accompanied by images of old-fashioned bakeries and dairies, and the advert encouraged the viewers to reminisce. For those who missed the flavours of their youth, Cadbury had the power to 'bring back that taste you'd almost forgotten'.[14]

Attempts to prompt memories of childhood among viewers were common throughout the seventies and into the eighties. An advert for Heinz cream of tomato soup from 1981 began with the injunction, 'Remember your very first soup bowl.' Footage of a child's soup bowl being filled with red liquid plays against the spoken slogan, 'You never forget the one you love.'[15] Similar tactics were employed by the blackcurrant drink Ribena in the 1970s, with an advert that featured an elderly woman reflecting, 'I remember my mother giving it to me all those summers ago.' The woman says, 'I still love the taste,' and the advert insists that Ribena is 'as much for you now as when you were a child'.[16] In 1982, Anchor butter released an advert with a jingle called 'Anchor days of childhood', which played over footage of a 1930s family picnic. It ends with, 'That's why you've always had a soft spot for it.'[17]

The idea that certain products had maintained their quality and stayed reassuringly the same while the world around them pitched and rolled was a theme that ran through advertising in this period. In the 1970s, journalists and sociologists were both arguing that the uncertainties of the age might be remedied or reassured by nostalgic reverie or reflection. In a 1974 commercial for the breakfast cereal Weetabix, the female narrator reminisces, 'My dad had one of those funny old cars and he'd take us to the country.' But things had changed: 'It's not the same today, what with the traffic jams and all! Everything is different today.' Except, that is, for Weetabix: 'Well, not everything,' she continues. 'Weetabix is still the same, of course.'[18] Household favourites like Ribena, Weetabix, Hovis and Anchor provided emotional ballast in the storms of social and political change. They were steadfast companions who could be relied upon, even when everything else seemed to shift beneath your feet.

The seventies might have been dubbed the 'second-hand' decade, but advertising companies also knew they were on to a lucrative strategy that could help them promote new products in an increasingly competitive marketplace. Nostalgia sold things, and they had no intention of abandoning Don Draper's emotional time machine. As a result, nostalgia would dominate TV adverts throughout the eighties, nineties, and into the new millennium. But with this nostalgia came a strange kind of amnesia. While nostalgia was a consistent presence on TV screens from the 1970s onwards, advertising executives and marketing researchers repeatedly rediscovered the emotion's power as a sales tool, insisting that each new decade was more nostalgic than the last. Seeming to forget the prevalence of the emotion in advertising in earlier decades, as the twentieth century turned into the twenty-first, marketing researchers identified a growing malaise twinned with what they understood to be a new and newly intense nostalgia. Inadvertently echoing the work of 1970s sociologists, they considered this *fin de siècle* – or 'end of century' – moment to be a time when people in the West were becoming increasingly and unusually 'uncertain and anxious about the future'.[19]

To capitalize on this supposedly new phenomenon, advertisers encouraged consumers to 'return to their pasts'. In the United States, nostalgic TV channels like Nick at Nite (the 'first classic TV network', airing programmes from the 1950s through to the early 1970s) and TV Land (launched in 1996, it was originally a spin-off of Nick at Nite) had a boom in popularity. In the UK, the Mini Cooper car was reintroduced in 1996, and there was a resurgence of 1980s television icons, such as Mr T. and ALF, as product spokespeople (or spokesalien, in the case of ALF).[20]

The nostalgia of the 1990s was thought to be particularly intense because the close of the twentieth century marked not only the end of a millennium but also an unprecedented demographic event. The largest group in the population, the baby boomers, born in the post-war decades, were hurtling towards middle age, and having to face up to their own mortality as a result.[21] The supposed nostalgia wave of the nineties was a collective mid-life crisis. In response, marketing executives adopted a specific permutation of nostalgia. They appealed to this ageing population by offering them mementos of their youth. According to psychologists, the fifty to sixty-five age group is especially likely to show attachment to possessions that evoke pleasurable memories. The reasons given for this are particularly bleak. Recollection of past joys supposedly escalates as the likelihood of future joys diminishes – nostalgic tendencies increase as someone approaches the end of their life.[22]

But this strategy only worked with one kind of nostalgia: personal nostalgia, which idealized an individual's own childhood and youth. It's sentimental, reassuring and secure. Of course, personal nostalgia does not depend on an actual happy childhood, but on a fictional, imagined one.[23] Nostalgia in advertising made consumer goods into things that could offer a taste of youth to older people. In seeking to command the baby boomers' attention, marketers turned to reminders of the 1950s and 1960s, reconnecting them with their childhood. Coca-Cola distributed its product in its original green-tinted glass bottles. In the words of one consumer, 'I drank these growing up – wouldn't it be great to share it with my son?' Other companies also revived old advertising campaigns. In 1991, the pharmaceutical company Bristol-Myers Squibb re-released their 1968 'Excedrin Headache' advert, featuring a busy mid-century housewife versus a washing machine let loose.[24]

These adverts, and their success, were based on the idea that, in youth, people form enduring preferences which they then return to throughout the rest of their lives.[25] The French perfume market has brands that are decades old, with hundreds of new products being released every year.[26] Younger consumers are more likely to change their preferred brand, whereas older ones are more likely to remain attached to the same product they have used for decades.

This is true across the board. In France, in 1998, 74 per cent of new car buyers seventy-five years of age and older purchased one of three well-established national brands that have been available for about a century, compared with only 49 per cent of consumers aged eighteen to thirty-nine. In 2007, French radio stations established before the 1981 deregulation had a 58 per cent share among the audience who were sixty years and older, versus a 30 per cent share among those thirty years and younger.[27]

Throughout the 1990s, historical nostalgia was a regular feature in adverts. Unlike personal nostalgia – a longing for your own childhood, for example – historical nostalgia meant a yearning for a past one never experienced. A desire to retreat from contemporary life by returning to a time in the distant past that might be viewed as superior to the present. The past in this instance was a place where good things happened, and where good people lived. The goal of such adverts was to enable consumers to 'bask in the glory of the past in the hope that some of it will magically rub off'.[28] Essentially, marketing and branding were trying to enrapture the consumer by turning the ordinary and the everyday into something emotionally charged. Even brown bread can be a portal to another world – something saturated in wonder. Some brands attempted, and continue to attempt, to do this, making claims for an illustrious heritage, sometimes even inventing a past that isn't true.

Twin City, a Swedish restaurant located in the city of Jönköping, was supposedly set up by identical twins who strategically located a chain of restaurants in twin cities – from Minneapolis and Saint Paul, to Tokyo and Yokohama – all over the world. The story is entirely made up, but it is all over their menus, on the corporate website and repeated by waiters to customers. Corporate heritage can be big business. A start-up gold-trading house in Germany acquired the name of a defunct 168-year-old heritage brand, Degussa. In doing so, they gave the impression of being part of almost 200 years of industry tradition. The company was convicted of misleading marketing and had to modify its use of the heritage brand.[29] Despite being inauthentic, and in some cases illegal, these strategies work because they make a company seem more appealing, allowing consumers to escape from the tedium of day-to-day life and engage in a tiny bit of time travel – what academics have called 're-enchantment'. Nostalgia as a marketing tool allows us to add something to the mundanity of shopping, eating and banking. Buyers can play at journeying back to a better, albeit lost, time and place.[30]

However, marketing experts do not universally agree about the benefits of using nostalgia in advertising, believing that personal nostalgia has minimal impact on purchasing choices.[31] While people definitely enjoy films, music and products associated with their youth, that doesn't necessarily mean they like adverts that overtly reference that past. If adverts don't chime with a person's own experiences or memories, if they seem inauthentic, they are not appealing. Nostalgia might be everywhere in advertising, but researchers in the early 2000s could find no empirical evidence that nostalgic commercials actually evoked nostalgic feelings in viewers, nor that those feelings would make them part with their money.[32]

Despite this scepticism, nostalgic advertising remains popular and nostalgia still seems to have at least some selling power. Some of the most popular television programmes of recent years have capitalized on viewers' fondness for the 1980s and 1990s. The new millennium also saw a particularly powerful and prevalent version of nostalgia marketing, one that dominated the British high street and capitalized on a unique national context and cultural tradition. In his book, *The Ministry of Nostalgia*, the writer and historian Owen Hatherley recalled walking around flea markets in the early 2000s, seeing a slow expansion of a very specific type of object for sale.[33] He increasingly came across wartime memorabilia and 'old tins, plates, tat of various sorts'. Record stalls stocked nothing produced later than the sixties, while the clothes on display dated from or emulated the 1940s and 1950s. And one particular item was everywhere: the ubiquitous poster bearing the slogan, 'Keep Calm and Carry On'.[34]

'Keep Calm and Carry On' was a motivational poster, in essence a piece of propaganda, produced by the UK government in 1939 in preparation for the Second World War. It was designed to raise the morale of the British public in the face of the widely anticipated mass air attacks on major cities. Nearly two and a half million copies of the poster were printed, but these were only very rarely displayed publicly during the war itself, and it was generally little known until a copy was rediscovered in 2000, in a bookshop in Alnwick, in Northumberland, England. In about 2008, it suddenly became omnipresent, evocative of a 1940s notion of the British stiff upper lip, and the stoicism, self-discipline and fortitude that was supposed to have been demonstrated by the wartime population.[35] First sold in London by the shop at the Victoria and Albert Museum, it was disseminated across a wide range of products. By the time the recession hit in 2008, it had become a 'middlebrow staple' and then grew from being a 'minor English middle-class cult object' into a global brand. Hatherley described the looming presence of the poster as that 'horror film-like feeling that I was being chased wherever I went by an implacable enemy'.[36]

That the popularity of 'Keep Calm and Carry On' exploded at the same time as the recession was no coincidence. The Blitz spirit has been exploited by British politicians since the 1970s. When members of both Conservative and Labour governments spoke of 'hard choices' and straitened economic times, they often invoked memories of wartime rationing. This kind of nostalgia served to legitimate the government position that resources were scarce and that spending should be limited. In the climate of austerity under the coalition government of 2010 to 2019, the 'Keep Calm and Carry On' slogan was particularly resonant. It made a virtue of good budgeting, prudent housekeeping, moderate expenditure and individual stoicism. It worked to keep the peace among a population facing unprecedented financial hardship, imploring them to suck it up and take their complaints elsewhere. 'Keep Calm and Carry On' encouraged the British public to admire a 'strong, struggling but basically deferent working class,' one that 'knows its place.'[37] It also, according to Hatherley, had another, equally malign consequence, which echoed the concerns and analyses of 1970s sociologists: 'The effect was as if pop music and the social revolutions of the 1960s – the struggles for sexual equality, and particularly, racial equality – had never happened.' 'Keep Calm and Carry On' appealed because it returned us to a 'preliberation era', before society had become more equal and forgiving.[38] This was the dark side of nostalgia marketing, playing on people's conservative desires for a retrograde world, and exploiting their anxieties over progressive change.

*

Today, both nostalgic marketing and nostalgic consumption continue. As one *Financial Times* journalist put it in 2022, 'we are living in an age of déjà vu', even if this age has now endured for almost half a century.[39] Vintage fashion still captivates and young people wear 'pieces of history' from new shopping sites and apps like Depop, Vinted and Poshmark, despite the production of more than a hundred billion new items of clothing each year.[40] Mid-century modern furniture still prevails in the world of interior design, and television programmes like the BBC's *The Repair Shop* capitalize on public interest in preserving, refurbishing and resurrecting old objects. One of the things that's particularly interesting about this iteration of investment in vintage, retro and reusing the old is that, unlike other versions of nostalgia that are repeatedly criticized as politically right-wing, constitutionally retrograde or socially conservative, instead it's part of a more progressive, environmentally conscious movement. Buying and using old clothes, furniture and decorative items is less about languishing in a bygone era (although *The Repair Shop* certainly does a fair bit of that, too) and more about cultivating sustainable practices and a rejection of fast fashion.

The popularity of second-hand or throwback style – mostly from the 1990s – has been aided by social media. As Michelle Freyre, global president of make-up brand Clinique, said, 'TikTok is a place that loves nostalgia.' And Clinique has exploited this trend. Launched in 1968, the company had been struggling to compete with newer brands in a notoriously fickle market. But a combination of 'nostalgia, TikTok and NFTs [non-fungible tokens]' helped elevate Clinique's profile among a younger demographic and increase sales. The brand's Black Honey lipstick, which originally debuted in 1970, was rediscovered by TikTok influencers in the summer of 2021. Clinique noticed that it was newly trending and enhanced the process with a bit of paid support. The company also launched its first NFT, also reliant on nostalgia, giving away three images of the brand's history and an assortment of products annually for a decade, to three people who submitted the most compelling personal stories about their own experiences with Clinique's products.[41]

In India, nostalgia has assisted the commercial success of a very different brand. In early 2022, Reliance Industries bought Campa Cola. In 1977, the country's maverick industries minister George Fernandes had ousted Coca-Cola. The home-grown brand Campa Cola's popularity increased to fill the void, until the early nineties, when both Coca-Cola and Pepsi were invited back to an India 'smitten with liberalisation and all that came with it', especially foreign brands and investment. Today, at a time when the nationalist Indian government is zealously promoting home-grown goods, Campa Cola – the product of jingoism and nostalgia – has been given a chance to rise again. As one journalist put it, 'You can never underestimate the emotional pull of the good old days, especially in times when complexities and uncertainties abound.'[42]

Nostalgia still dominates our television screens, too. In the streaming wars between services like Netflix, Amazon Prime, Disney+ and Apple TV, the nineties sitcom *Friends* has become one of the most valuable commodities. Titles on these streaming services look like an old multiplex cinema marquee, often featuring titles from the nineties, with films like *The Mighty Ducks* and *Hocus Pocus* back on our screens nearly three decades after their original premieres. In Hollywood, the old is new again – thanks to (another) wave of nostalgic programming. As we know, TV programmes and movies have been drawing on nostalgic themes since at least the 1970s, but the trend has become increasingly self-referential. Once again, people put this current wave of nostalgia down to the pain associated with rapid societal change. Executives, show creators and psychologists say that America's partisan political rifts, the 'psychic cost' of the Covid pandemic, and the war in Ukraine, which began in 2022, have contributed to the latest embrace of shows and films designed to make adults feel like kids again. Polls suggest that many Americans are unhappy, and, in response, Hollywood has flooded the market with nostalgic programming to soothe their collective unease. No wonder one of the top performers for Netflix over the past few years has been *Stranger Things* – a nostalgic if fantastical bask in the relative (and seeming) political and economic calm of the 1980s.

The media giant Disney's forthcoming titles include a new version of the late-eighties comedy *Three Men and a Baby*, starring Zac Efron, and a third in the series of Sister Act films. In 2022 – reaching back more than eighty years – they released a live-action reimagining of the classic 1940 cartoon *Pinocchio*.[43] At an investor day in late 2020, Disney previewed the programming they were yet to roll out. Of the sixty-three new shows and movies announced, forty-three drew on existing characters or were reboots or remakes of older titles. Also in 2022, Disney started advertising 1990s films, including *Cool Runnings* and *The Parent Trap* (the 1998 version), as part of a throwbacks collection on their streaming service, asking subscribers if they were 'feeling nostalgic?' 'Ah, the good old days,' their advertising read.

A similar strategy was being pursued by rival behemoth Paramount, where executives sifted through their back catalogue to see what they might be able to reimagine for the Paramount+ streaming service. Among the new shows they announced were a *Fatal Attraction* miniseries, a prequel to *Grease* (the original itself a nostalgic reimagining of the 1950s) called *Rise of the Pink Ladies*, and reinventions of the 1970s hit *Love Story* and 1980s blockbuster film *Flashdance*. Nicole Clemens, the executive overseeing the streaming service's scripted shows, said that nostalgia can pull in several age groups living under one roof. And, since the library of programmes can live on a streaming service forever, children who are now too young to watch a certain show or movie might discover it later in life. 'It will be there waiting for them,' she said.

In Australia, as the classic nineties soap opera *Neighbours* said goodbye (before being bought by Amazon to secure its return), the hotel booking site Booking.com sought to capitalize on a bit of TV nostalgia. They launched a 'Nostalgic *Neighbours* Finale Stay on Ramsay Street' campaign, offering fans the chance to book and win a two-night stay at 18 Ramsay Street, one of the houses on the show's set, for just twenty-eight dollars. Whoever managed to book the property first would win the stay. The company's regional manager Simon Clark told the newspaper *The Australian* that the site 'booked out within seconds'.[44]

The music industry tells a similar story. For the release of her album *30*, singer Adele persuaded the streaming service Spotify to disable the shuffle button on all artists' album pages, so that tracks would play in the chronological order of a vinyl record or CD. 'This was the only request I had in our ever-changing industry!' the singer tweeted. 'We don't create albums with so much care and thought into our track listing for no reason.' To emphasize her point, she also sells cassette-tape versions of *30* on her official website.

In 2019, Spotify published an editorial reflecting on the power of nostalgia to sell music and keep people tuning in. The company actively tries to cultivate the emotion among its listeners. They create playlists like #ThrowbackThursday and developed 'Your Time Capsule', which is a playlist full of songs designed 'to take you back in time to your teenage years'. The tool offers two hours of 'iconic throwback tracks – all picked just for you'. When these playlists launched, Spotify gained over 1.6 million followers and over half a billion streams respectively. This wasn't a huge surprise to Spotify, however, as they had conducted research into the relationship between nostalgia and music beforehand. Almost 70 per cent of the people they surveyed said that nostalgia can help 'change or improve their mood', and three quarters told the media company that 'nostalgia connects people, thanks to shared experiences and memories.' The survey also found that music is the number-one trigger for the emotion. Respondents said that they often turned to songs from their past to prompt fond memories, which offered a welcome break from modern-day stresses like constant connectivity and news alerts: 'There's a comfort in thinking of a time before inbox zero became an unattainable goal plaguing our workdays.'[45]

If nostalgia generally is everywhere, nostalgia for the nineties is particularly potent today. Carrie, Miranda and Charlotte (although sadly no Samantha) have reappeared as part of *And Just Like That . . .*, the sequel to the hit television programme *Sex and the City*. Early 2023 saw another nineties cultural touchstone return to TV screens. *That '70s Show*, a coming-of-age sitcom set in seventies Wisconsin, has a new, nostalgic spin-off: *That '90s Show*. While *That '70s Show* starred Ashton Kutcher and Mila Kunis, the new iteration has the children of the original programme's leads decked out in checked shirts and backwards baseball caps. This is comfort TV for a particular generation. One journalist called it 'edgeless and unthreatening', another 'a nostalgia turducken' (a monstrous, but edible hybrid of a roast turkey, chicken and duck). As another writer, Eloise Hendy, put it, the seventies nostalgia that made the original show so popular is now encased first by the nostalgia for that show, and for the nineties era it portrays, 'like a series of birds stuffed in bigger birds'.[46]

The video-game company Nintendo now gives users of its Switch Online console the opportunity to play classic games from Sega Genesis and Nintendo 64, including the fan favourite *Mario Kart 64*, first released in 1996. Amazon has its own nineties 'throwback' section, where you can buy replicas of original Aaliyah memorabilia, commemorating the singer who died tragically young, and Smashing Pumpkins CDs. The children's games company Hasbro makes 'grown-up' Play-Doh packs that smell like buttery popcorn, designed to transport people back to the ubiquitous Blockbuster video stores of the nineties. Fashion and culture researcher James Abraham created @90sanxiety, an Instagram account that curates images of everything from stills of Halle Berry from the 1997 film *B.A.P.S*, to early Xanax adverts. The handle now has more than two million followers.[47]

There are several reasons for this nineties revival. Those who are coming of age in the early 2020s were born in the nineties, and it's the last period before smartphones became ubiquitous, before social media, before digital cameras, before everything that makes life in the twenty-first century what it is. The fashion house Marc Jacobs released a line called Heaven, which is inspired by Sofia Coppola's 1999 cult film, *The Virgin Suicides*. According to the line's art director, Ava Nirui, 'The younger generation definitely romanticizes a time before the internet. The '90s were the most "advanced" pre-web era in terms of culture, which is why it might seem so appealing to those who didn't experience it.'[48] Lindsey Turner, the daughter of the creators of the original *That '70s Show*, Bonnie and Terry Turner, and an executive producer on the spin-off, said that the nineties 'was the last time that people were looking up; they weren't looking down at their phones.' She insists that the decade was the last time any 'real kind of engagement' was possible, when you had to 'make your own fun' and connect with other people.[49]

For James Abraham, nineties nostalgia is less to do with the internet and more about reassurance, commerce and even a lack of creativity: 'Everyone is cycling back to things that they might have seen or done, because they are safe and tested,' he said.[50] Nostalgia works in this way, supposedly, because it makes people feel good. The argument has been the same since the 1970s: particularly in a time of global unrest, like the one we are living through now, nostalgia is a grounding force, something that, provided we part with enough money, has the capacity to calm our nerves.[51]

The problem with this argument is that it doesn't explain the specificity of now. Since the seventies, sociologists, journalists, social critics, advertising executives and marketing academics have noticed the commercial power of nostalgia and claimed their particular moment in time as acutely and unusually backward-looking. Their explanation for their own version of the 'nostalgia waves' follows similar lines. Nostalgia was acute then – whether they're writing in 1975, 1995 or 2022 – because then was a time of unprecedented discontent and rapid social change. So, what should we conclude? That the world has been bad and uncomfortable to live in since the seventies, that every year is more disconcerting than the last? That nostalgia is on an irreversible trajectory up, as society plummets down? That argument sounds, to this writer at least, like a rather nostalgic one. It's not enough to explain a nostalgia wave by recourse to present-day conditions. Perhaps it would make more sense to see nostalgia as a more or less permanent condition in the anglophone West – something that happens regardless of the problems and promises of the age in which we live.

CHAPTER SEVEN

REINVENTING THE WORLD

Nostalgia has the power to make you buy things, but it can also change the world in which you live. For some, nostalgia is more than just a passing feeling. It prompts people to remake their surroundings – to take themselves back in time and live as their predecessors did, complete with Victorian dress, 1940s appliances or 1970s wallpaper. For some, the past has a particularly powerful allure that can reshape our lives and transform the landscape and infrastructure of our towns and cities.

In 1819, Walter Scott published, *Ivanhoe: A Romance*. A historical novel in three volumes, set in England in the Middle Ages, it became one of Scott's best known and most influential novels, kicking off a spate of performances, reconstructions and re-enactments. Adapted for stage and the circus, *Ivanhoe* allowed people to witness the Middle Ages first-hand (well, almost). In 1839, Archibald William Montgomerie, thirteenth Earl of Eglinton, organized a full-scale re-enactment of a medieval tournament at Eglinton Castle, his neo-Gothic family pile in Ayrshire. It was a spectacle on a grand scale. Despite the steady Scottish drizzle, members of the local nobility presented themselves as the Knight of the Dragon, the Knight of the Black Lion, or simply, the Black Knight. Each was supported by a retinue of men-at-arms, bannermen, pages, squires and trumpeters.[1] The Eglinton tournament was part of a vibrant new trend. Medieval tourism started in earnest in the Victorian era and medieval scenes were included in the numerous World Fairs of the second half of the nineteenth century. Medieval-style buildings proliferated, from Pugin's masterpieces to the new and restored Gothic churches, civic buildings, private residences and railway stations. Victorian musicians wrote and performed sacred tunes inspired by medieval and Renaissance precedents. Pre-Raphaelite paintings also resurrected an imagined medieval aesthetic tradition.[2] These artists depicted a bucolic version of early English life in representations containing assorted Arthurian motifs that appealed to fantasies of a harmoniously stratified feudal society.

As we know, nostalgia meant something very different in the nineteenth century. It was a disease, associated more with place than with time. Nonetheless, it is clear that the Victorians were drawn to the Middle Ages. They found the period alluring and they attempted to resurrect it, or at least their version of it. And, as with the nostalgia prevalent in the late twentieth century, the Middle Ages were invoked in order to criticize their own times. Medievalism was, for many, a reaction against the social, political, economic and cultural ravages, as they saw it, wrought by nineteenth-century industrialization.[3] The aristocracy and landed gentry, under threat from the new industrial middle classes, were experiencing a touch of status anxiety. And so, they turned towards a medieval fantasy world to reassert feudal ideals of a rigid social hierarchy. For the aristocracy, the Middle Ages offered security over autonomy, charity over opportunity, and hierarchy over equality. At the opposite end of the socio-economic spectrum, the working classes lamented their lost ancient rights and the erosion of long-standing liberties. They championed the rural England of small landholders and domestic craft, and feared the arrival of factories and workhouses. Middle-class social critics also found much to admire in the Middle Ages. Buildings such as Manchester's town hall were built by middle-class civic leaders, inspired by the free medieval cities that made up the Hanseatic Leagues. Artists and critics like William Morris and John Ruskin railed against Victorian capitalism, lamenting the machine that entrapped the worker, allowing him neither freedom nor pleasure in his industry. By contrast, or so they believed, the medieval craftsmen made beautiful things and enjoyed their labours.[4]

The appeal of the past persisted into the early twentieth century. Citizens across Britain succumbed to what historians have called 'pageant fever'.[5] Thousands dressed up in historical costumes and hundreds of thousands more watched them perform scenes from the history of their home towns and villages. While they didn't just re-enact the Middle Ages, pre-modern history was particularly alluring for pageant-goers. These pageants were incredibly popular and were performed in settlements of all sizes, from major cities to tiny hamlets. Community groups of all sorts took part, including schools, churches and Women's Institutes. Pageants were regularly featured in the popular press and in highbrow literature alike.[6] Often held at times of acute economic crisis (the Depression of the 1930s, for example), they were both celebrations and laments. Their creators simultaneously portrayed optimistic visions of the present and future, while also capturing the period's widespread anti-industrial feeling. People in small towns and villages feared expanding urban developments and the lengthening network of railways and roadways, and they channelled that anxiety into their pageants.[7]

But was this thing that scholars now call 'medievalism' really motivated by nostalgia? The Middle Ages were, of course, riven by war, pestilence and strife. Is there anything about that period – even in its fantasy form – that might appeal to people living centuries later? Why would anyone born in the age of railways, steamships, antiseptics – and, later, the era of antibiotics, chemotherapies and the internet – want to return to the so-called Dark Ages? And yet, despite the unpleasantness of the historical reality, the Middle Ages undeniably possessed a magic – one that could be continually reborn in new stories, new media and new histories. The medieval period still enthrals people. Take, for example, the immense popularity of the books and television series *Game of Thrones*. While admittedly set in a fantasy world, the *Game of Thrones* universe is clearly inspired by the European Middle Ages. And almost all versions of the Middle Ages resurrected today are something of an invention or fantasy of those born since.[8] Indeed, the lines between fact and fiction when dealing with this distant period of time are often blurred. From King Arthur and Robin Hood, through to battleground re-enactments and medieval-themed restaurants, the culture of the Middle Ages continues to surround us, and has done ever since the very concept was first invented by Renaissance scholars.[9]

One of the stranger things about the appeal of the Middle Ages is that it is perhaps felt most strongly in the United States of America. King Arthur and Robin Hood are English legends and the medieval culture recreated at re-enactments and on screen is a European one, albeit often heavily fictionalized. North America before European colonization did, of course, look very different from the continent on the other side of the Atlantic. But these geographically and chronologically distant cultures have exerted a powerful draw on American people, especially at the turn of the twenty-first century.

In 2002, the American author Lev Grossman charted the recent resurgence of fantasy in popular culture.[10] While the last quarter of the twentieth century had been dominated by sci-fi franchises like Star Wars, Independence Day and The Matrix, since the turn of the millennium a world of swords and sorcerers, knights and princesses, magic and unicorns had resurfaced. In 2001, *Harry Potter and the Chamber of Secrets* and *The Lord of the Rings: The Fellowship of the Ring* ranked first and second at the box office. In its first weekend, *Harry Potter and the Chamber of Secrets* surpassed $88 million. The books sold seventy-seven million copies in the US, while J. R. R. Tolkien's various works sold eleven million copies in 2001 alone. The online fantasy game *EverQuest* had half a million subscribers, collectively paying more than $5 million a month, and the fantasy card game Magic: The Gathering had seven million players. Fantasy had become a multibillion-dollar business. Grossman thought there was a reason for the revival, writing, 'Popular culture is the most sensitive barometer we have for gauging shifts in the national mood.'[11] He thought the early twenty-first century was characterized by a 'darker, more pessimistic attitude toward technology and the future'. Instead of looking ahead, Americans were preoccupied with fantasy and 'a nostalgic, sentimental, magical vision of the medieval age'.[12]

But, while there was a shift in the tastes of the cinemagoing American public at this time, as we've seen, popular preoccupation with the Middle Ages started much earlier. Grossman identifies its origins in the 1960s, when a paperback edition of *The Lord of the Rings* was first published in the US. It sold more than a million copies in its first year. 'Gandalf for President' badges appeared on late-1960s lapels, 'Frodo Lives' was graffitied on New York City subway cars, and Tolkien inspired an American insurance salesman named Gary Gygax to quit his job and create Dungeons and Dragons, a fantasy role-playing table-top game made famous again by another, much later, nostalgic popular-culture phenomenon, the TV show *Stranger Things*. But, for some aficionados of the Middle Ages, it is not enough to enjoy the past vicariously through a novel, film, piece of artwork or pageant; instead, they must (re)live this past them-selves.[13] They do this through live-action role playing, jousting, re-enactments and travel destinations such as Medieval Times Dinner and Tournament.

The Society of Creative Anachronism is the best-known and most dominant force in American medieval re-enactment.[14] Founded in Berkeley, California, in 1966, two years later the SCA was incor-porated as a non-profit education organization and today it claims around 30,000 members and remains an umbrella organization for hundreds of re-enactor groups across North America. The SCA's motto is 'Forward into the past!' and their motivations are distinctly nostalgic. Members long for a simpler time and wish to recapture or return to a period with clear moral values. They cite an anti-technology nostalgia and share a sense that honour, courtesy and chivalry are missing from contemporary society.

Many of those who choose to live medievally, however briefly or temporarily, attempt to find solutions to the problems of moder-nity in the distant past. Re-enactments allow them to experience the Middle Ages, but also escape the temporal constraints of their lives to live as 'avatars and alter egos' distinct from the day-to-day grind of school or work.[15] They can be whoever they want to be – a knight, a princess, a jouster, a sorceress – rather than an accountant, IT manager or investment banker.[16] In *Monster Camp*, a documentary detailing the behind-the-scenes manoeuvres of a Seattle-based group of live-action role-players (or LARPers), JP, who plays under the name of Sir Gregor, summarizes the allure of the game as a kind of escapism: 'There's a lot of people who [re-enact] to try – you know, the theme of "be all you *can't* be." So they're trying to be something they normally aren't in their lives to one extent or another.'[17]

Lev Grossman interviewed various SCA members for his article. Darren Chermack, also known as Sir Tristan von Eising, a proud nobleman of the Barony of Nordskogen, explained, 'I think our technology today has taken us further from morality and generous behaviour . . . I find that this lifestyle is a way to touch on something that I want to be as a person – the pursuit of courtesy, chivalry, and proper behaviour.'[18] 'There's a heavy anti-industrial streak there,' agrees Carrie Crowder, forty-one, a conservative Republican, mother of two and former SCA member. 'It's tied to the medieval, feudal landscape that is the backdrop for so much of fantasy.'[19] Author and active SCA member Michael A. Cramer agrees: 'The SCA is nostalgic for the Middle Ages. It is this nostalgia, the sense that somehow the Middle Ages were a better time than the present, that is the most prominent feature of the SCA.'[20] The SCA is not, of course, 'the real Middle Ages, nor is it an accurate picture of the real Middle Ages.' Instead, it is a 'pastiche', a collection of ideas about the Middle Ages, often, but not always, 'romantic and highly nostalgic'.[21] Although some theorists of nostalgia think that you can only feel nostalgic for a period within living memory, Cramer evidently disagrees.

But, while some of the nostalgia motivating SCA members is of the conservative, right-wing variety, the Middle Ages can be made to mean different things to different people. The SCA emerged out of the countercultural movements of 1960s California and its members are themselves countercultural almost by definition, if you take counterculture to encompass 'those people who reject the dominant values and behaviour of society'.[22] When it was founded, SCA members sought to reject self-interest, greed and modernism, and replace these values with a romantic notion of chivalry. But they were also aligned to the hippy movement and created an alternative utopian world where contemporary strictures and mores were relaxed. Indeed, medievalism in general, and the various different ways people seek to experience the Middle Ages in the present, isn't just driven by conservative, anti-bourgeois nostalgia. Charles Dellheim, a historian, denies that medievalism is simply, 'a conservative revolt against modernity'.[23]

Amateur medievalists, and particularly re-enactors, are regularly derided by both trained historians and by the general public. Both believe that historical expertise requires a degree of distance, a kind of objectivity that precludes immersive experiences or play. As a result, re-enactors and LARPers are seen as 'merely nostalgic, naively, uncritically, and irresponsibly yearning for an idealized past as escape from a present felt to be dismal and unpromising.'[24] At one time, the leading academic conference in the field, the International Congress on Medieval Studies, in Kalamazoo, Canada, tried to underscore the divide by asking the SCA not to participate in the event. But some modern medieval re-enactors deny nostalgia as a motivation altogether. Rather than emotionally identifying with their chosen period of time, these people justify their hobby along intellectual and rational lines – arguing that what they're doing is a kind of scholarship. Rather than simply reading history books or primary sources, this is a way of understanding the past – warts and all – through doing.

The lines between serious scholarship and re-enactment are blurry. Not only do many of the people engaged in communities like SCA research their costumes, adopted roles and the history of their chosen time period with great care and diligence, but there are entire sub-fields that cross over between what has traditionally been seen as professional and amateur history. Experimental archaeology, for example, attempts to generate and test historical and archaeological hypotheses, usually by trying to replicate or assess the feasibility of prior cultures performing various tasks or feats. Building the pyramids is a classic example. Other examples of this include Butser Ancient Farm in Berkshire, England, which recreates buildings from British archaeology to test theories of construction, use and materials. The farm still carries out long-term experiments in prehistoric agriculture, animal husbandry and manufacturing to test ideas posited by archaeologists. Another is the oldest open-air museum in Denmark, Lejre Land of Legends, a site that features reconstructed buildings from the Stone Age, Iron Age, Viking era and even the nineteenth century, and runs experiments on prehistoric and medieval lifestyles and technologies.

While these scholarly enterprises are in their own way inventions – they are certain archaeologists' 'best guesses' at what historical life was like – re-enactments and reconstructions can also be seen as laboratories of sorts. The Crossroads medieval village cooperative was an enterprise in New South Wales, Australia, established in 1992. They built a medieval village, including accommodation for sixty people, and established a permaculture farm featuring old animal breeds and plant varieties. Crossroads combined ideals of equality with sustainable ecology, demonstrating that nostalgia and research can coexist. The cooperative had aimed to construct a replica of a small French castle, but this more ambitious plan was never realized and the site was sold in 2018. Even when nostalgia does motivate re-enactment, it can be a version of nostalgia that prioritizes community, equality, a slower pace of life and a return to nature, not merely a resurrection of the hierarchy and patriarchal chivalry of the Middle Ages.

Another manifestation of medievalism emerged in tandem to re-enactments. In the 1990s, the British Marxist historian Raphael Samuel described how the past thirty years had 'witnessed an extraordinary and, it seems, ever-growing enthusiasm for the recovery of the national past'. Surveying the gamut from retrofitting old warehouses to saving steam locomotives, he noted that this 'preservation mania' had reached a point where the National Trust was and remains Britain's largest mass-membership organization.[25] History was the country's number-one growth industry. Early manifestations of this 'heritage industry' tended to be of the stately home variety, with an emphasis on preserving and gaining access to the homes of the elite. Exemplifying this, the vast majority of National Trust properties used to belong to the landed gentry. Indeed, other versions of British 'public history' also tend to focus on the wealthy and the elite. Think of *Downton Abbey* and *The Crown*, two of Britain's main historical, cultural exports. But, in the last decades of the twentieth century, both academics and heritage professionals were shifting their gaze from politicians and aristocrats to the ordinary and under-represented. The 1960s and 1970s were when social history, or history from below, first emerged and a kind of vernacular heritage sought to explore ordinary people's everyday lives, emphasizing particularly those of the working classes.[26]

It was in this period, then, that 'living history' destinations, museums and experiences became increasingly popular. The Canterbury Tales experience first opened its doors in 1987 and offered an 'interactive tour through Chaucer's tales'.[27] Visitors walked the darkened streets between London and Kent, meeting both waxworks and costumed characters along the way. It also ran after-dark and school-holiday events in which children enjoyed everything from medieval 'potion making' to sword fighting and storytelling. The Jorvik Viking Centre opened in York in 1984 and quickly became one of the most popular visitor attractions in the UK, with over eighteen million visitors since. This 'ground-breaking visitor experi-ence' involves taking a 'journey through the reconstruction of Viking Age streets' and experiencing 'life as it would have been in 10th century York'. Jorvik strives for authenticity with the help of '22 new animatronic characters' who guide visitors through the 'ride experience'. Everything from clothing and facial features to speech has been 'meticulously researched' to offer visitors 'a real insight into the lives of people who lived over 1,000 years ago'. The site attempts to reconstruct the sights, sounds and even smells of the distant past.[28]

Sometimes, immersive experiences of the Middle Ages make no claims to education and are used as pure, simple entertainment. Across the Atlantic, in Las Vegas, you can stay in a medieval-themed hotel and casino called Excalibur (after King Arthur's mythical sword). The building's facade is a stylized castle and, until 2007, a model of Merlin surveyed arriving visitors from a high turret. When it opened in 1990, it was the largest resort hotel in the world, with more than 4,000 rooms covering over seventy acres. Along similar lines, Medieval Times Dinner and Tournament is a 'family dinner theatre featuring staged medieval-style games, sword-fighting, and jousting'. It began in Spain, with two 'dinner/entertainment complexes' located in Majorca and Benidorm. The first North American venue opened in Florida in 1983 and it now has locations in California, Georgia, Illinois, Maryland, New Jersey, South Carolina, Texas and Toronto. Medieval Times' 'castles' have since entertained more than seventy-two million guests and it claims to be North America's '#1 dinner attraction'.[29] Guests are invited to a royal feast with the king and his family. They enjoy a fine, four-course dinner, while taking in the 'colourful medieval pageantry' and watching knights compete in jousting tournaments on horseback.[30] The website promises a fantasy experience 'that blurs the boundary between fairy tale and spectacle'. Guests 'travel through the mists of time to a forgotten age and a tale of devotion, courage and love.' Eveleena Fults, an experienced princess at Medieval Times in Orlando, told a researcher, 'creating the fantasy is my favourite part of the job.'[31] But it isn't all fun and games. 'The athletic stunts, jousting, and swordplay the knights perform are not fairy tale,' the advertisements say, 'they are very real, as you will see.'[32]

The website also advertises various job openings, including squires who are expected to 'assist all of His Majesty's Brave Knights'. Successful training and performance as a squire is a prerequisite for advancement to the role of knight. The role isn't, however, open to all: 'To preserve the authenticity and genuineness of the scripted role of Knights in the Medieval Times theatrical production, Knights positions are reserved for male performers.' Since knights positions are filled exclusively from the ranks of squires who have trained at Medieval Times, the role of squire is 'likewise reserved for male performers'. No parallel restrictions are placed on applicants to the role of queen.[33]

Medieval Times has been around since the 1980s, and as such pre-dates the recent revival and commercialization of jousting as a combat sport. Jousting has taken off in both North America and in

Europe. Contests are held at the Longs Peak Scottish Irish Highlands Festival in Estes Park, Colorado, the Sword of Honour in Leeds, England, the Tournament of the Phoenix in San Diego, and the Tournois du Lys d'Argent in Quebec.[34] But the style on either side of the Atlantic differs. The sport in America is just that, a sport, and its participants are often uninterested in the Middle Ages. One of the world's leading jousters, the American Charlie Andrews, claims to know and care nothing for history. He doesn't joust because he's attracted to 'romantic notions of honour and chivalry', nor because he has an affinity for the Middle Ages. He does it because he considers jousting, 'one of the most extreme sports ever invented'.[35]

In contrast, European jousting is more of a spectacle or performance, put on as part of medieval fairs or family days at historic castles. European jousting is also supposed to be more historically accurate. WorldJoust Tournaments, the company that sponsors European events, claims to be 'dedicated to the creation of historical tournaments and their development into an upscale, modern international sport'.[36] For some modern-day jousters, like Charlie Andrews, the sport appeals because of the skill and performance required. But others are motivated by an emotional connection to the Middle Ages. Jouster James Anderson, who earned a bachelor's degree in medieval studies in 2019, described its allure thus: 'I feel nostalgia for it even though I wasn't there . . . Some people are born with the medieval bug, and I have it.'[37]

Of course, living-history museums, events, tourism and re-enactments are not confined to resurrections of the Middle Ages. Re-enactors are numerous across the United States, Canada, the United Kingdom, Germany, Australia, Italy, Denmark, Sweden and Poland. Re-enacting the American Civil War began even before the real fighting had ended, and veterans quickly recreated battles as a way to commemorate their fallen comrades. The Great Reunion of 1913, celebrating the fiftieth anniversary of the Battle of Gettysburg, was attended by more than 50,000 Union and Confederate veterans, and included re-enactments of elements of the battle.[38] Modern re-enacting began during the 1961–5 Civil War centennial commemorations and grew in popularity during the 1980s and 1990s. In

1986, *Time* magazine estimated there were more than 50,000 re-enactors in the US. In 1998, the 135th anniversary re-enactment of the Battle of Gettysburg took place near the original battlefield. Estimates vary, but it was probably the largest battle re-enactment ever held anywhere in the world, with between 15,000 and 20,000 participants and 50,000 spectators.[39]

Some of those participants were incredibly earnest. 'If you want to understand this war, then you have got to know how the soldiers felt,' explained Thomas Downes, a machinist from Cleveland who had signed on as a captain with the 2nd New Hampshire Regiment. 'We cannot drink Cokes or Gatorade in the camp. It wouldn't be authentic. But if you can get whisky, that's all right. We are living historians. We have to do this to understand our forefathers.'[40] Harry Burgess, a history teacher from Michigan, said that partaking in such battles, 'gives us private time machines'.[41] Re-enactment societies weren't just around in the United States. The Sealed Knot, for example, is the oldest re-enactment society in the UK, and now the biggest in Europe. Founded in 1968, The Sealed Knot re-enacts the battles of the English Civil War.

When history and heritage became boom industries in Britain in the seventies and eighties, living-history museums also boomed. In 1973, the open-air museum Blists Hill Victorian Town opened. Located in the former industrial region of Shropshire, and one of ten interlinked museums in the area known as the Ironbridge Gorge, Blists Hill is an immersive museum that invites visitors to 'experience life as it was over 100 years ago through the sights, sounds, smells and tastes of a recreated Victorian Town'.[42] Reconstructing industrial life of the 1890s, Blists Hill shares many similarities with museums like Beamish in northern England, as well as Colonial Williamsburg and Plymouth Plantation in the United States. These sites promise visitors the opportunity to experience history in ways that lie outside of traditional museums and academic study. They offer the fantasy of time travel, via interactivity, simulation and make-believe.

In 2019, one visitor described Blists Hill as a place 'for those who love history and nostalgia'. Another tourist, from Mansfield, UK, left a review entitled, 'A walk through times long gone', and added that they 'thoroughly enjoyed the nostalgia'. For Tessy68, this was a 'trip back in time' and they enjoyed a very 'nostalgic and informative afternoon'. In 2018, nickthebottlewasher praised Blists Hill as 'not just a nostalgia trip for us old fogeys, but entertaining and educational for the school-age children too.' Similarly, John C J wrote, 'Nostalgic for older family members and an insight of the way it was for the younger ones.' Hawthorne21 titled their review 'Childhood memories' and called the village a 'place for nostalgia and remembering the good times'.[43]

Of course, none of these visitors, or the many hundreds more who mention nostalgia in their reviews, were alive in the 1890s, nor can they remember Victorian or even Edwardian life. Their nostalgia is, therefore, a more diffuse kind. Just like those motivated by nostalgia to recreate the Middle Ages, they're drawn to an illusion – a fantasy version of the past, in which precise chronology doesn't matter. Instead, it's an imagined version of what a particular period in history might have been like, and what it represents in the present. They're not interested in the past for its historical accuracy – or even the precise time period – but for the very personal feelings it has the capacity to evoke. It is this emotion – this nostalgia – that enables people to conflate the 1890s, decades before they were born, with the 1960s they grew up in. However much wartime re-enactors, professional jousters and Medieval Times employees might insist they're motivated by historical accuracy, for many consumers of these performances, it simply does not matter. The people behind Blists Hill might want to create an educational attraction – accurate in its resurrection of the 1890s – but that doesn't necessarily mean that's how visitors will experience it.[44]

For many cultural critics and professional historians, this nostalgia is deeply problematic. Codified into British law in 1980 and 1983 with the National Heritage Acts, heritage became not only big business, but a topic of heated political debate. Despite (or perhaps because of) its huge popularity among the general public, the British heritage industry faced accusations of promoting idealistic nostalgia, endorsing paternalistic, conservative values and sanitizing historical periods that were in reality unstable, dirty, unequal and exploitative. The poet and critic Tom Paulin deemed the industry 'a loathsome collection of theme parks and dead values', while the historian Robert Hewison argued that the English obsession with heritage was symptomatic of a culture mired in nostalgia, unable to look to its future.[45] The cultural historian Patrick Wright contended that 'heritage is the backward glance which is taken from the edge of a vividly imagined abyss.'[46]

In the 1980s, many academic historians were at best ambivalent about, and more often outrightly critical of nostalgia. As so many others have done, they characterized the emotion as a universal modern malaise, a contemporary epidemic of romantic bad faith. Almost all of us, they argued, were infected with a sense of exile from the past as a once familiar, but now foreign country. In the second phase of the disease, we become compulsive preservers and consumers of even the most trivial relics of our past. Just as the anxiety and unprecedented pace of change experienced from the sixties onwards produced a nostalgia wave in fashion and film, that same flood drove people to indiscriminately preserve as many traces of the past as possible. This fevered, uncritical nostalgia prompted us to collect trifling pieces of material culture and preserve pretty much anything for the sake of its past-ness. Many historians thought that this nostalgic preoccupation was unproductive, precluding progressive action and foreclosing the future.

This wasn't true for all academics. In 1994, the Marxist historian Raphael Samuel called this trend 'retrochic', a process by which people borrow from the past at random, but he also believed the enthusiasm for heritage was a good thing.[47] He saw the fascination with time-worn buildings, clothing and music as something that 'welled up from nowhere' – in the counterculture, collectors' clubs, local labour councils and grassroots efforts. This living history rejects epic narratives in favour of personal observation and local knowledge. It invites us to play games with the past and pretend that we're at home in it, ignoring the limitations of time and space by reincarnating it in the here and now. Samuel thought that retrochic offered something that dry historical accounts could not. It provided a sensory experience of the past that you could smell, touch and experience; one that was democratic, where no specialist knowledge was necessary, that was populated by amateur enthusiasts and obsessives. This was something to celebrate, 'not a reason for snark'.[48]

Indeed, as one of the major heritage centres in England, Blists Hill was the target of specific vitriol from academics who deemed the nostalgia-driven heritage industry facile and harmful. One historian devoted an entire article to accusing the attraction of promoting a spectacle of idealized Victorian work and another historian derided the museum as having the 'authenticity of a film set'.[49] But is that idealization and lack of authenticity a problem? Why does it matter if places like Blists Hill do evoke nostalgia in their visitors? After all, is a desire for escapism all that bad? And why must the past *not* be entertaining, evocative or fun?

*

For some people, visiting living-history museums or participating in historical battle reconstructions is insufficient. They want to entirely reconstruct the world in which they live, resurrecting past clothes, furniture, technologies, foods, buildings and habits. In 2015, Gabriel and Sarah Chrisman were hurtled into the public eye, going viral for living as if they had been sent back to Victorian times, a radical rebellion against modernity that had been going on since 2009. They live as much as possible as a couple in the late nineteenth century would. Sarah wears a corset and the flowing, formal skirts of the Victorian era. When he goes for a cycle ride on one of his big-wheel 'ordinary' cycles (penny farthings), Gabriel dons trousers that end above his ankles and wears a short tie, just as the Victorians did. They don't have phones or a computer or a television. Sarah writes historical fiction by filling up notebooks in longhand using a fountain pen. They sleep on a mattress Sarah sewed and read books by light from oil lamps or replicas of late-nineteenth-century light bulbs.[50]

Their house, on an anonymous street in the small, rainy town of Port Townsend, Washington, is a reminder that the Victorian era they've worked so hard to recreate was not a glamorous time. By modern standards, it is small, dark and quiet. A huge iron wood-burning stove dominates the kitchen. At the centre of their living room is a Wardian case, a small glass enclosure housing an ornamental fern. Their home is neat and full of books: nineteenth-century novels, more modern works of non-fiction or sci-fi, and magazines printed out from the Google Books archive and bound by hand so the couple can read nineteenth-century issues of *Cosmopolitan* without using a screen (Google Books is one of their few modern tech concessions.)[51]

The Chrismans are part of a broad and diffuse movement of people seeking to wrest back control from the phones and screens and algorithms that surround us. Many articles have been written declaring that our contemporary nostalgia for the nineties is a manifestation of a deep dissatisfaction with the pervasive nature of the internet.[52] But Gabriel and Sarah are unusually passionate and committed, driven by a zeal comparable to utopians of an earlier age. Like millions of people, they are unhappy with the way things are in the present day. And their solution is familiar: why not turn back the hands of time to return to 1980 or 1950 or 1890? Why can't we return to when things were good, whenever that might have been?

They aren't, of course, the only people who have registered that the technology that has been designed to improve our lives has hidden costs. Even executives at social-media companies suggest they wouldn't allow their own children access to the sites they manage, and have lamented the stress technology has placed on society. Tech giants are increasingly seen as organizations in need of constraint, and those in power have proposed 'right to repair' laws and monopoly-busting measures to curtail their influence. Ordinary internet users have boycotted Uber and Amazon for their working practices, and we routinely download apps to prevent us using our other apps (this book could not have been written without SelfControl). There are plenty among us who have sought to do something like the Chrismans have done, whether that's go entirely off grid or at least unplug from technology and the internet for a short while.

The Chrismans might be unusual, but they are certainly not unique. In early 2022, British journalist Johann Hari published *Stolen Focus*, which argued that our collective attention span is collapsing.[53] Hari claimed he was inspired by the steady shrinkage of his own attention span. Activities that required 'deep focus, like reading a book, or watching long films' were becoming more and more difficult.[54] He was not alone, he said. Everyone around him was experiencing something similar, particularly the young people he knew. Hari blames many things for this 'serious attention crisis' – pollution, big business, but most of all technology. He argues that our attention has not simply collapsed, but it has been stolen.

Hari packs his book with all sorts of shocking factoids. In the United States, teenagers can focus on one task for just sixty-five seconds at a time, while office workers average only three minutes. Citing a Carnegie Mellon University study, he insists that 'almost all of us with a smartphone' are losing 20 to 30 per cent of our brain power 'almost all the time'. Hari argues that there has been a gradual loss in our ability to concentrate, partly because of sleep deprivation. Since 1942, he writes, the amount of time a person sleeps has been 'slashed by an hour a night'. The reason for this, he says, is that 90 per cent of Americans look at a 'glowing device', like a phone, in the two hours before going to bed.[55]

The book sold well, and it features some glowing reviews on its cover. But its claims have been disputed. The journalist and broadcaster Matthew Sweet and others have argued that the evidence underpinning Hari's argument is flimsy, misrepresented and cherry-picked.[56] Nevertheless, much of it *feels* true and aligns with a cultural conversation that has been going on for decades. It also taps into an idea that underpins the motivations of many medieval re-enactors. Think of Sir Tristan von Eising, who explained his commitment to the Middle Ages in the early 2000s by saying, 'I think our technology today has taken us further from morality and generous behaviour.'[57] *Stolen Focus* is only the latest iteration of a relatively long-standing argument about the negative consequences of social media and the internet on our brains. In 2015, for example, *Time* magazine cited a study that claimed we now have even shorter attention spans than goldfish.[58] Every few months, there's a new spate of headlines alerting people to the latest studies on reduced attention. At least some of those studies were funded by authors or companies selling self-help books and products designed to solve the very problem they have supposedly identified.[59]

The demands on our attention that Hari pinpoints are part of a broader pathology of the contemporary age, as diagnosed by pundits, scientists and Luddites. The twenty-four-hour news cycle and the onslaught of information produced by smartphones, the internet and social media are supposedly making us sick. In the early months of the pandemic, researchers found that news consumed online and via social media was associated with increased depression, anxiety and stress – more than when people consumed the same news via more traditional media, like television or newspapers.[60] Other studies associate 'excessive' smartphone use with OCD, ADHD, substance misuse, difficulties in cognitive-emotion regulation, impulsivity, impaired cognitive function, social-media addiction, shyness, low self-esteem, sleep problems, reduced physical fitness, unhealthy eating habits, pain and migraines, and changes to the very volume and structure of the brain.[61]

In our current information age, or so the story goes, we suffer in new and unique ways. But the idea that modern life, and particularly modern technology, harms as well as helps, is deeply embedded in Western culture. In fact, the Victorians diagnosed similar problems in their own society. The kind of anxieties that motivate books like Hari's were also fundamental to an immense body of literature produced in the nineteenth century by English-language writers about the pace of social change, the pressures of new technologies and the emergent diseases of modern life. The parallels to the present are obvious: 'FOMO', phone addictions and the melancholia evoked by the constantly turning news cycle are the diseases of *our* modern life. But the Victorians had their own, too.

As we have seen, the late nineteenth century was a time, like ours, of hectic social and technological transformation. Telegraph cables, steamships, motor cars and eventually aeroplanes knitted the world more and more tightly together, and the pace of change felt unprecedented. It was an era of progress and technological innovation, but also a period of intense introspection and unease. With the new expediency of travel and communication came new diseases – physical, emotional and mental. Passengers were warned about 'train heart', a condition that afflicted too-enthusiastic users of the railways, and doctors complained about the emotional toll of being constantly contactable by this new-fangled thing, the telephone. In the 1860s, the doctor James Crichton Browne spoke of the 'velocity of thought and action' then required. He identified the consequences, all negative, of the amount of information the brain now had to process – more data in a month 'than was required of our grandfathers in the course of a lifetime'.[62]

Just as it is today, work was central to concerns about the diseases of modern life. Industrialization, professionalization and urbanization combined with the explosion of cheap printed material and a growing audience of literate men and women to turn labour of all kinds into a subject of acute medical concern. Many worried about the industrial hazards of factory work, while others fretted over the mental and physical health of what would now be termed white-collar workers – an expanding category of labour in the nineteenth century. Authors elaborated lengthy texts on the impact of distraction, mental strain and overwork on the professional man, claiming that these things harmed the psychological self as well as the physical body. In 1854, a concerned reader named John Marshall wrote a letter to the London magazine *The Spectator*, drawing attention to a little-known malady that he called 'overwork of the brain'. Victims might be able to walk, talk, eat, drink and 'at least partially' sleep, but they suffered a kind of 'nervous excitement' that rendered them fatigued, anxious and ultimately mad. They became alienated from friends and other normal social contact. Left untreated, overwork of the brain could cause permanent damage to a person's sanity. This was a new problem, unique to this 'age of boasted enlightenment' – an unintended product of progress. More people had easy access to literature, science, politics and art than ever before, and were, as a result of these distractions, sleepwalking to an early grave.

This was, Marshall insisted, one of the 'severest calamities' known to humankind.[63]

For many, these occupational anxieties were tied to new technologies. The main offenders were telegraphs, telephones and trains – things that had fundamentally altered the pace of life, with a range of pathological consequences. Railways were a source of special anxiety. Medical writers were concerned that the introduction of train travel introduced a degree of hurry into people's lives, reducing their quality of life and damaging their health. In 1868, a concerned physician wrote, 'In our old coaching time, there was none of that hurry and bustle which now characterizes our present mode of travelling by rail.'[64] While, in the age of coach travel, 'passengers leisurely took their places,' now, 'all alike hurry to one spot, with one object, to save the train.'[65] This wasn't just a cultural shift, but a biological one, too: 'Everything is changed, even our bodies are changing.'[66]

The same writer continued: 'All this striving to do certain distances in certain given times has engendered an irritability in our organs which has told upon thousands, and will tell upon thousands more.' Today, in the twenty-first century, the same sorts of pundits diagnose us as living through an 'age of productivity', with too little time for rest, reflection or leisurely tourism. As a remedy for our 'hyper-scheduled busy lives', people recommend 'slow living' and companies sell things like 'slow travel'. Similar anxieties prevail, albeit with different mechanisms for harm.

In 1845, the satirical magazine *Punch* described the threat of 'railway mania', a new disease provoked by proximity to, and obsession with, trains. Sending up contemporary anxieties rather than expressing genuine concern, *Punch* wrote of a disorder of the wits, 'principally incidental to those who live by them; but it is by no means unknown among capitalists possessed of less wit than money.' Caused by a 'tempting advertisement', propagated by 'the contagion of example' (nineteenth-century peer pressure or influencer culture), the first symptoms of the 'railway mania' were idleness, inattention and a neglect of study: 'The patient leaving good books to read the newspaper supplement.' As the condition worsens, 'reason is prostrated' and the moral feelings are 'perverted'. The sufferer becomes unable to take care of himself, while losing any sense of duty or obligation to others.[67]

Train travel was harmful, but it wasn't the only damaging element of nineteenth-century society. It was part of an entire culture of taxing, over-strenuous body and brain work. In an 1868 article, evocatively titled 'Hurried to Death', the author lamented, 'We must hurry, we must bustle, we must travel by railways, we must read, write, and otherwise work our brain all day long.'[68] Other new technologies were just as bad – particularly those designed to speed up and ameliorate communication. The electric telegraph was invented in 1837, and the first telephone patent was granted to Alexander Graham Bell in 1876. Pre-empting present-day anxieties about the negative consequences of always being contactable, Victorians worried about the new ease of communication. They were particularly concerned about the impact of the telegraph and telephone on doctors (perhaps because it was doctors themselves doing the worried writing). One such perturbed physician described the growing difficulties 'arising from the modern facilities for communication by the post, by the telegraph, and by the telephone'.[69] Advertisements began to appear, posted by doctors offering telephone consultations 'either by night or day'. One Pittsburgh practitioner had even devised a way of taking his telephone to bed: 'Should any calls come during the night, he can answer them without leaving his room.'[70]

There were obvious perks to these new technologies. They made telemedicine possible before the internet and gave some doctors a commercial edge over their rivals. But this hyper-connectivity had consequences. 'Advice and explanation', one physician argued, were too 'easily asked for'. Patients were now able to contact their doctors over any small, inconsequential matter which required the 'sacrifice of much time and labour from an overworked man'.[71] One late-nineteenth-century writer put the problem succinctly: 'Civilization (like success) has its penalty.' New technologies, new industries, new professions and new opportunities for travel were all seemingly marks of social and economic progress. But this progress had its drawbacks. In the Victorian era, anxieties about these consequences were tied up with concerns about civilization, racial supremacy and imperial overreach.

The almost comical concerns about train travel and telephones had a dark underside. As a body of literature, they fed into a discourse of social and biological degeneration, which flourished around the turn of the twentieth century. These texts dealt with the 'apparent paradox' that civilization itself might be the catalyst of – as much as the defence against – physical and social pathology.[72] 'Anglo-Saxon' and 'Teutonic' races had reached their pinnacle and were increasingly suffering from social disorders, physical and mental ill health, and moral deviancy. This kind of thinking also underpinned eugenics and its attempts to reverse degeneration and preserve the 'quality' elements of Western society.[73]

Clearly, pathologies of progress are not unique to today. As Matthew Sweet put it, Johann Hari's book is 'part of a long tradition that registers the pain of cultural and technological change – but over-reaches by telling you it is making you ill or stupid.'[74] Knowing that we've all been through this before might help alleviate some of the current worry. These Victorian writings make apparent the not unprecedented nature of it all, hopefully making it slightly easier to bear. Illuminating the processes by which progress is turned pathological can help us navigate our lives online. It also shatters one of the key assumptions that underpin so many Hari-esque anxieties about technology and its ills. We've experienced periods of rapid progress before, and humanity has survived. Knowing that ideas about civilization and degeneration lay behind Victorian diseases of modern life helps us understand those nineteenth-century texts. But it also helps with interpreting current concerns about the negatives of new technologies and the accompanying social transformations.

This isn't to say that those discussing the perils of the internet age are eugenicists or inspired by the same nineteenth-century concerns about progress and decline, race and empire. But it might, at least, prompt us to look beneath the current deluge – to dig through the present-day discourse in search of its own motivations

15. Historian Joachim Fest's bestselling biography, *Hitler: A Career*, was turned into a film in 1977.

16. The original 1939 poster was only rarely displayed during the Second World War and was little known until a copy was rediscovered in an English bookshop in 2000.

17. Hovis released their iconic advert, 'The Bike', in 1973.

18. Medieval dress in the 1907 Oxford Historical Pageant.

19. The Medieval Times building in Lyndhurst, New Jersey.

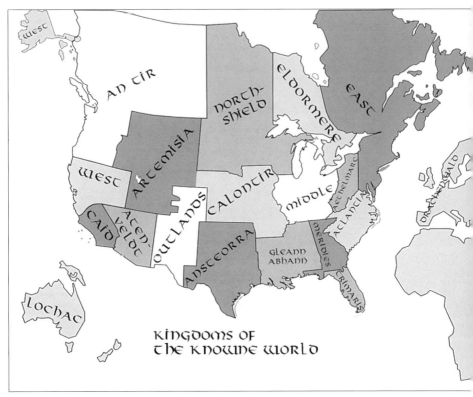

20. The Society for Creative Anachronism's 'Kingdoms of the Known World', as of 2015.

21. Members of the Society for Creative Anachronism in Emporia, Kansas.

22. Dioramas at Jorvik Viking Centre in York, England.

23. A street in the open-air museum Blists Hill Victorian Town, in Shropshire, England.

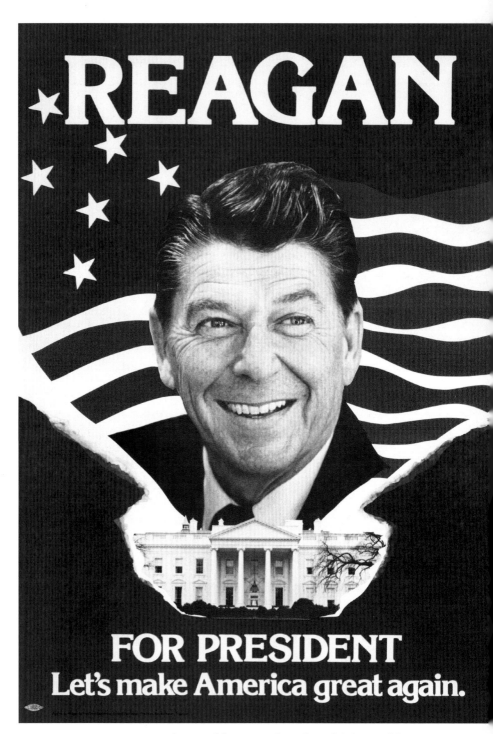

24. A 1980 poster for Republican presidential candidate Ronald Reagan, featuring the slogan 'Let's Make America Great Again'.

25. Signs supporting then American president Donald Trump in Washington DC, September 2017.

26. Gift shop selling German Democratic Republic memorabilia in Weimar, Germany.

ТЕЛЕКАНАЛ
NOЅ̶ALЬГИЯ

27. Logo for the Russian TV Channel, Nostalgiya.

28. Nurses in 1950s dress dance in the 2012 London Olympic Games opening ceremony, directed by Danny Boyle.

and driving forces. It suggests that a degree of scepticism might be useful. Does the scale of concern match the scale of the problem, or is it more about misplaced nostalgia than real ill health? Concerns about the pace of life and all its attendant pathologies are often shot through with the idea that society today has lost something it once had – something ephemeral, but nevertheless fundamental. A belief that, at some point in the not-too-distant past, people felt, behaved and worked better. That lives were more relaxing, communication less hurried and society more genial. But history suggests otherwise.

We are only ever able to interpret our lives according to the contexts in which we live. The nineteenth century felt hurried and pressured for those who experienced it. Many of its technologies were met with enthusiasm, but also with anxiety and stress. This is true for then, for today, and even for some aspects of the seventeenth century. Take this entry in Samuel Pepys' diary, written in May 1665. He had just had his pocket watch mended. It could only tell him the hour – it didn't do minutes or seconds – but nonetheless he could not 'forbear carrying my watch in my hand in the coach all this afternoon, and seeing what o'clock it is one hundred times'. His addiction was so acute, he was 'apt to think with myself, how could I be so long without one'.[75]

People who re-enact the past almost always get something wrong about the history they're trying to reconstruct. They might collapse different time periods together, romanticize unpalatable elements or – in the case of the Chrismans – fail to appreciate the peculiar pathologies of distant centuries and decades. An element of nostalgia underpins a variety of different attempts to resurrect the past, whether it's military re-enactments, restaged medieval jousting tournaments or homes kitted out with Victoriana. Sometimes that nostalgia has a slightly troubling set of motivations. Sarah Chrisman, for example, has written fondly of a society where women, considered the 'morally superior sex', had more control over the 'home and private sphere'.[76] She has reservations about modern feminism more broadly, writing, 'I think that in a lot of the efforts that women have made to try to prove they're the same as men, a lot of the power that women used to have has gotten lost along the way.'[77]

But these 'amateur' historians aren't the only ones who get things wrong about the past, and they're also often meticulous, accurate compilers of evidence. People hold retrograde, socially conservative and archaic views all the time, even those who don't immerse themselves in the past. And if re-enactors, living-history museum attendees and the Chrismans find pleasure and meaning in the past, then why should historians or critics resent or deny them that joy? Nostalgia, for all its flaws, at least has the power to enchant, to lure people into the past and allow them to stay a while, enjoying everything history has to offer.

CHAPTER EIGHT

POLITICAL NOSTALGIAS

In 2016, Donald Trump won the USA's presidential election. It was a campaign saturated in nostalgia, and his slogan – 'Make America Great Again' – contained both an implicit critique of America today and a yearning for an America past, rooted in a sneaking suspicion, on behalf of many American citizens, that things had somewhere, somehow gone wrong. The 'MAGA' motto, and its performance at rallies and emblazonment on merchandise, lacked specificity, but that gave it an emotional capaciousness that perhaps only made it even more effective.

Trump's victory is just one of the many relatively recent perceived political sins blamed on nostalgia. For the writer Grafton Tanner, nostalgia is the defining emotion of our contemporary age, and he isn't pleased about it.[1] In the first few decades of the twenty-first century, political leaders worldwide have repeatedly promised a return to yesteryear. Nostalgia's power, according to Tanner, lies in its defence against and embodiment of our unstable time. With little faith in a present of economic anxiety and a future of climate collapse, many have turned to nostalgia for solace, while powerful elites exploit it for their own, sometimes nefarious, gains. From Trump to Britain's 'Brexit' from the European Union, commentators argue that nostalgia has shaped recent political life and altered electoral trends in profound and sometimes troubling ways. Even the EU chief negotiator, Michel Barnier, used something of a tautology to blame Brexit on Britain's 'nostalgia for the past'.[2]

As we know, throughout the twentieth century, most people thought that nostalgia was a fundamentally small-c conservative emotion, one indulged in by those who would rather avoid engaging with the sometimes messy modern world. It is, as one sociologist phrased it, 'the latest opiate of the people'.[3] This belief continued into the new millennium, when the historian George K. Behlmer suggested that someone's nostalgic bent could easily 'lapse into cloying sentimentality'. He cautioned, a little too late, against the trend towards 'commercialising the fond backward gaze'.[4] He thought that nostalgia closed off the future, allowing people to reject the possibility and potential of productive, fruitful social, cultural and political change.[5]

Tanner insists we live in a peculiarly nostalgic time. And he is not alone. This idea is implicit, and sometimes explicit, in many of the discussions about politics and nostalgia that circulate today. In 2021, the former Observer columnist Nick Cohen concurred – himself making a very nostalgic claim. He asserted that the contemporary 'politics of nostalgia' were a sure sign of 'present-day decay'. Maintaining that 'Confident countries are not nostalgic', he described how Britain's decline was accompanied by 'the sound of sighs for a lost country'.[6] This assertion – that now is very nostalgic – is bolstered by research and supported by polls. In 2018, a study done by the left-leaning think tank Demos found that Britain, France and Germany were all 'gripped by a kind of malaise, a sense that something is fundamentally rotten at the heart of their societies'.[7] The study's authors argued that nostalgic narratives had recently become a key component of contemporary politics. At around the same time, the European public opinion research agency Eupinions was conducting a very similar study. Its report, 'The Power of the Past', was based on a survey of 10,885 EU citizens and it classified the majority of the European public as nostalgic.[8] Their findings mostly chimed with that of Demos's research, but they went into much greater detail. While 67 per cent of Europeans surveyed thought the world used to be a better place, nations varied in the intensity of their feelings. Italians were by far the most nostalgic, whereas Polish people were the least. About equal numbers of French, German and Spanish respondents harboured feelings of nostalgia, but rates varied between the young and the old.

Throughout Europe, the under-twenty-fives were the least likely to express nostalgia, men were more likely to be nostalgic than women, and 53 per cent of those who felt nostalgic at the time of the survey placed themselves to the right of the political spectrum. By contrast, 58 per cent of those who did not feel nostalgic identified as politically left-wing. European nostalgics also tended to share more negative opinions of immigration and the EU: 78 per cent thought that recent immigrants to their respective countries did not want to fit into society and 53 per cent believed that immigrants were taking away the jobs of 'natives'. While 82 per cent of non-nostalgics wanted to remain in the EU, fewer nostalgics – 67 per cent – felt the same. Nostalgics were also more likely to be unemployed and to identify as working class. The report concluded that these demographic dynamics suggest that nostalgia is triggered in response to 'increased anxiety and fear fuelled by processes of rapid personal, economic, or societal change'.[9] In other words, the report concluded with very familiar findings. Nostalgics tended to be older, anti-immigration, and were more likely to want to leave the EU, vote for right-wing political parties and identify as working class.

*

These assumptions underpinned much of the rhetoric around Brexit. Shortly after Britain voted to leave the European Union in 2016, commentators both at home and abroad diagnosed the nation with 'nostalgia for empire'. British writers thought their nation was beset with 'postcolonial melancholia', driven by 'a nostalgic yearning for lost colonies – and the wealth and global influence that came with them'.[10] Headlines like 'The Empire Strikes Back' were everywhere, and, for *The New York Times*, Brexit marked 'England's Last Gasp of Empire', the 'diseased reaction' of a nation 'sickened by nostalgia'.[11] As the legal scholar Nadine El-Enany put it, the terms of the entire referendum debate were 'symptomatic of a Britain struggling to conceive of its place in the world post-Empire'.[12] She goes on to observe how Theresa May, then Home Secretary, referred to the Commonwealth as evidence of Britain's 'unique and proud global relationships', insisting that Brexit was the country's opportunity to 'rediscover its role as a great, global trading nation'.[13]

Much of the rhetoric around Britain's place in the world in the run-up to the referendum traded in praise for the nation's former empire. The then secretary of state for international trade, Liam Fox, said, 'The United Kingdom is one of the few countries in the European Union that does not need to bury its twentieth-century history.'[14] Turning the myths of empire on their head, the Leave campaign adopted the language of 'national liberation', framing Britain's voluntary decision to leave the EU, an organization it opted to join in the first place, as 'an existential struggle between oppressor and oppressed'.[15] In Brexit's aftermath, imperial nostalgia continued. As El-Enany observed, in his first major speech after the referendum, the then foreign secretary Boris Johnson insisted that 'Brexit emphatically does not mean a Britain that turns in on herself.' He described British colonialism as a manifestation of 'astonishing globalism, this wanderlust of aid workers and journalists and traders and diplomats and entrepreneurs'. He mused over whether 'the next generation of Brits will be possessed of the same drive, the same curiosity, the same willingness to take risks for far-flung people and places.' He promised that post-Brexit Britain would be 'more outward looking and more engaged with the world than ever before'.[16]

This benign image of empire was shared by non-politicians too. A 2016 poll conducted six months prior to the referendum found that 44 per cent of the British public were proud of Britain's colonial history and 43 per cent considered the British Empire to have been a good thing.[17] These sentiments were not a product of Brexit. El-Enany quoted then Conservative PM David Cameron, who, back in 2011, had stated that 'Britannia didn't rule the waves with armbands on.'[18] She also noted that, before him, in 1997, the Labour PM Tony Blair had insisted that he respected British history enormously, and that he felt the British Empire should elicit neither 'apology nor hand-wringing' and should be used to enhance Britain's global influence.[19] These politicians say nothing of empire's 'violences and humiliations' or its 'fantasies of cruelty, subjugation and supremacy'.[20] And the historian and cultural theorist Paul Gilroy called Britain's failure to deal critically with colonialism and imperialism 'an unhealthy and destructive post-imperial hungering for renewed greatness'.[21]

Ever since the nineteenth century, and even in its earlier iterations as a kind of homesickness, nostalgia has had ties to patriotism. And this isn't just the case in Britain. In 2021, and in the process of figuring out a new 'taxonomy' of the emotion, the psychologist Anna Maria C. Behler and her colleagues determined a specific type: 'national nostalgia'. In their sample of American voters, Behler et al. found that high levels of national nostalgia not only predicted more positive attitudes towards President Donald Trump, they also correlated with racial prejudice.[22] Right from the beginning of his 2016 presidential campaign and through his failed 2020 re-election efforts, Trump repeatedly invoked the American past, ranging from the 'salient nostalgic reverie' of 'Make America Great Again', to policies and political rhetoric that offered white working-class Americans a return to earlier, more affluent times.[23]

As one journalist put it, during his first campaign, Trump's favourite word was 'again'. Denigrating the secularization of American life, he promised, 'If I'm elected . . . we're all going to be saying "Merry Christmas" again.' His predilection for 'again' was only matched by his fondness for 'bring back', and he repeatedly committed himself to resurrecting manufacturing jobs, steel and coal production, 'law and order' in the cities and the waterboarding of terrorists. This 'mission of restoration' underpinned Trump's 2016 campaign, and he ran on the promise that he would reverse what he portrayed as years, if not decades, of American decline.[24] These appeals worked because they touched on what some journalists diagnosed as the 'pervasive sense of loss' among many of his constituents – the belief that the 'changes moulding modern America have marginalized them economically, demographically, and culturally.' Trump evoked a rose-tinted time in American history, when life was easier and more affluent for the white blue-collar workers among his supporters. With nostalgia, he built a powerful emotional connection, one that would sustain him through the many scandals that might otherwise have harmed his ultimate electoral victory.[25]

Since 2016, then, this national nostalgia has preoccupied the collective imagination – seven years, at the time of writing. It seems to saturate the populist politics of the present and has seeped into other more mainstream elements of social and conventional media, as well as public life. There is some logic to this idea that the twenty-first century is a peculiarly nostalgic age. It helps explain the flourishing of the far Right and the trenchant culture wars over statues, museum exhibitions and other kinds of public history ongoing right now. But nostalgia is no twenty-first-century phenomenon. It is not solely a condition of modern life, and it certainly is not a product of the twenty-first century. Not only has nostalgia been felt, diagnosed and worried about for many centuries before either the European Union or Donald Trump existed, but this critique of populist politicians and their followers as fools living in denial has also been around for decades. Think of the post-war psychologists who dismissed the chronic nostalgic as living in a state of arrested development. And, as discussed, every new era since at least the nineteenth century has had its own nostalgia wave, or nostalgia panic, and many of those have been political in nature.

For example, in 1959, *The New York Times* accused the British Conservative Party of being nostalgic for the nineteenth century, and they illustrated their article with a strangely familiar election poster. The Conservatives were campaigning in advance of the October election – which they won – and they used their version of a now infamous slogan. Across an illustration of a British bulldog were emblazoned the words: 'Make Britain Great Again.'[26] Similarly, in 1964, America's own conservative revival was explained by 'a sense of frustration with the state of the world and a yearning for easier days'.[27] Indeed, in 1970, J. Daniel Mahoney, New York State chairman of the recently formed American Conservative Party, said, 'We do believe, with a sense of nostalgia, in all the old American verities and values. Our meetings have always started with the Pledge of Allegiance, we're not too sophisticated to take pride in our flag. And we're for self-dependence, individual effort, hard work – all the square virtues.'[28]

But also, and perhaps even more importantly, nostalgia is not just a condition of the political Right. The Left has its own emotional baggage and its own nostalgic commitment to the past – to events like the Paris Commune, the Soviet Union, America's New Deal, and Britain's welfare state and the 'golden age' of social democracy. In the electoral battle fought between Donald Trump and Joe Biden in 2020, Trump might have deployed his own brand of nostalgia to great effect, but Biden also played on the trope of an industrial America of yesteryear, when people worked hard and contributed to their communities in a nation untainted by division. Historians argue that nostalgia has defined the identity of Britain's Labour Party, which remains committed to an 'era of heroic male industrial working-class struggle'. It is, according to Richard Jobson, nostalgic for a world that, 'in social and economic terms, no longer exists'.[29]

Also in Britain, the idea that imperial nostalgia underpinned Brexit has become something of a trope – present in almost all left-wing or Remain analysis of the Brexit referendum. But this is precisely one of the problems with this analysis – it implies that it is only Leave voters who are, as historian Robert Saunders put it, 'haunted by the ghosts of Empire'.[30] Imperial nostalgia is, therefore, supposedly something that only happens to other people. But, in fact, lamenting the loss of Britain's global power was a key part of Remain discourse too. In 2018, the outgoing head of Europol mourned the country's 'loss of influence' post-Brexit: 'the seat at the table will be either fully gone or half gone . . . and that means there will be a loss of British influence, and I think it's a shame for the UK.' He was particularly concerned that Britain would lose sway over international policing and security.[31] 'We are no longer "Great" Britain,' tweeted the Remain-voting former Conservative MP Anna Soubry on Christmas Eve, after the trade deal was announced. Leaving the EU, she added, 'diminishes our country, will make us all a little poorer & narrow our horizons.' As Saunders explains, 'One of the legacies of the imperial past is the assumption that Britain should punch above its weight in the world, that it should be a global player and an influencer and a leader.' But, 'that idea has been just as present in pro-European thought as it has been in anti-European thought.'[32]

This is true today, and it was also true when Britain voted to *join* the EU in the 1970s. As Labour's Chancellor of the Exchequer Roy Jenkins complained in the 1960s, politicians were both passionate about the European project and held 'an attachment to imperial commitments worthy of . . . Joseph Chamberlain, Kitchener of Khartoum and George Nathanial Curzon'.[33] For the Labour foreign secretary, George Brown, Europe offered a new opportunity to lead the globe. The *Daily Mail* celebrated the nation's entry into the union in 1971 with the headline, 'Now we can lead Europe!' while the *Sun* told readers that membership offered 'an unrepeatable opportunity for a nation that lost an empire to gain a Continent'.[34]

There are elements of left-wing politics and ideologies that seem antithetical to nostalgia. The Left's very identity is built around progress and the future, and it has shaped itself in opposition to some of nostalgia's supposed tendencies. Barack Obama's 2008 slogans were starkly different from those of both Biden and Trump. 'Change we can believe in' and the chant 'Yes we can' worked because they projected an air of possibility about the future. Left-wing movements and wider society alike have tended to identify nostalgia with conservatism. After all, if the Left is about progress, change and utopian visions of what is to come, then nostalgia ought to have little role to play in its design, politics and rhetoric. Left-wing politics are characterized instead as forward-looking, radical and, by definition, anti-nostalgic, un-nostalgic or even nostophobic.

In 1988, the Fabian Society issued a short pamphlet, written by Raymond Plant, a politics professor at Southampton University, England. A British socialist organization founded in 1884, the society's nine founding members included Frank Podmore, an author and sceptical spiritualist, and Edith Nesbit, the children's author. Other illustrious members were George Bernard Shaw, H. G. Wells, Ramsay MacDonald, Emmeline Pankhurst, and Sidney and Beatrice Webb. In 1895, the society founded the London School of Economics. Throughout its history, the Fabian Society has regularly published pamphlets expressing the views of its members, reflecting on left-wing politics and policies.

In his pamphlet, Plant insisted that 'nostalgia is not a good basis for political thinking and particularly for a radical party.'[35] The radical party in question was Britain's mainstream left-wing political party, Labour. Neil Kinnock, Labour's then leader, called on his political allies to desist from their tendency to 'wallow in nostalgia for the old days of terraced housing, minimal healthcare and few educational opportunities'. For Kinnock, only those who never really knew the past could long for it: 'Socialism is dedicated to progress.'[36] But Kinnock failed to understand something fundamental about progressive culture. Even Raymond Plant, in the very pamphlet in which he rejected nostalgia, yearned for the post-war neighbourhoods of Grimsby, a port town in the north-east of England, where he had grown up. He lamented the decline of 'community'. And, while he conceded that perhaps the community he yearned for was far from the idyll which his rose-tinted spectacles made it seem, he none-theless expressed his own regrets about the decline and fracture of working-class life. Indeed, despite what progressives like Kinnock might insist, people everywhere can be nostalgic about left-wing pasts, just as they can yearn for periods of cosy conservativism. Even revolutionaries and socialists can be nostalgic sometimes.

*

The Paris Commune was a radical, egalitarian and insurrectionary experiment in government. In March 1871, after the withdrawal of German forces at the end of the Franco-Prussian war, Paris demo-cratically elected a Commune council. The council ruled the city for seventy-two days and passed measures such as the abolition of night work, free secular education, the separation of Church and State, and the cancellation of rent arrears. In May, the Commune was brutally defeated during a week of bloodshed. More than 10,000 Communards were killed. Karl Marx, in his *Civil War in France*, called the Commune, 'The first revolution in which the working class was openly acknowledged as the only class capable of social initiative, even by the great bulk of the Paris middle class – shopkeepers, tradesmen, merchants – the wealthy capitalists alone excepted.' Just ten years after the Commune, in 1881, the German socialist newspaper *Freiheit* (Freedom) called for 18 March to be celebrated as the anniversary of the Commune, saying that it should be held henceforth as a holiday by the 'working men of the world'.[37] Lenin himself was particularly fond of drawing parallels between the Commune and the abortive Russian Revolution of 1905. Each year that the Russian Revolution of 1917 outlived the Paris Commune, Lenin is said to have counted in 'Commune plus one', and, when he died, his body was wrapped in a Communard flag.[38] As the historian Edward S. Mason wrote in the 1930s, this left-wing history of the Commune was 'almost pure myth', but this did little to dampen the nostalgic flames. In 1931, American journalist Louis Stark said that the 'Marxian interpretations' of the Commune were 'polemics . . . that stir their revolutionary ardour to the quick.'[39]

Even after the Second World War, when other revolutions might have replaced it in the popular psyche, the Paris Commune lived on. In June 1955, the Yugoslav parliament reconvened to plan their path towards 'pure socialism' via self-administered communes. These communes, each made up of around 10,000 people, would be governed according to the political needs and rights of the people, and not from the state. This idea, the government said, was inspired by the short-lived Commune of 1871.[40] As one historian in the 1960s put it, the Commune 'left martyrs and a myth for revolutionaries to feed on which has remained green'. When the first three-man team of Soviet astronauts went up into the atmosphere in 1964, they took with them, besides pictures of Marx and Lenin, a ribbon from a Communard flag.[41] In the summer of 1966, and in January 1967, China's Chairman Mao said the Cultural Revolution would result in a type of government modelled after the Paris Commune.[42]

In France itself, however, the myth and memory of the Commune was almost immediately quashed through vigorous censorship. Ever since, there has been a prolonged struggle over the commemoration of the Commune. Since the 1880s, but most enthusiastically between the 1920s and 1960s, the Mur des Fédérés (the wall in Père Lachaise

Cemetery against which thousands of Communards were shot in the experiment's final days) was the location of a commemorative ritual for the Parti communiste français (PCF). At the end of every May, on the anniversary of the Semaine Sanglante (the week of bloodshed), people process to the Mur des Fédérés, deliver speeches, sing songs and fly red flags. Between the two world wars, during the years of the Popular Front, this ritual reportedly attracted hundreds of thousands of people.[43]

Despite some of the contradictions, it makes sense for communists and socialists to look back at long-dead political allies for encouragement, connection and a galvanizing mythology. While left-wing politics are supposed to be progressive – all about the future – history can offer profound inspiration for new movements. But what about people who are supposed to have left these political beliefs and political regimes behind? Long after the fall of the Soviet Union, people living in Russia and many Eastern European countries expressed, and continue to express, their own nostalgia for the socialist systems of the past. The transition from state socialism to liberal democracy has been a long and bumpy ride. Severe unemployment, lack of job security, economic instability and stagnating economic growth were hallmarks of the 1990s and early 2000s as much as they were of previous twentieth-century decades. Despite its promise, the failures and uncertainties of capitalism seemed to turn people's attention to the real and imagined past.

Survey data from the 1990s indicates that more than half of the adult population in the entire East European region gave a positive assessment of the socialist economic system. The highest support came from Ukraine and Belarus, at 90 per cent and 78 per cent respectively. This was a significant increase from the amount of support communism had in 1991 (36 per cent). The further they got from 1989, the more nostalgia for the economic stability and equality of the communist past increased. In 2018, a poll showed that 66 per cent of Russians regretted the fall of the Soviet Union, setting a fifteen-year record. Today, 66 per cent of Romanians also claim they would vote for their former communist dictator Nicolae Ceauşescu, who was ousted during the 1989 revolution, and 81 per cent of Serbians believe that they lived best under their dictator, Tito. In 2020, the number of Russians who claimed that the Soviet era was 'the greatest time' in the country's history had risen to 75 per cent.

According to Kristen Ghodsee, a historian of post-communist Eastern Europe, this nostalgia is a product of the dramatic changes to daily life experienced by people living in the former USSR. While they might not want to revive twentieth-century totalitarianism, there is a desire for a collectively imagined, more egalitarian past. She argues that nostalgia for communism is a 'common language', one used by ordinary men and women to express disappointment with the shortcomings of parliamentary democracy and neoliberal capitalism today. According to various polls, people mainly miss the Soviet Union because they have lost a general feeling of belonging and community, a shared identity with other parts of the USSR, and the sense of prestige associated with living in a great power. Some Russian writers call it a decline in a feeling of 'familiarity', or rather a collapse of collectivist sentiment and solidarity. However, the most significant thing motivating this epidemic of nostalgia is the straitened economic circumstances of Eastern Europe's poor. A strong majority of Russians believe that 'there used to be more social justice and that the government worked for people.' A 2019 Levada Centre poll found that 59 per cent of Russians felt that, unlike today, the Soviet government of the twentieth century 'took care of ordinary people'.[44]

The year 2009 marked the twentieth anniversary of the end of the Polish People's Republic. Museums and temporary exhibits celebrated the Solidarity movement, a broad, anti-authoritarian social movement from the 1980s, and displayed the wretchedness of life under the Soviet Union. But, clearly, not all Poles remember the middle decades of the twentieth century in quite the same way. Rather than rejecting their communist history entirely, many older people in Poland yearn for some sort of connection to and remembrance of their lives then. In general, the transformation from communism to capitalism has not worked to the advantage of older Poles. For them, 'the "bad old days" of oppression and fear' have become 'the "good old days" when they had steady jobs and free medical care'.[45]

Zofia Niczke, founder and director of the Emeryt's Foundation, an organization that improves the lives of Warsaw's elderly citizens, pointed out that she was in a much more financially secure position under communism. Before the reforms of 1993, pensions were 7 per cent higher and medicines and healthcare were more affordable and accessible. Niczke admits that 'things weren't great under socialism', and remembers standing in long lines for basic necessities. She recognizes that capitalism has improved the diversity and abundance of products to buy, but, because of her straitened financial circumstances, she is 'only able to look at these products through the shop window'. Nostalgia for communism and socialism was not, however, just about money and political systems, but food, culture and aesthetics too.[46]

In 2004, the television channel Nostalgiya, its logo featuring stylized hammer-and-sickle imagery, was launched in Russia. The channel broadcasts to almost all the former USSR and Yugoslavia, as well as countries with large Eastern European immigrant populations, like the United States, Germany and Israel. Nostalgiya attempts to recreate the daily television schedules of the Soviet era, running news programmes and weather forecasts from the period. The channel also broadcasts talk shows, documentaries and vintage television programmes and films.[47] Similarly, the 1960s Polish series, *Czterej pancerni i pies*, or 'Four Tank Drivers and a Dog', has been repeated six times since 2001. With each rerun, over a million viewers watch Polish infantrymen battle alongside the Red Army. Among the country's older generation, there's also ample brand loyalty to vintage products like Ludwik dishwashing and laundry soap, Inka coffee substitute and SDM butter. In 2005, and at the request mostly of women in their fifties, grocery stores reintroduced processed meats with tastes loyal to original 1970s recipes. These products, distributed by the supermarket chain Stół Polski, sold incredibly well under the label *Wędliny jak za Gierka*, or 'Sausages like they were under Gierek'. The slogan refers to Edward Gierek, the Polish Communist Party's first secretary in the 1970s. Natalia Lewicka, Stół Polski's marketing and advertisement specialist, explained that the company's aim was to 'recapture that bygone flavour, one resembling the ones made in the "better days" that are so close to the heart of our parents'.[48]

In her article, 'Art of Nostalgia', the Polish art critic Katarzyna Pabijanek explains that collecting toys, knick-knacks, art, film, food and music from the time of communism 'does not simply indulge in melancholia for an idealized communist or welfare state of the past'. Instead, 'it heightens the awareness that something is missing from the present.'[49] The forty-four years of Polish history under communism have been simplified by recent public histories and political accounts, reduced to a bleak caricature. It is as if the personal narratives of individuals have been erased and replaced with a dark collective memory. As one Polish writer put it, 'those who grew up in the PRL [Polish People's Republic] played with friends, fell in love, went to school, worked, cooked dinner every night.'[50] Their personal biographies are continuous, even if the political systems under which they lived fractured, collapsed and were replaced. Nostalgia in this context is, therefore, an effort to make sure that people's lives up until 1989 were not rendered entirely meaningless by the coming of capitalism, and cannot just be subsumed beneath a political monolith.[51] In other words, nostalgia is an act of resistance, one that insists on people's ability to find something positive in history, even if the popular narrative of their shared past is one of personal misery, economic stagnation and political repression.

The famous dissident writer Christa Wolf described this strange feeling in her autobiographical account of life in the German Democratic Republic. After the fall of the Berlin Wall, she had become 'spiritually homeless', an exile from a country that no longer existed. Besides the official 'monumental history' of communism, there was an alternative account. Under communism, people wrote about the everyday experiences of left-wing life and recounted a series of 'successful, radical, radiant' revolutions, including the Paris Commune, the Spanish Civil War, the Cuban Revolution and May 1968. After the shock of November 1989, however, these other stories vanished, 'buried under the debris of the Berlin Wall.' The downfall of state socialism flattened the history of socialism itself. The experience of this period of the recent past was reduced to its totalitarian aspects, no room for joy, friendship, or the tedium of the day-to-day.[52]

In German culture, *Ostalgie* is a kind of nostalgia for aspects of life in communist East Germany. The portmanteau of the German words *Ost* (east) and *Nostalgie* (nostalgia) was coined by the stand-up comic Uwe Steimle in 1992, and it takes many forms. Brands of East German food have been resurrected, old state television programmes are sold again on VHS and DVD, and the once widespread Wartburg and Trabant cars have started to reappear. One particularly visible example of *Ostalgie* was the effort to save the 'Eastern Traffic-Lights Man' (*Ost-Ampelmännchen*), an illuminated image of a man wearing a hat in pedestrian-crossing lights (inspired by a summer photo of the leader of the GDR, Erich Honecker, in a straw hat). Many German cities in and near the former East German border, including Berlin, Lübeck and Erfurt, still use the *Ost-Ampelmännchen* in all or some pedestrian crossings, and souvenirs are sold which feature the iconic image. This is all part of what some call communist chic, whereby elements of popular culture such as fashion and commodities use communist symbols and other things associated with the political past. Typical examples include T-shirts and posters with Alberto Korda's iconic photo of the Cuban revolutionary Che Guevara.

In 1998, on the 150th anniversary of *The Communist Manifesto*, the radical British publisher Verso produced an 'upscale edition' of the revolutionary classic, 'self-consciously marketed towards sybarites'. The plan was to make the text succeed as a fashion item as well as a political creed by collaborating with expensive boutiques in London and New York. Simon Doonan, then creative director at the department store Barneys, was excited: 'People are forgetting the Gulag and Stalin and the negative imagery . . . So it could be time for it to come back as pure style.' He continued, 'It's a great idea. The idea of carrying a book instead of a handbag. Hmm . . . does it have a string or wrist wrap? No? That's okay. An accessory that requires a high level of motivation. I like it.'[53] The irony of making a luxury commodity out of a book written by Karl Marx was not lost on journalists covering the reissue. But even some hard-line lefties were keen. 'Cool,' exclaimed Terrie Albano, spokesperson of the Communist Party USA, while Stanley Aronowitz, a labour sociologist in New York, said, 'This is the name of the game for knowledge and distribution. I don't cry over that stuff.'[54]

*

But communism is not the only left-wing political tradition with plenty of nostalgic pageantry and popular culture attached. Social democracy, and specifically Britain's National Health Service, exerts its own emotional hold over people. The 2012 London Olympic Games opening ceremony mythologized the foundation of the NHS and used the service as a symbol for Britain and its historical achievements. The ceremony's director, Danny Boyle, drew on images of a bygone and romanticized era of universal healthcare to tell a grandiose story of national pride. Nurses in 1950s dress danced around metal hospital bedframes and battled with childhood villains like Harry Potter's adversary Voldemort and the Child Catcher from the film *Chitty Chitty Bang Bang*. An NHS worker said, 'I couldn't help but smile when we first saw the bit when the monsters came out. Are they supposed to be the managers or the politicians?'[55]

The NHS is an important British institution. It is more than just a health service; it is central to the nation's identity, a key site of interaction between the public and the state, and the country's largest single employer. As the one-time Conservative MP Nigel Lawson put it in 1992, 'the National Health Service is the closest thing the English have to a religion.'[56] Boyle presented the NHS and its role in the British national psyche as unequivocally positive – 'an amazing thing' – and the opening ceremony was generally very well received. Combining historical props and costumes with childhood characters, Boyle put forward a nostalgic vision of the NHS that profoundly resonated with a large swathe of the British population.

However, Boyle was also criticized for his portrayal of this treasured institution. And that criticism settled on his nostalgia. In an article published in the right-wing newspaper *The Mail on Sunday*, shortly after the opening ceremony, the journalist Ian Birrell, who was also Conservative PM David Cameron's speech writer, decried those who elevated doctors to 'deities' and deemed our health service 'sacrosanct', and he insisted that those who possessed a 'misty-eyed myopia' about the NHS prevented 'real reform'.[57] Birrell lambasted 'the dancing doctors, the nurses in their old-fashioned uniforms, the cute children bouncing on 300 luminous beds that spelt out those sacred three letters: NHS.' He thought that Britain's 'senti-mentality' over its health system was damaging, an 'ultimately self-defeating national tragedy'.[58] At around the same time as the Olympic Games were held in London, the BBC television drama *Call the Midwife* was becoming increasingly popular. The series is set in 1950s London and fictionalizes the harrowing experiences of women giving birth and the heroism of those that cared for them. The nostalgia of both *Call the Midwife* and Boyle's opening ceremony was attributed by critics to the austerity policies imposed by the coalition government and the straitened financial circumstances of the welfare state in 2012.[59]

Much like in Russia and Eastern Europe, these shows resonate with a nostalgic desire for the perceived stability and 'fairness' of post-war Britain, as embodied by the NHS. Nostalgia is so prevalent in discussions about the NHS that it has become part of the service's fabric; it permeates the language of its supporters and is invoked at almost every turn. In 2018, a patient at Bassetlaw Hospital in Worksop entertained staff with anecdotes of his time spent as a chef at the site in the 1950s. He regaled his doctors and nurses with stories from what he described as the 'good old days', remembering how he would bake 300 cakes a day for the patients and at weekends make one for the staff on each ward. He harked back to a bygone era of hospital life, a time when doctors and nurses had their own dining rooms, and when Matron and her maid were served tea in her study.[60] On 5 July 2018, the NHS turned seventy. Celebrations were held at hospitals across the UK. NHS Tayside in Scotland shared information about their commemorations on their website: 'As the much loved institution turns 70 on 5 July, NHS Tayside is encour-aging everyone to join in the celebrations that have been planned to mark this historic occasion.'[61] Staff and visitors to Ninewells Hospital in Dundee were invited to visit their 'Trip Down Memory

Lane' display: 'If you want to see some of the old hospitals again or reminisce about the "good old days" then this nostalgic photographic display is definitely not to be missed.'[62]

In addition to such happy reflections, nostalgia is also regularly used as part of social-media pleas to 'save our NHS' from under-funding and government caprice. Twitter user Sue (using the tag '#NHSLove') tweeted in 2022, 'If people don't wake up soon & come to their senses – the NHS will be history. Workers' rights will be the good old days. The gap between the haves and have nots will be beyond measure. There will be no social services & no social care.'[63] Nostalgic lines of attack are often, therefore, used to level critique at the current state of the NHS. Domestic cleaner Rona McFarlane has worked at Whipps Cross Hospital for thirty-two years. She insists that the 'good old days' of the NHS are in the past. 'Under the NHS, you felt proud to help people and in those days you had the time to talk to patients,' she said. 'Then, if a nurse was busy and a patient needed a glass of orange juice, you could go and get it for them, as long as you asked the nurse first, of course.' But, 'things have changed . . . You are so busy now you don't have the time to listen.' Sixty-year-old Rona first came to the UK from Jamaica in 1961. She settled in East London and started her public-sector career almost immediately. But, with the outsourcing of hospital cleaning services, her role has since been contracted to an external private company. Rona has seen her role change from a public servant, working as part of what she calls the NHS 'family', to becoming an employee of a company primarily interested in profit.[64]

However, the political identity of these nostalgic reflections is not necessarily straightforward or obvious. While many of the nostalgic critiques of current healthcare policy or practice were made by people with explicit left-wing leanings, and the NHS has largely been co-opted by the British Left as a talisman of progressive poli-tics, the service also has broad cross-party support. There might be plenty of disagreement over whether actions always match right-wing words of commitment, but people on both sides of the political spectrum campaign for the health service's protection. There's also, therefore, plenty of NHS nostalgia in the right-wing press. Meg Henderson wrote to *The Sunday Times* in 2007 to say that she'd worked in the 'medical world' since the late 1960s, and 'everybody thinks their younger days were a golden era but I know mine were.'[65] In letters to the newspapers, current or past NHS workers yearn for a bygone era, one characterized by clear hospital hierarchy, by the bedside training and well-ironed uniforms. As Jill Parkin wrote in the *Daily Mail* in 2005: 'With a rustle of her starched cap and a disapproving look at what was to come after her, Matron vanished from our hospitals sometime in the 1970s. She left behind her spotless wards, respectful nurses and a faint whiff of carbolic.'[66]

Former nurse Claire Rayner also lamented in the *Daily Mail* that she was once regarded as an 'angel of mercy': 'We weren't paid lavishly, but our status could not have been higher.'[67] The splendidly named Dr Max Gammon, a retired doctor, wrote a letter to *The Times* in 1999. He recommended a return to the 'old system of an apprenticeship on the wards' and suggested that the principal entry requirement for the nursing profession ought to be 'the desire and ability to care for sick people'. He, as a retired medical practitioner, was 'confident that there would be no lack of well-qualified nurses who would be eager to return to hospital life'.[68]

But, just as NHS nostalgia is neither inherently right- or left-wing, as with other political nostalgias, it is not confined to the twenty-first century either. Instead, nostalgia is something of a constitutional condition of the NHS, regardless of when in its seventy-five-year history you look. It is, after all, an institution in constant need. Since its foundation in 1948, the NHS has been subjected to periodic funding constraints, managerial reforms and administrative restructuring. It is a service in a state of perpetual crisis and has been leveraged as ammunition by politicians since its very inception.

This state of constant flux means that people who work in the health service always have something to look back on, and this was particularly apparent in the aftermath of the first major reorganization of the NHS, in 1974. Five years later, in 1979, the Royal Commission on the National Health Service was published. Since 1976, it had been gathering evidence and had received 2,460 written submissions, held fifty-eight oral sessions and had met and spoken informally to about 2,800 individuals.[69] According to the commission's chairman, Sir Alec Merrison, it was 'appointed at a time when there was widespread concern about the NHS' following 'a complete reorganisation of the service' in 1974, which few had greeted as an 'unqualified success'.[70] The published report reflected a profoundly polarized set of opinions about the condition of the health service. Descriptions of the state of the NHS ranged from 'the envy of the world' to it being 'on the point of collapse'.[71]

Many of the people who submitted evidence waxed lyrical about a time before the reorganization, and they were deeply nostalgic about the NHS of the 1950s and 1960s. Mrs Nora Brown wrote to the Royal Commission offering up her ideas for how to help 'both the Health Service and the ailing country . . . get back to once again be Great Britain as of the old days'. Keith A. Mallinson lamented the passage of time and the impact of big policy changes, saying, 'I see around me a great deal of dedicated service, given by the doctors and nurses and other staff within the hospital, however, one thing which is more than apparent is the excessive bureaucracy. It seems that since reorganisation our hospitals have become over administered, and this is a cause of unrest among staff.'[72]

Just like today, people commenting on the NHS were nostalgic for some mythic time before bureaucracy. The surgeon A. J. N. Phair wrote in 1976 that 'Bureaucracy used to be a term to define the most efficient office procedures.' Now, it could only be used 'in its pejorative sense of red tape, buck passing and considerable inexcusable delays which is partly caused by administrators shying away from their responsibilities and receding into the management structure cocoon.'[73] Sir George Godber, a prominent Conservative and chief medical officer from 1960 to 1973, had a similar gripe about administrative overkill. In the notes for a 1974 article, he identified two major obstacles to the NHS being the 'envy of the world' (as Britons liked to claim): 'Ministers (i.e. politicians) and Civil Servants (i.e. bureaucrats).'[74] What this pair had done over the last ten years, or so he insisted, had been 'greatly to the detriment of the service to the sick'. In charged tones, he lamented the administrative and bureaucratic burdens shouldered by hospital workers: 'The best nurses no longer attend the sick. They walk around the hospital corridors clutching sheafs of papers and demanding coffee from the overworked ward sister.' And he lambasted the amount of 'office work' clinical staff now had to do.[75]

In an addendum to this article, handwritten in January 1975, he wrote, 'All the ideals of the best in the profession of medicine and the profession of nursing seem about to vanish, probably for ever. It is sad for me to have to report this opinion and to see the ruin of what was the finest Service in the world.'[76] His words were drenched in nostalgia. The NHS he knew was 'living on its momentum from the halcyon days of yore'. He compared the health service 'as it was and promised to be' with the NHS of today, and called the transformation 'tragic'.[77] Godber had played an instrumental role in the foundation of the NHS and had only recently left the Department for Health and Social Care. His nostalgia was probably both personal and professional. He lamented changes to the health service but was also wistful, basking in his own memories of over-hauling the service in the 1960s.

Staff who referenced the 'good old days' of the NHS were every-where in the 1970s and 1980s – and they complained regardless of whether the Labour Party or the Conservatives were in power. A surgeon wrote to the Labour PM James Callaghan's government in 1976 with a complaint. He balked at the 'faceless uniformity' of the health service, lacking in professional opportunities and diversity of work. He ended his letter with a note of grief: 'I am dispirited, disappointed and embittered. The NHS is an idol with feet of clay.'[78] In the same year, nurse Pamela M. Jefferies wrote an article in the *British Medical Journal*. She was angry about the Salmon reforms to nursing training and practice. These reforms were supposed to further professionalize nursing, elevate the status of nurses and offer them opportunities for promotion. The problem was that this meant more and more nurses were taking on what George Godber called 'office work', or administrative or managerial roles in the hospital, taking staff away (as critics saw it) from the more important business of patient care. Nurse Jefferies was nostalgic about a pre-Salmon era: 'it is somewhat disconcerting to cast one's mind back over the last ten years and see the changes which have taken place in the profession during that time.'[79] Despite good intentions, the Salmon reforms were deeply unpopular. One hospital administrator called them 'disastrous' and 'dangerous'. In some ways, these nostalgic complaints are very much like the familiar, small-c conservative reflections that are now everywhere, and they are not particularly radical. But they are also ambiguous. They might be populist, but they're not right-wing, and certainly not party-politically so.

The surveys done by Demos and Eupinions in 2018 determined that nostalgic people tended also to be anti-immigration, patriotic and politically right-wing, and the research was driven by the premise that the emotion was particularly prevalent in the late 2010s and seemed to be a condition of the heady political climate in and around 2016. However, that version of nostalgia is just one of many. For much of nostalgia's lengthy history, it has been the preserve of both right- and left-wing activists, politicians, writers and workers. Its aesthetic and emotional appeal draws people in from across the political spectrum and is as often politically ambiguous as it is straightforwardly conservative or liberal. Political nostalgias have also been around for a while, and nostalgia's deployment in new reforming as well as populist movements well predates the cataclysmic electoral events of 2016. Language eerily similar to that used by Donald Trump appears in 1960s Conservative Party rhetoric, but nostalgic appeals have also been embedded in the twentieth-century revolutions and state politics of socialism. If 'politics of nostalgia' are a sign of what Nick Cohen calls 'decay', then the decline has been going on for quite some time.

CHAPTER NINE

THE NOSTALGIC BRAIN

By 1970, a sixty-three-year-old woman had been living in the Beth Abraham Hospital, in the Bronx, in NewYork, for twenty-four years. Since the age of eighteen, she had had something called progressive postencephalitic parkinsonism. Parkinsonism is a group of chronic neurological disorders characterized by a progressive loss of motor function resulting from the degeneration of neurons in the brain. Some people develop parkinsonism after encephalitis, or inflammation of the brain, which is sometimes caused by a viral infection. Just after the First World War, there was a pandemic of encephalitis lethargica (sleeping sickness). Rather than recovering, some of the patients developed postencephalitic parkinsonism. This woman's condition had caused her to descend into an almost continuous 'trance', necessitating her institutionalization for more than two decades.

But, in 1970, she underwent a remarkable recovery. After being treated by a pair of neurologists with a drug called l-dopa, she experienced a rapid release from her parkinsonism symptoms and her trance, and was once again able to speak and move. She also experienced a surge of intense, joyful nostalgia. She requested a tape recorder and, over the course of a few days, recorded innumerable 'salacious songs, "dirty" jokes, and limericks, all derived from party-gossip, smutty comedians, night-clubs, and music halls.' Nobody was more astonished than the patient herself. 'It's amazing,'

she said, 'I can't understand it. I haven't heard or thought of those
things for more than forty years. I never knew I still knew them.
But now they keep running through my mind.'This surge of nostalgia
soon passed. But it seemed to have served its purpose. The woman
remained articulate, but instantly forgot all those early memories
and was never again able to recall a single line of the songs she had
recorded.[1] This bizarre case was written up in the form of a letter
to the British medical journal *The Lancet*. One of the letter's authors,
and one of the patient's neurologists, was Oliver Sacks, who would
go on to become an eminent writer, retelling this story in his book
The Man who Mistook His Wife for a Hat.[2] For our purposes, the story
marks a new chapter in the biography of nostalgia. It was one of
the first suggestions that nostalgia might be involved in recovery
from illness. Not only was nostalgia no longer a sickness, it could
now help alleviate troubling symptoms and even make people better.

Seventies sociologists, early-twentieth-century psychoanalysts and
Victorian medical professionals all thought about nostalgia slightly
differently, and their conceptualizations changed over time. However,
for much of the emotion's history, it has consistently been seen as
dysfunctional. In the 1990s, however, scientists – including their old
enemies, the psychologists – started to rehabilitate nostalgia. They
understood the feeling to be elicited by a variety of triggers, such
as objects, events or people, music or songs, photographs, odours
and tastes. They decided that it was prevalent (i.e. people experience
it several times a week), universal (as in, occurring in many cultures
across five continents) and observed in people of all ages (older
children, teenagers and adults).

Due to this rehabilitation, in scientific circles at least, nostalgia
is now seen as a predominantly positive, albeit bittersweet, emotion
that arises from personally salient, tender and wistful memories of
one's past. But nostalgia is more than just benign; it is now actively
therapeutic. The emotion has recently been reconfigured as a
powerful and pervasive psychological resource that provides people
with a variety of benefits. It can boost self-esteem, increases meaning
in life, fosters a sense of social connectedness, encourages people
to seek help and support for their problems, enhances psychological

health and well-being, and attenuates loneliness, boredom, stress or anxiety. Nostalgia can even now be used as an intervention to maintain and improve memory among older adults, enrich psychological well-being and ameliorate depression.

*

The study of the emotions began in earnest in the nineteenth century, when psychology turned into a fully fledged scientific discipline. Blending the tools of physiology (the study of the body's normal functions) and neurology (the anatomical investigation of the nervous system, including the brain), psychologists searched for the physical basis of fear, anger and sadness. Scientists tried to develop taxonomies, classifications and categories of emotion, and to do so they looked for the physical fingerprint of specific feelings. Ever since Phineas P. Gage had half a teacupful of his brain ejected from his skull by a tamping iron in 1848, scientists have been interested in the relationship between emotions and the brain. Which parts of the brain, or neural circuit, they asked, were associated with which emotion? By the end of the Victorian era, psychologists had concluded that emotions inhabited the most ancient part of the brain, the 'limbic system', or our 'inner beast', which controls the body. In contrast, thoughts or cognitions were assigned to the cortex – the 'more evolved' bit of our brain. This dichotomy is now a famous one. Emotions are base, animalistic and traditionally feminine. Whereas thoughts, reason and rationality are humane, advanced and conventionally male. But, in the first half of the twentieth century, the brain fell out of view as scientists focused instead on the biology of behaviour. Emotions were no longer considered purely mental phenomena. They were recast as states of the nervous system that caused specific behaviours or physical reactions. For example, rather than being located in a bit of the brain, fear was now the act of freezing, fleeing or fighting, while anger became the expression of rage – ranting, raving and going red in the face.

In the 1950s and 1960s, trends changed again and the brain was reinstated as a topic of scientific inquiry. However, because psychologists did not yet have a tool to observe the mind in action, they employed the newly popular and increasingly widespread computer as the driving metaphor. Emotions were recast again – this time as computations. But still they were equated with behaviours. Rather than looking at the experience of emotions, scientists focused on the processes that caused them and how they made living creatures behave. Part of the rationale for this was that animals (as in, non-human ones) clearly have emotions, but they do not necessarily have emotional *experiences* (which require language and culture and other things unique to human beings). Scientists wanted a cross-species explanation for emotions so that they could generalize their findings from rats, to meerkats, to dogs, to monkeys, to humans.

But, in the late seventies, a new technology finally allowed scientists to witness the live brain doing its thing. Magnetic resonance imaging (also known as MRI) started to be widely used by academics and clinicians in the 1980s and, by the nineties, cognitive neuroscience, and then affective neuroscience (the neuroscience of the emotions), emerged as new disciplines. Cognitive neuroscience is a branch of both neuroscience and psychology, concerned with the study of the biological processes that underlie thought or cognition. Cognitive neuroscientists are interested in the neural connections or circuits in the brain which are involved in various mental processes. Much like their nineteenth-century predecessors, but with updated technologies at their disposal, these new scientists sought the underlying mental origins for different emotions. The idea was that each emotion is caused by its own dedicated neural circuit. And, at first, as neuroscientific studies of emotion accumulated, it looked as if scientists might be able to locate the specific regions of the brain responsible for anger, sadness and fear. This supported the pre-existing basic emotion theory, in which emotions are thought to be innate, biologically bound and recognizable across cultures, communities and even species.

As the science of emotions developed, becoming more robust and more comfortable with the new technologies at its disposal, some researchers turned their attention to nostalgia specifically. Most of these studies relied on the assumption that nostalgia was a relatively stable category. Even if they hadn't yet found the bits of the brain responsible for the feeling, scientists worked with the idea that people, generally, had a shared understanding of what nostalgia was, how it felt and what words should be used to describe it. In 1995, the American psychologist Krystine I. Batcho developed the Nostalgia Inventory, a questionnaire designed to measure how often and how deeply people feel nostalgic. It asks participants to consider what they miss about when they were younger and prompts them to rate how much they miss it, on a scale of one (not at all) to nine (very much). The Inventory is scored by averaging the ratings given to the various items. The higher the score, the more nostalgic a person tends to be. The items include 'Family', 'Not having to worry', 'Someone you loved', 'Toys', 'School', 'The way society was' and 'Not knowing sad or evil things'.[3]

The Inventory was originally completed by 210 respondents − 88 men and 122 women − ranging in age from five to seventy-nine years old. For much of the twentieth century, psychologists, psycho-analysts and sociologists thought that nostalgic tendencies were more common in people dissatisfied with the state of the world and with their lot in life. In contrast, the Inventory found that, while high-scoring subjects rated the past more favourably than those who scored low, both held the present and future in similar regard. More nostalgic people were not necessarily less happy or optimistic than less nostalgic respondents to the questionnaire. Individuals who scored highly tended to rate themselves as more emotional, with stronger memories, a greater need for achievement and a more consistent preference for activities with other people, but not as risk or thrill seeking, religious, logical, easily bored, confident of success or less joyful. In a second study, 113 undergraduates − thirty-two women and eighty-one men − completed measures of nostalgia, memory and personality. High-scoring subjects weren't better at remembering things in general, but were more able to quickly recall more people-oriented autobiographical memories. Individuals who scored highly on this iteration of the Nostalgia Inventory were also no more optimistic, pessimistic or negatively emotional, but were more emotionally intense.[4]

Back in the 1970s, Fred Davis had distinguished between what

he called 'private nostalgia' and 'collective nostalgia'.[5] Whereas the
former was what the individual felt about their own personal past
– their childhood memories, for example – the latter captures the
social dimensions of nostalgia, an emotion potentially shared by
many people. 'Collective nostalgia' could be expressed at religious
events, political rituals or demonstrations. Batcho made a very similar
argument and one of her key findings was that there were multiple
varieties of nostalgia. In the 1990s, she homed in on two in particular:
personal and historical nostalgia. Personal nostalgia involves longing
for, or feeling good about, aspects of your life that you have already
lived through and can remember. In contrast, people who experience
historical nostalgia might have an emotional attachment to, or
yearning for, times in history that predate their own birth. Take, for
example, the man we met in Chapter Five, from 1970s Iowa, who
was desperately nostalgic only for the period between 1752 and
1768, more than a century before his likely birth. Crucially, Batcho's
data indicated that someone might be experiencing a lot of one type
of nostalgia and not that much of another. She argued that personal
and historical nostalgia were 'relatively non-correlated or independent phenomena'. The two types were not really the same thing
at all.[6]

But both depended on imagination and a kind of invention. Of
course, nostalgia for a period of time many decades before you were
born obviously requires a degree of reconstruction, however
grounded in solid historical research. But personal nostalgia also
rests on relatively insecure foundations. Personal nostalgia relies on
memory, but we have decades of cognitive research to show that
people's memories are inaccurate. The process of retrieval, whether
that's recalling what we did last weekend or remembering what our
childhood was like, is selective and incomplete. If someone is asked
to remember the 1950s, they will only ever be able to dredge up a
partial impression of the decade. As they reminisce, someone might
become nostalgic about that time, but only because they're selectively
remembering the things they loved and enjoyed. They might recall
their friendships, their romantic relationships, the freedom they felt,
the joy they experienced, a life lived before back pain and interrupted

sleep. But they might forget or fail to retrieve less positive aspects of a period of time, like political unrest, economic hardship or social inequity. Baby boomers, for example, might be nostalgic for the sixties, not for the Vietnam War or the race riots, but for Woodstock and smoking pot.

Batcho's Inventory has now been translated into multiple languages, made available as an app, and has been used in numerous research studies. In the twenty-first century, cognitive and affective neuro-scientists started to investigate the physiological mechanisms of nostalgia, and many of these studies used brain-scanning technology. In 2022, a team of researchers outlined the consensus.[7] Nostalgia involves four main brain regions. One: the region associated with self-reflection (the medial prefrontal cortex, posterior cingulate cortex and praecuneus). Two: the region related to autobiographic memory, long-term memory and the recall of factual details from the past (the hippocampus). Three: the region related to the regu-lation of emotions (the anterior cingulate cortex and the ventrolateral prefrontal cortex). And four: the region related to reward processing (the striatum, substantia nigra, ventral tegmental area and ventromedial prefrontal cortex). These various regions make up the so-called 'nostalgic brain'. It is this 'nostalgic brain', according to these studies, that works to produce nostalgia when it encounters nostalgic cues or stimuli.

So, every time nostalgia is experienced, a part of the brain is activated. The performance and activity of the brain's reward and memory system are altered through stimulation. When the reward systems in the brain are triggered, a chemical called dopamine is released (similar to l-dopa, which was given to Oliver Sacks's 'trance' patient in 1970). Experiments using MRI scanners have suggested that, when nostalgia is felt, the dopamine deposits itself in the hippocampus, which significantly improves the ability of the person to recall specific memories and events. This helps explain why it is that people are better able to remember things in detail when it is associated with some kind of reward. For example, if you scored highly on an exam and were given a gift to celebrate by your parents, then you're more likely to remember the event many years later, whereas, if you weren't rewarded, you're more likely to forget that the achievement ever took place.

The experiments done to reach this consensus were eclectic, and sometimes slightly strange. For example, one group of researchers conducted an electroencephalography (EEG) study to examine the neural basis of nostalgia. People watching a Double-A Minor League Baseball game were asked to report their level of nostalgia every twenty minutes, while their brain activities were measured by EEG. The study found that the attendees' brainwave frequencies, which are indicators of self-reflection, increased when they reported more nostalgia. In other words, introspection correlated positively with the feeling of nostalgia. Another study, this time using MRI scanners, used images rather than sport to elicit nostalgia. Participants were shown two images: one from their youth and the other a neutral control image. The nostalgic pictures made regions of the brain involved in autobiographic memory (the hippocampus) and the reward system (substantia nigra, ventral tegmental area and striatum) light up on the scan. The more highly a person rated the emotional and personal significance of the pictures, the more strongly the relevant regions of their brains were activated.

One of the major findings of this era of nostalgia science was that smells were more powerful even than old photographs when it came to triggering memories. Just a whiff of a certain odour could take an adult back to early childhood. According to Dr Simon Chu at the University of Liverpool, 'Odours are incredibly good reminders. Smell recalls memories that are more detailed, more emotional and go back further than those that are recalled by any other sense.'[8] To test the link between odour and memory, the Liverpool researchers exposed groups of volunteers to smells, including cloves, petrol, cheese, coffee, whisky, mustard, wine, coconut, curry, paint and ink. For one participant, the smell of fruit transported him back to when he fell out of a tree as a child. For another, the smell of boot polish reminded him of the day a long-lost relative knocked at the family door. The smell of vinegar reminded another volunteer of the first time he had ever had fish and chips by the seaside. Dr Chu is adamant that 'We now know that there are certain smells which remind people very vividly of some previous experience.' But, perhaps most interestingly, what is different about odour as a sense is that one is not making any attempt to remember something, but rather 'the remembering is forced upon you.'[9] The area of the brain involved in smell – the olfactory bulb – is close to other regions responsible for memory.

As a result, experiments that use odours to elicit nostalgia are very popular among emotion scientists. In one such study, participants not only reported being flooded with positive, happy feelings after sniffing certain smells, they were also better and more accurately able to remember events from their past. Positive emission tomography (PET) scans of their brains also found that nostalgic odours activated the brain's reward system and the areas responsible for autobiographical memory (including the hippocampus). A similar series of MRI studies used music rather than smells to evoke nostalgia, but again they found that the emotion activated the reward system and the bits of the brain responsible for autobiographic memory, self-reflection, emotion regulation and positive mood.

The conclusions of these various experiments on the nostalgia brain are consistent with other neuroimaging studies of so-called basic emotions (e.g. fear, anger, sadness, happiness, disgust and surprise) which also show that each feeling involves multiple networks in the brain, rather than being specifically related to a single brain region.[10] Indeed, early neuroscientific studies of emotion struggled to isolate the specific neural basis – or individual underlying physical structure – to an emotion and to distinguish it consistently from other feelings. Take, for example, the case of patient S. M., who lost both her amygdalae to Urbach-Wiethe disease, a rare genetic disorder. Amygdalae are a pair of small almond-shaped regions deep in the brain which help us regulate our emotion and encode memories. They are supposed to be particularly linked to fear. In theory, then, without her amygdalae, S. M. ought not to have been able to experience fear at all. And in many circumstances – watching scary films or visiting haunted houses – that proved to be the case. She also had difficulty learning from prior errors and interpreting physical signals, like when she'd sweat in response to unexpectedly loud sounds. However, in everyday life, she was capable of what scientists call 'aversive learning', or 'fear learning'. For example, she didn't want to break the law for fear of getting in trouble, and she reported feeling worried. She was capable of learning fear in the real world, and avoided seeking medical treatment and visiting the dentist because of pain she'd experienced on past occasions. Thus, an intact amygdala – the bit of the brain supposedly responsible for fear – does not appear to be necessary for someone to respond to perceived threats.

In general, recent neuroscientific research does not reliably prove the hypothesis that an individual emotion can be consistently localized to a specific bit of brain tissue. As a result, as we have seen, many neuroscientists argue that emotions are linked to multiple interacting parts of the brain, or networks. However, it has also prompted some neuroscientists, like Lisa Feldman Barrett, to go even further. She suggests that we should move away from what she calls essentialism when it comes to the study and understanding of emotions. She's not so keen on basic emotion theory and calls instead for a more 'dynamic, contextual' approach to the psychological world.[11] Emotions do not, she argues, appear to have a set of universal markers irrespective of the person under investigation. Our brains do not work in exactly the same way. Our behaviours, and even our facial movements, differ from one another. Scientific studies should, then, attempt to capture this variety, exploring feelings in all sorts of different people and contexts.

Indeed, evidence seems to suggest that, when it comes to emotion, variety is the norm. Some people smile when they're sad, cry when they're angry and scream when they're happy. A person can 'tremble, jump, freeze, scream, gasp, hide, attack, and even laugh', all in the face of fear. There is, therefore, an ongoing debate in the world of emotion science. At the beginning of this book, I described some of the flaws in basic emotion theory and quoted the psychologist James A. Russell, who maintains that 'different languages recognize different emotions. They carve up the domain of emotion differently.'[12] Evidently historians and psychologists generally have quite different opinions on what constitutes an emotion and, more specifically, what constitutes nostalgia. There are also scientific versions or definitions of nostalgia and more general or colloquial ones. Since the 1980s, more and more psychologists agree about what nostalgia is and how it ought to be defined. However, as the work of people like Lisa Feldman Barrett and James A. Russell indicates, the very identity of emotions – whether they are wholly biological or at least partly cultural – is still up for debate. This is true for fear, and it is also true for nostalgia.

*

Despite the ongoing debates over the science and psychology of nostalgia, there does seem to be a consensus emerging over the feeling's positive potential. One of the key things that psychologists were interested in finding was the trigger that prompts nostalgia in people. In their studies, they asked volunteers to describe how they were feeling when they become nostalgic. Mostly, they reported feeling low, saying things like, 'I think of nostalgic experiences when I am sad as they often make me feel better', and, 'if I ever feel lonely or sad I tend to think of my friends or family who I haven't seen in a long time.'[13]

In one, more in-depth study, British undergraduates were asked to read one of three news stories, each based on real events, that were designed to influence their mood. They read articles about the 2004 Indian Ocean earthquake and tsunami, about the January 2005 landing of a space probe on one of Jupiter's moons, and about the 2004 birth of a polar-bear cub in a zoo. The first was supposed to make them sad, the second was supposed to be emotionally neutral and the third was designed to be uplifting. They were then asked to complete a measure of nostalgia, rating the extent to which they missed eighteen aspects of their past (such as, 'holidays I went on' or 'someone I loved'). The study concluded that participants who had read about the tsunami – the sad cohort – were more nostalgic than their more cheerful peers.[14] In another study, researchers induced loneliness by giving participants false feedback on a 'lone-liness' test. Again, the subjects were asked to rate how much they missed eighteen aspects of their past. The lonelier the person, the more nostalgic they felt. The study was repeated for nine- to fifteen-year-old Chinese children, Chinese undergraduates and Chinese factory workers, all with similar results.[15]

These various experiments concluded that negative feelings can trigger nostalgia. But, perhaps more importantly, researchers also found that nostalgia can make people happier and more content. When triggered, the emotion can ameliorate loneliness and lessen people's fears of death. For those who feel emotionally detached and dissatisfied, nostalgia can be used as a tool to create a sense of meaning and purpose. Nostalgia is, therefore, a kind of emotional armour. It can protect us from various psychological and physical threats by making our brains regulate our emotions better and process rewards more effectively and efficiently. Researchers in China have found that loneliness is not just about being alone, but about a general perceived lack of social connection or support. If you feel well loved, then being alone for a short while does not make you feel lonely. Nostalgia, on the other hand, is a social emotion. One psychologist said that, during nostalgic reflection, 'the mind is "peopled".'[16] The emotion affirms symbolic ties with friends, lovers and family; close others come to be 'momentarily part of one's present.' People with a greater tendency towards nostalgia feel more loved and protected, have reduced attachment anxiety and avoidance, and report having better social skills. Nostalgia can be therapeutic, serve as a coping function, and is capable of counteracting the negative effects of loneliness.

Nostalgia is also supposed to imbue life with meaning; it helps people cope with existential threat and alleviates anxieties around our inevitable death. In one study, American undergraduates were reminded of their mortality (researchers described a gruesome dental procedure), and those who were more prone to nostalgia (determined by a survey), or who had received nostalgic triggers (as part of the study), had fewer death-related thoughts. Another set of studies, conducted about ten years later, found that adverse weather conditions can prompt nostalgia, but that this 'weather-evoked' emotion confers psychological benefits and the feeling became a source of comfort amid stormy skies.[17]

Since the early twentieth century, nostalgia has been an emotion about the past. But, paradoxically, it has also been found to have remarkable implications for one's future. Psychologists argue that it raises optimism, makes people feel inspired and boosts creativity. Far from being a kind of escapism from the present, nostalgia offers people an attainable future. But it was the sociologist Fred Davis who might have been the first to suggest that nostalgia, strangely enough, may promote a sunny outlook on the future. He wondered, 'If [nostalgia] reassures us of past happiness and accomplishment; and, since these still remain on deposit, as it were, in the bank of our memory, it simultaneously bestows upon us a certain worth, irrespective of how present circumstances may seem to question or obscure this. And current worth, as our friendly bank loan officer assures us, is entitled to at least some claim on the future as well.'[18]

Nearly forty years later, psychologists set about testing Davis's hypothesis. One hundred and two University of Southampton under-graduates (ninety-two women, ten men) opted to participate in a study for a course credit. They were randomly split up into a 'nostalgia condition' group and a control group. Participants in the control group were asked to read a description of a scenic spot and to briefly reflect, in writing, on the scenery and their feelings. The nostalgic ones were instructed to 'bring to mind a nostalgic event in your life. Specifically, try to think of a past event that makes you feel most nostalgic.' They were then given five minutes to write about the event and describe how it made them feel. Their narratives were then transcribed and analysed using software that calculated the relative frequency of different predetermined categories of words. The descriptions in the 'nostalgia condition' group were found to contain a significantly higher proportion of 'optimism expressions' (words in the 'optimistic' category), suggesting that the experience of nostalgia makes people feel more optimistic.[19]

Another experiment studied the relationship between nostalgia, inspiration and creativity. The researchers triggered nostalgia among the participants, who were then assessed on their inspiration and determination to pursue their goals. Subjects reported feeling 'filled with inspiration' and expressed a desire to 'put more time and effort into my goal[s]'. Participants were also given thirty minutes to compose a short story that involved either a 'princess, a cat, and a race car' or a 'mysterious noise on a cold winter evening'. The stories were independently coded for creativity (the academic articles do not explain exactly how this was done) and the more nostalgic participants wrote more creative stories than the controls. Nostalgia is not, therefore, 'simply a past-oriented emotion'. Instead, its scope extends into the future – and, in particular, 'a positive future'.

These emotion scientists collectively argue that their findings not only have the capacity to transform our understanding of nostalgia, but potentially have implications for clinical practice. Knowing what they now know about the regions of the brain responsible for nostalgia means that neuroscientists could help develop therapies for various kinds of psychological illness or distress. And reconfiguring nostalgia as a positive, forward-looking feeling means that it might confer emotional protection – protection that could perhaps be used in the treatment of psychological disease. Indeed, in stark contrast to historical views, nostalgia is no longer a disease itself, but instead a remedy for dysfunction.[20]

Nostalgia is now regularly used as part of interventions among older adults with dementia. One experiment used something called activity reminiscence therapy (ART) in a care home in Japan. Reminiscence therapy is when people discuss events and experiences from the past to evoke memories, stimulate mental activity and improve a person's well-being. *Activity* reminiscence therapy has similar aims, but, rather than just talking, people participate in tasks. In this study, the older adults with dementia were given the tools required to do a series of familiar and enjoyable things. For one hour a week, for twelve weeks, they were given a rice kettle, furnace, measure and charcoal, and were asked to cook rice; they used an earthenware pot, salt and water to pickle vegetables; they were given a tub, washing board and washing powder to wash some clothes; and they used a pot, rolling pin and board to make noodles. Cognitive tests were administered before, during and after the intervention, and the care home's staff and families were interviewed to assess whether the patients seemed to have changed in any way. The study found that the 'nostalgia brought about by using these familiar tools' improved people's memory, communication, social interaction, emotional functions and behaviour.[21]

Nostalgia not only has the capacity to lessen the symptoms of dementia and improve people's memories, it can also help enrich psychological well-being and ameliorate depression.[22] In 2009, a group of academics conducted a randomized control trial (the 'gold standard' in research) in which they recruited ninety-two elderly people, aged sixty-five years and older, who were living in care homes. The participants were randomly assigned to two groups. In one group, the people received reminiscence therapy eight times over the course of two months. Three months later, the researchers found a significant improvement in the participants' depression, psychological well-being and loneliness, as compared to those who received no therapy at all.[23] These studies have been going on since the early nineties. An experiment conducted in 1994 found that 'nostalgic reminiscence' could restore a sense of self, bolster people's identities and enhance personhood by helping to reweave 'the broken threads of life history'.[24]

Of course, just because psychologists have worked hard to rehabilitate nostalgia and strip the emotion of its pathological associations does not mean that there are no hangovers from its history as a disease and dysfunction. The vestiges of this past are still apparent in disagreements over the therapeutic value of nostalgia and the possibility that at least some forms might still be harmful or pathological. As we have seen, studies have repeatedly shown that recent refugees report psychosomatic symptoms as a result of a malignant, place-based form of nostalgia – a profound homesickness. This is sometimes referred to as 'maladaptive nostalgia', which involves the repetitive reconstructions of bittersweet memories, rather than the creative reminiscence of past experiences.[25] These involuntary memories prevented people from learning new things or adapting to their present circumstances, and made them depressed, anxious and unhappy.

Nostalgia can, though, be many things to many people simultaneously. One of the main ways that the rehabilitated, therapeutic version of nostalgia has been put to use in the last few years is in business. Organizations of various sizes have tapped into nostalgia's feel-good factor. Companies have deployed the emotion in their efforts to improve workforce well-being. Most of the recent psychological literature surveyed here focused on personal nostalgia. But, nevertheless, some of the findings are relevant to organizational life. Researchers noticed that nostalgia is a by-product – and often a benign one – of places of work where employees have spent many years, especially where the employer is central to the community, such as a coal mine or a university. The sociologist Yiannis Gabriel was the one of the first to coin the term 'organizational nostalgia.'[26] He interviewed workers from various organizations, who volunteered nostalgic stories about departed managers or colleagues and reminisced over old office buildings. They lamented interior-design changes and complained over new buildings that lacked character, were too noisy, or where you weren't able to open the windows yourself. Later studies looked at universities and hospitals specifically and found that organizational nostalgia strengthened professional identity among academics, doctors and nurses.

Some research on organizational nostalgia found that the emotion could, as in society more broadly, be deployed as a personal psychological resource. For example, some psychologists found that nostalgia at work helps employees cope with what they call 'interactional injustice', which basically means being poorly treated by your boss. Or, in their words, 'being subjected to disrespectful, impolite, or untruthful treatment by organisational authorities'. Nostalgia acts as an emotional buffer, allowing employees to maintain a feeling of motivation. A bad boss might not feel nice, but, because of nostalgia, they aren't allowed to compromise someone's intrinsic commitment to their job or dedication to an institution.[27] Despite the frustrations of, say, being denied a voice in important organizational decisions, researchers found that personal nostalgia provided an 'alternative route to social connectedness', which meant that employees remained cooperative and compliant.[28] In universities, studies found that organizational nostalgia stopped staff from feeling bad about radical structural changes.[29] And, when medical professionals were faced with threats to their autonomy by new ways of working, they could draw on nostalgia to make themselves feel better and reassert their commitment to the profession and to their patients.[30]

For employers and managers, this is all great news. One of the biggest challenges facing large organizations and industries is getting people to forgo self-interest and contribute to the collective instead.[31] Because personal nostalgia reminds people of their social relationships and can foster feelings of connectedness, it's supposed to make them more willing to engage in behaviour that benefits their colleagues and the organization they work for as a whole.[32] This is true even when the behaviour might come at some personal cost.[33] Research has found that nostalgia not only makes workers feel better, but it also ameliorates the symptoms of burnout and improves staff retention.[34]

The implications of these studies are obvious. Organizational nostalgia is not just a happy by-product of working somewhere, it can also be used as a management tool. If managers can strategically cast an organization's past in a nostalgic light, then perhaps they can reap the emotion's business benefits. Marketers have long been using nostalgia to impact consumer decisions and advertise a company's products, but the same approach could also improve staff satisfaction. One sociologist found that the managers of British Rail deliberately reflected on the glory days of the British railway industry in order to strengthen employee commitment, even while the organization was undergoing substantial change that could, in theory, make it a less pleasant place to work.[35]

This is also the situation in the National Health Service. Nostalgia is a chronic condition that has reached epidemic proportions in the NHS. Staff are almost universally nostalgic for more plentiful and better-trained colleagues, less bureaucracy and limited managerial control; but also for a more resource-rich working environment and for a different kind of emotional community – one that offered the support, care and comradeship required in a pressurized and sometimes traumatic workplace. Doctors I've interviewed almost all reflect on an age of long working hours that was made bearable by the emotional support provided by their colleagues and the compassionate connections they could form with their patients when they were able to maintain some form of continuity of care. These healthcare workers were nostalgic for a sense of professional cama- raderie – what one surgeon called the 'strong feeling of belonging and commitment' that characterized his younger days in the NHS.

In an article published in the *British Medical Journal* in 1999, the author – a doctor – described one of his twenty-four-hour shifts in the hospital's emergency department. It was the busiest day of the year, but strangely he enjoyed it – it was just like the 'good old days'.[36] He characterized these 'good old days' as an era when resources were more plentiful, staff turnover was lower and work was more enjoyable. Doctors are generally also nostalgic about a different management culture and landscape. In the past, they say, the specialist knowledge and skills possessed by doctors – which allowed for healthcare's smooth and effective delivery – were acknowledged by managers, who acted in a supportive role to medical professionals. One surgeon reflected, 'The process in which I grew up in the early days was one whereby the medical profession . . . had a lot more of a say in running the hospital.'[37] One surgeon said, in emotive terms, 'In spite of the pressures in the eighties and nineties, a sense of being in control of one's own destiny mitigated against much of the stress. I have lived through thirty-five years of erosion of autonomy and a burgeoning weight of governance, that, in turn, contributes to a sense of jeopardy and peril.'[38]

This nostalgia could be corroding the happiness of healthcare profes- sionals in the NHS. But, if we take the tenets of organizational nostalgia seriously, this same emotion could be the very thing that keeps doctors returning to their jobs, day after day, despite the erosion of their autonomy, time and resources. This casts the popular NHS nostalgia machine in a very different light. The 2012 Olympic Games opening ceremony was not only a celebration of the National Health Service, but a management tool. Of course, Danny Boyle was not in the pocket or on the payroll of NHS managers. But, if nostalgia has the capacity to make you feel good and offers a kind of psychological protection, then feel-good stories in the local press about your local hospital, period dramas portraying 1950s midwives, and dancing paediatric nurses are all helping the NHS to continue to survive.

CHAPTER TEN

REHABILITATING NOSTALGIA

Nostalgia is certainly not what it used to be. Over the course of the last 300 years, it has changed a great deal. When the term was first coined in the late seventeenth century, even the word 'emotion' did not yet exist. But that didn't matter much, because its inventor, Johannes Hoffer, was not inventing a new emotion. He was a physician creating a new diagnosis, a new disease. But even that didn't help people reach or maintain a consensus. Nostalgia the disease was unstable, and different doctors elaborated alternative causes, characteristics, symptoms, prognoses and possible cures depending on the variety of the condition they encountered in their clinics. These early versions of nostalgia were very different from the one we're familiar with today, and it is tempting to seek out what seventeenth-century patients *really* had. But diseases – indeed, like emotions – are unstable things. Medicine likes to make itself seem like a universal, ahistorical truth. And yet, nostalgia shows us that sickness is as susceptible to the whims of society as is anything else.

Diseases and the world they inhabit have a mutually dependent relationship. Nostalgia's various transformations tell us much about how the world has altered since 1688. Nostalgia, like many other diseases, flexed according to different social and political environments. It melded itself in response to the European wars of the eighteenth century, the professionalization of doctors in the nineteenth, the development of Victorian-era imperialism and the increasing depend-ence of global powers on migrant workforces. While it was still a disease, nostalgia embodied and helped to enforce rigid racial and imperial hierarchies, but also reflected the hypocrisies central to these systems. Nostalgia was simultaneously a marker of white upper-class British superiority – an indicator of genteel patriotism and feminine sensitivity – and also a disease specific to the supposed inherent instability of people of colour, who were seen as constitu-tionally unsuited to the macho and robust adventuring and travel of so-called Anglo-Saxon men.

But it also shifted according to more subtle changes in society and culture. The rise and fall of wet-nursing, for example. As the practice fell out of favour in France after the Enlightenment, babies became less vulnerable to the sickness of nostalgia. The development of relatively reliable international postal services (ah, the good old days) offered not only a potential remedy for homesickness – putting émigrés in semi-regular contact with loved ones – but also meant that people now had a medium in which they could *record* their homesickness. It made the emotional consequences of distant travel not only legible in texts for future historians to see, but it also turned such feelings into shared social phenomena – things with expectations attached and the trappings of respectability and etiquette.

Nostalgia was also the preserve of a varied cast of professionals and intellectuals, all of whom took ownership of the malady at different times, overlaying their own assumptions about the normal and pathological states of humankind. In the late nineteenth century, psychologists and psychoanalysts – new professionals, keen to make their mark – conducted a land grab, taking hold of nostalgia and in the process transforming it from a physical condition (admittedly, one with emotional qualities) into a feeling or psychological state. That, coupled with the denigration of nostalgia and its fraternal twin, homesickness, in a climate of rapacious imperialism and capi-talism, slowly transformed nostalgia from a deadly disease into a relatively benign, even positive, emotion.

In the early twentieth century, then, nostalgia settled into the form we now recognize. But it remained malleable, and particularly vulnerable to the professional interests and perspectives of the various academics and clinicians who subjected it to their studies. For early psychoanalysts like Nandor Fodor, while it was no longer a disease that could kill, it remained malevolent. Rather than being something that could cause harm, it became something that indicated defectiveness in the person who felt those familiar feelings of longing and regret. For understandable reasons, Fodor and his émigré colleagues were sceptical of backward-looking people, and suspicious of patriotism and nationalism. Nostalgia was an ill-fitting addition to the world of scholarly cosmopolitanism they all inhabited.

In the 1970s, journalists and cultural theorists took hold of nostalgia, and, while they didn't diagnose their non-existent patients with the emotional tendency, they understood it in a very similar way to the psychoanalysts. They also saw it as a feeling that only certain types of people were prone to. Nostalgia was the preserve of retrograde, conservative and sentimental folk. Folk unlike the savvy liberal reporters and intellectuals who wrote for *The New York Times* and the *New Statesman*. This conceptualization of nostalgia has lasted, and it is still deployed in the pages of mostly left-leaning publications. Writers lambast those who voted for Donald Trump and Brexit for their nostalgic tendencies, characterizing them with the same broad dismissive sweeps used by interwar psychoanalysts. It remains, strangely, a kind of diagnosis – an explanation for what the critic sees as wayward or irrational acts. As the historian Robert Saunders put it, in reference to the 2016 Brexit vote, 'the appeal to "imperial nostalgia" marks out the Leave vote as a psychological disorder: a pathology to be diagnosed, rather than argument with which to engage.'[1] This kind of snobbery is also directed towards history enthusiasts, medieval re-enactors and the people who have opted to remake the world around them in seeming self-indulgent mimicry of the past.

But there have been surprising defenders of nostalgia too, or at least people who have recalibrated the moral or cultural meanings of nostalgia, transforming it, once again, from a marker of spiritual pathology into a neutral, even benign, universal experience. The psychologists who took up research into the emotion with renewed enthusiasm in the nineties changed the scientific consensus on nostalgia. They argued that it was felt by everyone, regardless of their political or aesthetic proclivities. Rather than potentially causing harm, the psychologists' version of nostalgia confers a range of psychological benefits.

These various transformations and the unstable nature of nostalgia makes it difficult to write about. But it also makes it much more interesting. It offers us a crucial and illuminating case study of how the meanings and experiences of feelings mutate over time. And it acts as an alert system. When we see nostalgia in public, scientific and political debate, we should pay attention. What do we find when we really look at nostalgia? What experiences is it being used to long for and lament? Who do its invocations serve? And what does its deployment and expression tell us about what society and individuals value at any given time?

For this reason, at least in part, I've become fond of nostalgia. Despite the efforts of recent psychologists, in the twenty-first century, nostalgia remains dogged by associations with populism and intellectual vacuity. But perhaps it needs some broader, more mainstream rehabilitation. Psychologists and historians, like myself, have very different visions of emotions generally, and of nostalgia in particular. Most, but not all, emotion scientists think that emotions are biological, bound to specific locations in the brain, or neural networks. Everyone feels the same thing, regardless of when or where you lived or live. Historians, in contrast, tend to think that emotions depend much more on the company we keep. But nostalgia's history does support some aspects of the psychologists' interpretation of feeling. One of the key interventions made by emotions science in the late twentieth century was that nostalgia was everywhere, felt by almost everyone, all the time.

*

In and around 2016, the press obsessed over nostalgia. Headlines included, 'Brexit, nostalgia and the Great British fantasy', 'The Toxic Nostalgia of Brexit', 'Brexit has been driven by England's nostalgia for an imagined past' and 'Nostalgia and the promise of Brexit'.[2] In the US, journalists were similarly preoccupied. 'Trump has made America nostalgic again for a past that never existed', declared one publication.[3] Another titled an article, 'Trump's Rhetoric of White Nostalgia'.[4] And, in 2017, a writer for Vox wrote, 'empty nostalgia dominated 2016. Our popular and political cultures kept returning to the idea that the past was somehow better.'[5]

But the trouble with such claims is that they've been made before, again and again. While nostalgia might have changed, headlines like this are remarkably constant. Diagnoses of a particular decade as especially nostalgic simply do not hold up, especially for the last fifty years, ever since the nostalgia wave was first identified (if not first experienced) in the so-called second-hand seventies. And yet, all these writers and cultural commentators must have reasons for insisting that this time or that was a particularly nostalgic one. There are several ways to interpret this recurrent journalistic trend. First, and this is the version that might appeal to psychologists, the way people feel – or rather, the actual rates and prevalence of nostalgia – has stayed more or less consistent over the course of the past century or so. Journalists keep noticing nostalgia because it's always there. After all, as recent brain scientists and psychologists argue, nostalgia is a regular and universal experience, consistent across time and space. Even if people called nostalgia something quite different in the nineteenth century, it must still have been around because the human mind has remained more or less the same for millennia. The journalists' error, then, is not alerting us to the prevalence of nostalgia *now*, but that they forget it was also every-where *before*.

The explanation for the various supposed nostalgia waves – waves that seem to lap over our shores with increasing frequency – is precisely this universality. Nostalgia is an appealing target for both writers and politicians because it taps into a perennial anxiety: ageing. The sense that one's childhood is increasingly distant, and that the fond memories we have for infancy are at risk of being eroded, is a very human and humane condition. Nostalgia is, then, always around for the taking. Journalistic and political trends are more about other things than they are about an actual change in the amount of nostalgia. If papers, both physical and online, are trying to sell their wares, then it makes sense to appeal to an ubiquitous experience or emotion. It also offers an explanation for potentially troubling political trajectories, ones that don't easily align with either media consensus, progressive ideologies or teleological understandings of history. Things like Brexit and Donald Trump's political success go against prevailing notions that Western society at least ought to be moving in a certain direction, away from nationalism and towards international cooperation and political liberalism. Nostalgia offers a relatively straightforward explanation, one that does not require a deep probing of the validity of some of those assumptions, or the potential harm they might do.

The other way to interpret the persistence of nostalgia as a media and political talking point is to accept that maybe the world actually *is* getting worse. That, since the late-twentieth century, the social fabric has torn apart, that people now live more solitary and lonely lives, that technology and social media are rending our communities asunder, that traditional values made people happier and their dissolution is the cause of much irreversible harm. Nostalgia is a condition of modern life, and modern life is rotten to the core.

While both interpretations have their merits, I fall somewhere between the two. For me, nostalgia has been a near-constant feature of our collective lives for quite some time now. A lot of people feel nostalgic, in one way or another, pretty frequently. There is, of course, a spectrum. And it is much more accurate to speak of many nostalgias, rather than just one. Some experience the emotion fleetingly, rarely, occasionally. Others are intense nostalgics, and the feeling has fundamentally shaped the environments in which they live, the hobbies they pursue and the politics they support. But, regardless, nostalgia is everywhere, if not universal. The difference between me and the neuroscientists and psychologists is that I don't believe nostalgia is stable, universal or hardwired into our brains. Rather, it is a profoundly social phenomenon, something that bends and flexes depending on the languages we speak, the technologies we use, the social lives we live and the culture we consume.

Nor do I think the world has got worse. The changes lamented by the vehemently nostalgic populist Right are things that I – and many others – see as concrete improvements to society. Changes that have slowly and unevenly loosened the hold of the patriarchy, organized religion, white supremacy, the colonial order, heteronormativity and traditional notions of the family over the lives we live are positive ones. Nonetheless, nostalgia is indubitably a condition of modern life. The history of the emotion shows us that it emerged in response to the broad social and political forces that constitute modernity, like capitalism, migration, colonialism, industrialization, global warfare and the professionalization and widespread faith in science that solidified in the late nineteenth century. Nostalgia is a condition of modern life, but that modern life was made a long time before anyone living today might be able to recall. The modern life that made nostalgia began in the nineteenth century, at around the same time that nostalgia transformed from a disease into an emotion. The problems of modern life are old ones. They didn't begin in the seventies, or the nineties, or the early 2000s, or even in 2016. They are much older inheritances.

But, regardless of when nostalgia first emerged, we should move away from seeing those with a tendency towards nostalgia as sick, sentimental or stupid. Partly because of its prevalence. It has less potency as an invective if the person pointing the finger also feels nostalgic for a world left behind. The accusation then becomes less about the emotion experienced, and more about what people do with that emotion. Nostalgia can do real good in the world. Maybe it confers personal benefit – it might make us feel good, protect us from other more negative or harmful emotions, or improve social bonds – but it can also have positive cultural and political consequences.

Nostalgia can help us re-enchant the past. Academic historians often see nostalgics, re-enactors and sentimentalists as intellectually vacuous amateurs – people unable or unwilling to reckon with the atrocities of history, of which there are certainly many. We can see this derision in the disdain shown by academics and public intellectuals towards the heritage boom of the eighties, in the frequent eviscerations of popular period dramas for their historical inaccuracies, and in the refusal of specialist academic conferences to allow re-enactors to bring their swords and muskets along.[6] But history is a broad church and there ought to be space for different ways of doing it.

Even straightforwardly 'academic' historians are beginning to acknowledge the importance of the kind of 'affective history' being done by so-called amateurs motivated by nostalgia. Emily Robinson, for example, argues that we should be better at understanding the appeal of historical work – 'its pleasures'.[7] Historical research, despite what some might say, is not just an intellectual pursuit, but an emotional experience. The divides that we erect between the work of 'professionals' and 'enthusiasts' are not so absolute as they might seem. All historians, whatever their credentials and wherever and however they work, have to deal with a 'maddening paradox'.[8] Archives, for instance, are places where historians can literally touch the past, but in doing so are 'simultaneously made aware of its unreachability'.[9] It is in this tricky place that nostalgia thrives. You know just enough about the past to be intrigued, but also enough to know you can never return.

Re-enactors and amateurs are largely unashamed of their commitment, their feelings, but professional historians are mostly embarrassed to admit their own emotional relationship with the past. Indeed, an admission that historians are excited by the past 'seems to leave them dangerously open to charges of sentimentalism'. A 'sturdy barrier', Robinson argues, 'has been erected between "memory" [or nostalgia] and "history"'.[10] The first is emotional, the second 'critical and dispassionate'.[11] There are, of course, differences between academic and amateur history. History is a discipline with certain constraints, assumptions, methods and skills. It requires training. But historians know, deep down, that the emotional barrier erected is mostly fiction. Who would be a historian, in this economy, if they didn't feel something for the past?

But it isn't simply that the border between professional and amateur history is more porous than it might seem, it's that this thing some call 'affective history' is good, productive and helpful.

Re-enactors and living-history enthusiasts help us animate the past, and they help us animate the past of people who tend to be left out of mainstream history books. Popular history books might be mostly about kings, queens and Nazis, but places like Blists Hill Victorian Town educate the public about and recreate the world of people who tend not to be the subjects of school curricula. In addition, so-called amateur historians also do crucial work for and with professional academics. They collect dates and data, spend time in archives (genealogists, for example) and try out new ideas. They have both time and enthusiasm – two things sorely lacking in the world of academia.

These arguments are mostly relevant to academic historians, a small and frequently self-indulgent community. But they do also matter for broader society. History matters, and it increasingly carries political currency. To see this, you only need to look to debates over whether statues of colonialists and Confederate generals ought to be removed, whether objects like the Benin Bronzes ought to be returned to West Africa, whether the National Trust should present the colonial sources of wealth that funded their stately homes and whether the United States should date their history from 1619 (when the first enslaved Africans arrived in the English colony of Virginia) or 1776 (the year the country declared independence from Britain).[12] How history is done, whose stories are told, who gets to tell those stories and what emotions the past is supposed to elicit are all topics for discussions that now increasingly take place in the mainstream media and in political circles.

In these debates, nostalgia has a particularly poor reputation among those advocating more progressive uses and narratives of the past. Indeed, the idea remains latent that nostalgia is a disease. It is still a pathology that you can identify in others. In the present, and particularly in the kinds of 'history wars' detailed above, nostalgia is marginalized.[13] It is treated as a fundamental and mal-evolent failure to adapt. In this modern stereotype, nostalgia is cast as merely a 'paralysing structure of historical reflection'.[14] But nostalgia is not just the preserve of the Right, and it need not be a stultifying, stagnating emotion. It does, admittedly, retain links to socially and politically conservative agendas. But racism, sexism and nationalism are not products of nostalgia. Prejudice and hate are not created by an emotion – and especially not an emotion that is so ubiquitous. If nostalgia was all that was needed for the seed of right-wing politics to take hold, then how do you explain all the left-wing nostalgics out there? What about all those fans of eighties movies, medieval battles and period dramas who *aren't* racist, homophobic or sexist? What people *do* with their nostalgia is far more important than the experience of the emotion itself. And what people choose to do is about so much more than how they feel about the past. Nostalgia isn't an explanation for harmful views, it's more a way people choose to channel their hatred, a product or manifestation rather than a cause of reactionary politics. And it also depends deeply on the kind of nostalgia they experience and instrumentalize. Because, if nothing else, the biography of nostalgia reveals its shapeshifting nature and its multiple, varied forms.

Nostalgia itself can be radical and reforming, not just retrograde. It is not necessarily reactionary, but can be strongly 'progressive' – serving the needs of a community keen to change – and it can galvanize its public into positive action oriented towards the present and the future. Even in its more reactionary forms, nostalgia is not just a rose-tinted vision of a static past that ignores or attempts to deny the realities of the contemporary world. It is (or can be) a creative tool deployed as part of a broad arsenal of reform. The visionary writer, artist and social theorist Svetlana Boym suggested that nostalgia even has a utopian dimension, and that, while nostalgia and progress are – like Jekyll and Hyde – emotional alter-egos, they are nonetheless two sides of the same coin. She suggests, and I agree, that nostalgia is 'not always about the past, it can be retrospective or also prospective.'[15] She dissects nostalgia into different parts. There's 'restorative' nostalgia and 'reflective' nostalgia, and the second is more critical and open-ended than the first.[16] Nostalgia can be a tool used to redefine the past and win support for change.[17]

Left-wing writers about left-wing nostalgias tend to argue that this style of nostalgia – *their* style of nostalgia – with all its capacity for revolution and reform, is different from the nostalgia felt and exploited by their right-wing counterparts. Leftist nostalgia might look backwards, but it does not fixate on a political cause lost to a previous epoch, or so they say. It reanimates the revolutionary past to serve the needs of the present. This is what makes it different from 'left-wing melancholia' – a far more static tendency.[18] In other words, rather than looking back just at the tradition of the Left, it sees these past moments as recoverable – things to use in their present-day efforts to change the world. Of course, right-wing nostalgics could, and sometimes do, make very similar arguments, and it is much too easy to lapse into reasoning that characterize left-wing nostalgia as the 'good' kind, whereas right-wing nostalgia is all bad.

But it doesn't really matter what I say, what caution I advise. Because people will, regardless, continue to diagnose their social, political and cultural enemies with nostalgia. Subeditors will continue to write shocked and sensationalist headlines about the latest nostalgia wave, politicians will continue to level accusations of nostalgia at their rivals, and historians will still attempt to undermine the people supposedly encroaching on their intellectual territory with allegations of sentimentality. And this is because nostalgia's power lies in its ability to move, mould and to be many things, to many people.

ACKNOWLEDGEMENTS

Writing a book, despite what it might say on the front cover, is always a collaborative endeavour. And so, while any error or failing is entirely my own, I would like to thank, in no particular order: my agent, Oli Munson; George Morley, Rosie Shackles, Marta Catalano and everyone else at Picador who helped turn my words into a book; Kristin Hussey for her editorial eye; my family, Rebecca Jewell, Jake Arnold-Forster, Theo Arnold-Forster and Dora Arnold-Forster for their love and comments on early drafts; Caitjan Gainty and Lindsey Fitzharris for being relentless supporters of my work both in and beyond the academy; the Society of Authors for giving me a Foundation Grant; staff at the Wellcome Library, the British Library and Senate House; my friends Bronya Arciszewska, Phoebe Arnold, Isabel Asquith, Rita Conry, Isabelle Fraser and Francesca Wade for the good food and early and continuous enthusiasm for the project; and my partner Ben Westhead, for everything. This book is dedicated to my son Nye. He was born in May 2023 and, unlike the rest of them, has hindered rather than helped.

NOTES

INTRODUCTION

1   'Nostalgia', Merriam-Webster Dictionary, accessed 30 January 2023, https://www.merriam-webster.com/dictionary/nostalgia
2   Erica G. Hepper et al., 'Odyssey's End: Lay Conceptions of Nostalgia Reflect its Original Homeric Meaning', *Emotion*, 12(1), 2012, pp. 102–19, p. 114.
3   Kristen A. Lindquist et al., 'The Brain Basis of Emotion: A Meta-Analytic Review', *Behavioural Brain Science*, 35(3), 2012, pp. 121–43.
4   Paul Ekman, 'Universals and Cultural Differences in Facial Expressions of Emotion', in J. Cole (ed.), *Nebraska Symposium on Emotion and Motivation* (Lincoln, NE: University of Nebraska Press, 1971), pp. 207–83; Paul Ekman, 'An Argument for Basic Emotions', *Cognition and Emotion*, 6, 1992, pp. 169–200.
5   Paul Ekman, 'Basic Emotions', in T. Dalgleish and M. Power (eds.), *Handbook of Cognition and Emotion* (London: John Wiley & Sons, 1999), pp. 45–60.
6   Thomas Dixon, *The History of Emotions: A Very Short Introduction* (Oxford: Oxford University Press, 2023).
7   Richard Firth-Godbhere, *A Human History of Emotions* (London: HarperCollins, 2022).
8   Leonard Mlodinow, *Emotional: The New Thinking About Feeling* (London: Penguin, 2022).
9   Jean L. Briggs, *Never in Anger: Portrait of an Eskimo Family* (Cambridge, MA: Harvard University Press, 1970), pp. 74, p. 329. Cited in Thomas Dixon's article, 'What is the History of Anger a History of?', *Emotions: History, Culture, Society*, 4(1), 2020, pp. 1–34.
10 Agnes Moors, 'Integration of Two Skeptical Emotion Theories: Dimensional Appraisal Theory and Russell's Psychological Construction Theory', *Psychological Inquiry*, 28(1), 2017, pp. 1–19; James A. Russell,

'Core Affect and the Psychological Construction of Emotion', *Psychological Review*, 110(1), 2003, pp. 145–72.

11 Lisa Feldman Barrett, 'The Varieties of Anger', *The New York Times*, 12 November 2016, https://www.nytimes.com/2016/11/13/opinion/sunday/the-varieties-of-anger.html

12 Mlodinow, *Emotional*.

13 Dixon, 'What is the History of Anger a History of?'.

14 Quoted in Laura Miller, '"Sehnsucht" as Spiritual Exercise: C. S. Lewis and the Achievement of the Real in the Chronicles of Narnia', *The Lamp-Post of the Southern California C. S. Lewis Society*, 22(3), 1998, pp. 16–27, p. 16.

15 Anna Wierzbicka, '"Sadness" and "Anger" in Russian: The Non-Universality of the So-Called "Basic Human Emotions"', in Angeliki Athanasiadou and Elżbieta Tabakowska (eds.), *Speaking of Emotions: Conceptualisation and Expression* (Berlin: Mouton de Gruyter, 1998), pp. 3–28.

16 Jonathan L. Zecher, 'Acedia: The Lost Name for the Emotion we're all Feeling Right Now', *The Conversation*, 27 August 2020, https://the conversation.com/acedia-the-lost-name-for-the-emotion-were-all-feeling-right-now-144058

17 Dixon, 'What is the History of Anger a History of?', p. 17.

18 Martha C. Nussbaum, *Anger and Forgiveness: Resentment, Generosity, and Justice* (New York, NY: Oxford University Press, 2016), pp. 14–56.

19 Dixon, 'What is the History of Anger a History of?', p. 3.

20 'Last word', *The Times Higher Education Supplement*, 12, 1 February 1974, p. 4.

21 Johannes Hofer, 'Medical Dissertation on Nostalgia', trans. Carolyn Kiser Anspach, *Bulletin of the Institute of the History of Medicine*, 1934, pp. 376–91, p. 376.

22 Michael S. Roth, 'Dying of the Past: Medical Studies of Nostalgia in Nineteenth-Century France', *History and Memory*, 3(1), 1991, pp. 5–29, p. 6.

23 Thomas Dodman, *What Nostalgia Was: War, Empire, and the Time of a Deadly Emotion* (Chicago, IL: University of Chicago Press, 2018).

24 Susan J. Matt, *Homesickness: An American History* (Oxford: Oxford University Press, 2011).

25 Jennifer Craig-Norton, 'The Untold Stories of the Jewish Women who became Domestic Servants in Britain to Escape the Nazis', British Academy (website), 19 July 2019, https://www.thebritishacademy.ac.uk/blog/untold-stories-jewish-women-domestic-servants-britain-es-cape-nazis/

26 Linus W. Kline, 'The Migratory Impulse vs. Love of Home', *American Journal of Psychology*, 1898, pp. 1–81.

27 Edward Alsworth Ross, 'Social Control. XV. Custom', *American Journal of Sociology,* 5(5), 1900, pp. 604–16, p. 606.
28 Cited in Tobias Becker, 'The Meanings of Nostalgia: Genealogy and Critique', *History and Theory,* 57(2), 2018, pp. 234–50, p. 239.
29 Alvin Toffler, *Future Shock* (New York, NY: Random House, 1970), p. 407.
30 Sara Peterson, 'Victorian Era-Inspired Momfluencers Are Taking Over Instagram', *InStyle,* 25 March 2021, https://www.instyle.com/lifestyle/momfluencers-nostalgia-instagram
31 Jennifer Rankin, 'EU Chief Negotiator Blames Brexit on "Nostalgia for the past"', *The Guardian,* 30 May 2019, https://www.theguardian.com/politics/2019/may/30/eu-chief-negotiator-blames-brexit-on-nostalgia-for-the-past-michel-barnier
32 Yiannis Gabriel, 'Organisational Nostalgia: Reflections on the Golden Age', in S. Fineman (ed.), *Emotions in Organisations* (London: Sage Publications Ltd, 1993), pp. 118–41.

CHAPTER ONE

1 Johann Georg Zimmermann, *A Treatise on Experience in Physic* (London: G. Wilkie, 1778), p. 286.
2 John George Keyssler, *Travels through Germany, Bohemia, Hungary, Switzerland, Italy, and Lorrain,* vol. 1 (London: A. Linde and T. Field, 1756), p. 141.
3 Ibid., p. 145.
4 Ibid.
5 Johannes Hofer, 'Medical Dissertation on Nostalgia', trans. Carolyn Kiser Anspach, *Bulletin of the Institute of the History of Medicine,* 1934, pp. 376–91, p. 376.
6 Ibid., p. 380.
7 *Literary Memoirs of Germany and the North* (London: J. Warcus and J. Ross, 1759), p. 51.
8 Hofer, 'Medical Dissertation on Nostalgia', p. 386.
9 Ibid., p. 382.
10 Ibid., pp. 382–3.
11 L. D. Kubzansky and I. Kawachi, 'Going to the Heart of the Matter: Do Negative Emotions Cause Coronary Heart Disease?', *Journal of Psychosomatic Research,* 2000, pp. 4–5.
12 Elena Carrera, 'Anger and the Mind–Body Connection in Medieval and Early Modern Medicine', in Elena Carrera (ed.), *Emotions and Health, 1200–1700* (Leiden: Brill, 2013), pp. 95–146.
13 Ibid.
14 Quoted in L. Hill Curth, 'Lessons from the Past: Preventive Medicine in Early Modern England', *Medical Humanities,* 2003, p. 19.

15 Ibid.
16 Richard Saunders, *Apollo Anglicanus* (London: M. Clark, 1681).
17 Ibid., p. A7.
18 James Johnson, *Practical Researches on the Nature, Cure, and Prevention of Gout* (London: Highley & Son, 1819), p. iv.
19 Hofer, 'Medical Dissertation on Nostalgia', p. 388.
20 Ibid., p. 390.
21 Nandini Das, 'Early Modern Travel Writing: English Travel Writing', in Nandini Das and Tim Youngs (eds.), *The Cambridge History of Travel Writing* (Cambridge: Cambridge University Press, 2019), p. 83.
22 Keyssler, *Travels through Germany etc.,* vol. 1, p. 141.
23 'Gantlope, n.', Oxford English Dictionary Online, Oxford University Press, https://doi.org/10.1093/OED/3642162449, accessed December 2020.
24 J. J. Rousseau, *A Complete Dictionary of Music*, trans. William Waring (London: J. Murray, 1779), p. 267.
25 Lisa O'Sullivan, 'The Time and Place of Nostalgia: Re-situating a French Disease', *Journal of the History of Medicine and Allied Sciences*, 2012, p. 640.
26 Susan Youens, *Schubert's Late Lieder: Beyond the Song-Cycles* (Cambridge: Cambridge University Press, 2002), p. 156.
27 Jonathan Harle, *An Historical Essay on the State of Physick in the Old and New Testament* (London: Richard Ford, 1729), p. 70.
28 Keyssler, *Travels through Germany etc.,* vol. 1, pp. 140–1.
29 Thomas Arnold, *Observations on the Nature, Kinds, Causes, and Prevention of Insanity, Lunacy, or Madness*, vol. 1 (London: G. Robinson and T. Cadell, 1782), p. 271.
30 Quoted in Jonathan D. S. Schroeder, 'What was Black Nostalgia?', *American Literary History*, 2018, p. 658.
31 Zimmermann, *A Treatise on Experience in Physic*, p. 286.
32 John Trusler, *The Habitable World Described,* vol. 1 (London: Literary Press, 1787), p. 231.
33 Andrew Duncan, *Medical Commentaries: Exhibiting a Concise View of the Latest and Most Important Discoveries in Medicine and Medical Philosophy*, vol. 1 (Edinburgh: C. Elliot & Co., 1787), pp. 343–8.
34 Stephen Pender, 'To Lose the Physician', The History of Emotions Blog, 21 November 2019, https://emotionsblog.history.qmul.ac.uk/2019/11/to-lose-the-physician/
35 Susan J. Matt, *Homesickness: An American History* (Oxford: Oxford University Press, 2014), p. 5.
36 Tiffany Watt Smith, *The Book of Human Emotions: An Encyclopedia of Feeling from Anger to Wanderlust* (London: Profile Books, 2016).

CHAPTER TWO

1 'Howgate a Free Man', *Evening Star,* 28 December 1900, p. 5.

2 H. W. Howgate, 'The Polar Colonization Plan', *The American Naturalist,* 11(4), 1877, pp. 193–256, p. 227.

3 Ibid., p. 227.

4 Nostalgia was not the only emotional or psychological threat that faced Arctic explorers. In the nineteenth century, the frozen north was frequently imagined as otherworldly, strange, a place of dreams and ghosts that held supernatural, spectral power. Shane McCorristine, *A History of Dreams and Ghosts in Polar Exploration* (London: UCL Press, 2018).

5 Howgate, 'The Polar Colonization Plan', p. 231.

6 'Capt. Howgate is Guilty', *The New York Times,* 22 June 1895.

7 Kathryn Schulz, 'Literature's Arctic Obsession', *The New Yorker,* 17 April 2017.

8 Nostalgia was not the only 'polar pathology'; others included 'polar insomnia' and 'kayak fever'.

9 Michael F. Robinson, *The Coldest Crucible: Arctic Exploration and American Culture* (Chicago, IL: University of Chicago Press, 2006).

10 While nineteenth-century thinkers were anxious about the threat of nostalgia, historians today think that perhaps a version of nostalgia or homesickness, or at least positive memories of home, offered emotional support for explorers during overwinter expeditions, especially at Christmastime. Shane McCorristine and Jane S. P. Mocellin, 'Christmas at the Poles: Emotions, Food, and Festivities on Polar Expeditions, 1818–1912', *Polar Record,* 52(5), 2016, pp. 562–77.

11 As analysed by historian Michael S. Roth, in 'Dying of the Past: Medical Studies of Nostalgia in Nineteenth-Century France', *History and Memory,* 3(1), 1991, pp. 5–29.

12 Ibid., pp. 5–6.

13 Marilyn Yalom, *A History of the Breast* (Lewes: Rivers Oram Press, 1998), p. 111.

14 Roth, 'Dying of the Past: Medical Studies of Nostalgia in Nineteenth-Century France', p. 10.

15 'Homesickness as a Disease', *Scientific American,* 38(17), 27 April 1878, p. 266.

16 'Grief from a Medical Standpoint', *Scientific American,* 72(18), 4 May 1895, p. 283.

17 Thomas Dodman, *What Nostalgia Was: War, Empire, and the Time of a Deadly Emotion* (Chicago, IL: Chicago University Press, 2018), p. 4.

18 Ramesh Mallipeddi, '"A Fixed Melancholy": Migration, Memory, and the Middle Passage', *The Eighteenth Century,* 2014, p. 236.

19 'Slave Trade: Dreadful Narrative', *The Observer,* 7 January 1822, p. 1.

20 'British and Foreign History for the Year 1821: Chapter IV', *The New Annual Register, or General Repository of History, Politics, Arts, Sciences, and Literature, for the Year 1821* (London: Longman, Hurst, Rees, Orme, and Brown, 1822), p. 221.

21 Thomas Trotter, *Observation on the Scurvy* (London: T. Longman, 1792), p. 62.

22 Ibid., p. 62.

23 Quoted in Jonathan D. S. Schroeder, 'What was Black Nostalgia?', *American Literary History*, 2018, p. 660.

24 Quoted in Jose Maria Aguilera-Manzano, 'Slavery and Medicine in the Caribbean at the End of the "Ancien Regime"', *Social History*, 2008, p. 387.

25 Quoted in Schroeder, 'What was Black Nostalgia?', p. 662.

26 Katia M. de Queiros Mattoso, *To be a Slave in Brazil, 1550–1888* (1979), trans. Arthur Goldhammer (New Brunswick, NJ: Rutgers University Press, 1986), p. 140.

27 'Buxton on the Slave Trade', *The Times*, 12 August 1839, p. 6.

28 William Wordsworth, 'The Brothers', in William Angus Knight (ed.), *The Poetical Works of William Wordsworth*, vol. 2 (London: Macmillan and Co., Ltd, 1896), pp. 184–203, p. 197. Although, as scholar Jonathan D. S. Schroeder points out, after Winterbottom, anglophone writers never again called the enslaved people's 'spectacular death' nostalgia. Schroeder, 'What was Black Nostalgia?', p. 660.

29 Edward Long, *The History of Jamaica or, General Survey of the Antient and Modern State of that Island: with Reflections on its Situation, Settlements, Inhabitants, Climate, Products, Commerce, Laws, and Government*, vol. 2 (London: T. Lowndes, 1774).

30 Dodman, *What Nostalgia Was*, p. 4.

31 Jeremy Valentine MacClancy, *To Kill a Bird with Two Stones: A Short History of Vanuatu* (Vanuatu Cultural Centre, 2002), p. 48.

32 Frederic W. Farrar, 'Aptitudes of Races', *Transactions of the Ethnological Society of London*, 5, 1867, pp. 115–26, p. 122.

33 Boyle T. Somerville, 'Ethnological Notes on New Hebrides (continued)', *Journal of the Anthropological Institute of Great Britain and Ireland*, 23, 1894, pp. 363–93, p. 364.

34 J. M. Vermont, *Immigration from India to the Straits Settlements* (London, 1888), p. 7.

35 Farrar, 'Aptitudes of Races', p. 122.

36 While the term 'Anglo-Saxon' is sometimes used today as a phrase to describe the inhabitants of early England, it is historically inaccurate. According to historians Mary Rambaran-Olm and Erik Wade, the Anglo-Saxon 'myth' perpetuates a 'false idea of what it means to be "native" to Britain'. Today, the term 'exists as a supremacist dog whistle', is used as a 'euphemism for whiteness' and is frequently 'weaponized to promote far-right ideology'. Mary Rambaran-Olm and

Erik Wade, 'The Many Myths of the Term "Anglo-Saxon"', *Smithsonian Magazine*, 14 July 2021, https://www.smithsonianmag.com/history/many-myths-term-anglo-saxon-180978169/

37 Frederick Manson Bailey, 'Botany of British New Guinea', *Proceedings of the Royal Society of Queensland*, 13(1), 1898.

38 Arthur T. Holroyd, *The Quarantine Laws, Their Abuses and Inconsistencies. A Letter Addressed to the Rt. Hon. Sir John Cam Hobhouse* (London: Simpkin, Marshall & Co. Stationers' Hall Court, 1839), p. 3.

39 Ibid., pp. 28–9.

40 Dodman, *What Nostalgia Was*, p. 4.

41 Lisa Gabrielle O'Sullivan, 'Dying For Home: The Medicine and Politics of Nostalgia in Nineteenth-Century France' (Ph.D. dissertation, Queen Mary, University of London, 2006).

42 'Results of Emancipation: The Immigration Scheme', *The Eclectic Review*, 23, 1848, pp. 208–09.

43 Richard F. Burton, *Zanzibar: City, Island, and Coast* (London: Tinsley Brothers, 1872), p. 183.

44 Alison Blunt, 'Imperial Geographies of Home: British Domesticity in India, 1886–1925', *Transactions of the Institute of British Geographers*, 24(4), 1999), pp. 421–40, p. 421.

45 *Calcutta Review*, 1886, p. 359. Cited in ibid., p. 422.

46 Ibid.

47 *British Parliamentary Papers*, 1887, p. xx. Cited in Blunt, 'Imperial Geographies of Home', p. 421.

48 Roberts Bartholow, 'Sanitary Memoirs of the War', in Austin Flint (ed.), *Contributions Relating to the Causation and Prevention of Disease, and to Camp Diseases; Together with A Report of the Diseases etc. Among the Prisoners at Andersonville GA.* (New York: US Sanitary Commission by Hurd and Houghton, 1867), p. 22.

49 Bartholow, 'Sanitary Memoirs of the War', p. 21.

50 J. M. Guinn, 'The Pony Express', *Annual Publication of the Historical Society of Southern California and Pioneer Register*, 5(2), 1901, pp. 168–75.

51 William Cullen, *Nosology* (Edinburgh: C. Stewart and Company, 1800), p. 164.

52 Bartholow, 'Sanitary Memoirs of the War', p. 22.

53 'Home-Sickness as a Malady', *Scientific American*, 2 April 1864, p. 215.

54 Dodman, *What Nostalgia Was*.

CHAPTER THREE

1 'Calderdale History Timeline 1810–1850 ad', Calderdale Council (website), https://www.calderdale.gov.uk/wtw/time-line/1810-1850/1810-1850-1.html

2   David Ward, 'Immigration: Settlement Patterns and Spatial Distribution',
    in Stephan Thernstrom, Ann Orlov and Oscar Handlin (eds.), *Harvard
    Encyclopaedia of American Ethnic Groups* (Cambridge, MA: Harvard
    University Press, 1980), pp. 496–508.

3   Ibid.

4   Ibid.

5   Ellis Island Oral History Project, Series KECK, no. 0044: Interview of
    Arnold Ambler by Edward Applebome, 10 October 1985.

6   Susan J. Matt, *Homesickness: An American History* (Oxford: Oxford
    University Press, 2014).

7   Ibid.

8   This is not true for strictly academic accounts of immigration, which
    have covered the emotional landscape of migration in great detail. Not
    least, Susan J. Matt's book, *Homesickness: An American History*.

9   *Counsel for Emigrants, and Interesting Information from Numerous Sources
    Concerning British America, the United States, and New South Wales*, third
    edition (Aberdeen: John Mathison, Union Street, 1837).

10 Ibid., p. iii.

11 Ibid., p. ix.

12 Ibid., p. 21.

13 Ibid., p. 58.

14 Frederick Julius Gustorf, 'Diary of Frederick Julius Gustorf, October,
    1839', in *The Uncorrupted Heart: Journals and Letters of Frederick Julius
    Gustorf 1800–1845* (Columbia, MO: University of Missouri Press,
    1969), pp. 78–92.

15 Adolf E. Schroeder and Carla Schulz-Geisberg (eds.), *Hold Dear, As
    Always: Jette, a German Immigrant Life in Letters*, trans. Adolf E. Shroeder
    (Columbia, MO: University of Missouri Press, 1988), p. 5.

16 Ibid., p. 10.

17 Ibid.

18 Ibid., p. 245.

19 Susan J. Matt, 'You Can't Go Home Again: Homesickness and Nostalgia in
    U.S. History', *Journal of American History*, 94(2), 2007, pp. 469–97, p. 470.

20 Roxana Galusca, 'From Fictive Ability to National Identity: Disability,
    Medical Inspection, and Public Health Regulations on Ellis Island',
    Cultural Critique, 72, 2009, p. 144.

21 Emma Lazarus, 'The New Colossus', in Emma Lazarus, *Selected Poems
    and Other Writings* (Peterborough, ON: Broadview Press, 2002).

22 Ellis Island Oral History Project, Series KECK, no. 0113: Interview of
    Ememrich Gorozdos by Nancy Dallett, 19 December 1985.

23 Ibid.

24 Ellis Island Oral History Project, Series KECK, no. 0043: Interview of
    Bertha Devlin by Dana Gumb, 19 September 1985.

25   Hannah Arendt, *The Jew as Pariah: Jewish Identity and Politics in the Modern Age* (New York, NY: Grove Press, 1978), p. 60.

26   Gail Tolley, 'When you Can't Return Home', Wellcome Collection (website), 22 October 2020, https://wellcomecollection.org/articles/X3sHRxAAACcAWFfA

27   Ellis Island Oral History Project, Interview of Julia Israel Schueler by Paul E. Sigrist, Jr., 18 June 1992.

28   Anne C. Schenderlein, *Germany on Their Minds: German Jewish Refugees in the United States and their Relationship with Germany, 1938–1988* (New York, NY: Berghahn Books, 2020), p. 212.

29   Jennifer Craig-Norton, 'The Untold Stories of the Jewish Women who became Domestic Servants in Britain to Escape the Nazis', British Academy (website), 19 July 2019, https://www.thebritishacademy.ac.uk/blog/untold-stories-jewish-women-domestic-servants-britain-escape-nazis/

30   Ibid.

31   'Homesick', *The Youth's Companion*, 63(42), 16 October 1890, p. 536.

32   'Our Prize Stories for Children: When Nancy Was Homesick', *Congregationalist and Christian World*, Boston, 87(23), 7 June 1902, p. 825.

33   'Children in Happy Exile: Homes Across the Atlantic', *Times Educational Supplement*, 1(357), 3 May 1941, p. 205.

34   'Boy, 15, Refugee From Germany Hangs Himself', *New York Herald Tribune*, 17 July 1938, p. 12.

35   Theodore O. Reyhner, 'Camp for Junior?', *The Phi Delta Kappan*, 27(9), 1946, pp. 267–9, p. 267.

36   'Any Questions?', *British Medical Journal*, 2(4941), 1955, p. 747.

37   Jennifer Hassan, 'Books by one of Britain's most Famous Children's Authors Branded Racist', *The Washington Post*, 17 June 2021, https://www.washingtonpost.com/world/2021/06/17/enid-blyton-books-racist/

38   Matt, 'You Can't Go Home Again', p. 493.

39   Edmund S. Conklin, *Principles of Adolescent Psychology* (New York, NY: Henry Holt & Co., 1935), pp. 209–16, p. 216, quoted in Matt, 'You Can't Go Home Again', p. 493.

40   Willis H. McCann, 'Nostalgia: A Descriptive and Comparative Study', *Journal of Genetic Psychology*, 62, 1943, pp. 97–104.

41   Ibid., p. 98.

42   Reyhner, 'Camp for Junior?', p. 268.

43   Maria M. Tewater, 'Some Sociological Aspects of Parent–Child Relationships as they appear in Behavior Problems of Children' (MA dissertation, University of Southern California, 1927), p. 37.

44   Ibid., p. 53.

45   Margaret Stroebe et al., 'Homesickness Among Students in Two

Cultures: Antecedents and Consequences', *British Journal of Psychology*, 93(2), 2010, pp. 147–68.

46 McCann, 'Nostalgia', p. 104.

47 Gail Tolley, 'The Complex Longing for Home', Wellcome Collection (website), 1 October 2020, https://wellcomecollection.org/articles/X2yCNBEAAOQpPZUV

48 Susan J. Matt, 'The New Globalist Is Homesick', *The New York Times*, 21 March 2012, https://www.nytimes.com/2012/03/22/opinion/many-still-live-with-homesickness.html

49 Stuart Hall, 'Cultural Identity and Diaspora', in Linda Mcdowell (ed.), *Undoing Place? A Geographical Reader* (Abingdon: Routledge, 1999), p. 236.

50 Meredith B. Linn, 'Elixir of Emigration: Soda Water and the Making of Irish Americans in Nineteenth Century New York City', *Historical Archaeology*, 44(4), 2010, pp. 69–109, p. 101.

51 Dieu Hack-Polay, 'When Home Isn't Home: A Study of Homesickness and Coping Strategies Among Migrant Workers and Expatriates', *International Journal of Psychological Studies*, 4(3), 2012, pp. 62–72.

52 Ibid., p. 63.

53 Ibid.

54 M. A. Van Tilburg, A. J. Vingerhoets and G. L. Van Heck, 'Homesickness: A Review of the Literature', *Psychological Medicine*, 26, 1996, pp. 899–912, p. 903.

55 'Refugees and asylum seekers: statistics', Mental Health Foundation (website), 2023, https://www.mentalhealth.org.uk/explore-mental-health/statistics/refugees-asylum-seekers-statistics

56 Alison McCook, 'Immigrants more depressed than those who stay', Reuters (website), 4 April 2011, https://www.reuters.com/article/us-immigrants-more-depressed-than-those-idUSTRE7335VJ20110404; Matt, 'The New Globalist Is Homesick'.

57 Tolley, 'When you Can't Return Home', Wellcome Collection (website), 22 October 2020.

58 Colin Freeman, 'Should we expect Syrian asylum seekers to be grateful?', *The Telegraph*, 13 November 2014, https://www.telegraph.co.uk/news/worldnews/middleeast/syria/11226965/Should-we-expect-Syrian-asylum-seekers-to-be-grateful.html

59 Dina Nayeri, 'The ungrateful refugee: "We have no debt to repay"', *The Guardian*, 4 April 2017, https://www.theguardian.com/world/2017/apr/04/dina-nayeri-ungrateful-refugee

60 Quoted in Tolley, 'When you Can't Return Home'.

CHAPTER FOUR

1   Sara Rimer, 'Cavendish Journal; Shielding Solzhenitsyn, Respectfully', *The New York Times*, 3 March 1993.

2   John Martyn Harlow, 'Recovery from the Passage of an Iron Bar through the Head', *Publications of the Massachusetts Medical Society*, 1868, pp. 327–47.

3   John Martyn Harlow, 'Passage of an Iron Rod Through the Head', *Boston Medical and Surgical Journal*, 1848, pp. 389–93.

4   Malcolm B. Macmillan, 'Inhibition and Phineas Gage: Repression and Sigmund Freud', *Neuropsychoanalysis*, 2004, pp. 181–92.

5   P. Ratiu et al., 'The Tale of Phineas Gage, Digitally Remastered', *Journal of Neurotrauma*, 2004, pp. 637–43.

6   Harlow, 'Recovery from the Passage of an Iron Bar through the Head', *Publications of the Massachusetts Medical Society*, 1868, pp. 327–47.

7   Katherine Pandora, 'The Permissive Precincts of Barnum's and Goodrich's Museums of Miscellaneity: Lessons in Knowing Nature for New Learners', in Carin Berkowitz and Bernard Lightman (eds.), *Science Museums in Transition: Cultures of Display in Nineteenth-Century Britain and America* (Pittsburgh, PA: University of Pittsburgh Press, 2017), p. 36.

8   Harlow, 'Recovery from the Passage of an Iron Bar through the Head', *Publications of the Massachusetts Medical Society*, 1868, pp. 327–47.

9   'Scientist, n.', Oxford English Dictionary Online, Oxford University Press, accessed 2 December 2021, https://www.oed.com/view/Entry/172698?redirectedFrom=scientist

10 Matthew Cobb, *The Idea of the Brain: The Past and Future of Neuroscience* (New York, NY: Basic Books, 2020).

11 Ibid.

12 Thomas Dixon, *From Passions to Emotions: The Creation of a Secular Psychological Category* (Cambridge: Cambridge University Press, 2003), pp. 109–27.

13 Thomas Dixon, '"Emotion": The History of a Keyword in Crisis', *Emotion Review*, 2012, pp. 338–44, p. 339.

14 Ibid., p. 338.

15 Ibid., p. 340.

16 Charles Bell, *The Anatomy and Philosophy of Expression as Connected with the Fine Arts* (London: John Murray, 1847).

17 Charles Darwin, *The Expression of the Emotions in Man and Animals* (London: John Murray, 1872).

18 William James, 'What is an Emotion?', *Mind*, 1884, pp. 188–205.

19 Linus W. Kline, 'The Migratory Impulse vs. Love of Home', *American Journal of Psychology*, 1898, pp. 1–81.

20 Ibid., pp. 73–4.

21 Paul Carus, 'The Nature of Pleasure and Pain', *The Monist*, 1896, pp. 432–42, p. 434.

22 Joanna Timms, 'Phantasm of Freud: Nandor Fodor and the Psychoanalytic Approach to the Supernatural in Interwar Britain', *Psychoanalysis and History*, 2012, pp. 5–27, p. 5.

23 'Sigmund Freud's Famous Psychoanalytic Couch', Freud Museum London (website), accessed 3 December 2021, https://www.freud.org.uk/about-us/the-house/sigmund-freuds-famous-psychoanalytic-couch/

24 Raymond Buckland, *The Spirit Book: The Encyclopaedia of Clairvoyance, Channelling, and Spirit Communication* (Canton Charter Township, MI: Visible Ink Press, 2005), p. 144.

25 'Nandor Fodor, 69, A Psychoanalyst; Author of Theory to Explain Poltergeists Is Dead', *The New York Times*, 19 May 1964.

26 Julian Holloway, 'On the Spaces and Movement of Monsters', *Cultural Geographies*, 2017, pp. 21–41, p. 31.

27 'The Ghost of a Weasel', *The Observer*, 11 October 1936, p. 13.

28 Christopher Josiffe, 'Gef the Talking Mongoose', *Fortean Times*, December 2010.

29 Judith Robinson, 'Manx Mystery Mongoose', *The Globe and Mail*, 19 December 1936, pp. 1–2; 'The Mystery of the "Man-Weasel": Strange to Relate', *South China Sunday Post*, 4 October 1970, p. 37.

30 Harry Price, *Confessions of a Ghost-Hunter* (New York, NY: Putnam, 1963); Harry Price and Richard Lambert, *The Haunting of Cashen's Gap: A Modern 'Miracle' Investigated* (London: Methuen & Co. Ltd, 1936).

31 Alison Light, 'Astral Projection', *London Review of Books*, 17 December 2020.

32 'Medium Sentenced For Fraud', *The Times*, 4 April 1944, p. 2.

33 A. Conan Doyle, 'Fairies Photographed', *Strand Magazine*, December 1920, pp. 462–8.

34 Hereward Carrington and Nandor Fodor, *Haunted People: The Story of the Poltergeist Down the Centuries* (New York, NY: Dutton, 1951).

35 Nador Fodor, 'I Psychoanalyze Ghosts', *Mechanix Illustrated*, September 1949, p. 150; Carrington and Fodor, *Haunted People*.

36 Fodor, 'I Psychoanalyze Ghosts', p. 150.

37 Nandor Fodor, 'Varieties of Nostalgia', *Psychoanalytic Review*, 1950, pp. 25–38.

38 Anna Neima, *The Utopians* (London: Picador, 2020).

39 Nandor Fodor, *The Search for the Beloved: A Clinical Investigation of the Trauma of Birth and Pre-Natal Conditioning* (New York, NY: Hermitage Press, 1949).

40 Fodor, 'Varieties of Nostalgia', p. 26.

41 Ibid., p. 27.

42 Ibid., p. 30.

43 Ibid., p. 31.

44 Ibid., p. 36.
45 Alexander R. Martin, 'Nostalgia', *American Journal of Psychoanalysis*, 1954, pp. 93–104, p. 103.
46 Ibid., p. 103.
47 Ibid., p. 98.
48 Dominique Geahchan, 'Deuil et Nostalgic', *Revue Francaise de Psychanalyse*, 1968, pp. 39–65.
49 Fodor, 'Varieties of Nostalgia', p. 25.
50 M. Nawas and J. Platt, 'A Future-Oriented Theory of Nostalgia', *Journal of Individual Psychology*, 1965, pp. 51–7.
51 'Nandor Fodor, 69, A Psychoanalyst; Author of Theory to Explain Poltergeists Is Dead', *The New York Times*, 19 May 1964.
52 David S. Werman, 'Normal and Pathological Nostalgia', *Journal of the American Psychoanalytic Association*, 1977, pp. 387–98.
53 Alvin Toffler, *Future Shock* (New York, NY: Random House, 1970), p. 407.
54 Horst-Dieter Ebert, 'Jene Sehnsucht nach den alten Tagen . . .', *Der Spiegel*, 29 January 1973, pp. 86–99, p. 86.
55 Michael Wood, 'Nostalgia or Never: You Can't go Home Again', *New Society*, 7 November 1974, pp. 343–6, p. 343.

CHAPTER FIVE

1 Alvin Toffler, *Future Shock* (New York, NY: Random House, 1970), p. 407.
2 Harry Sosnik, 'Nostalgia! Nostalgia! But Where's Originality?', *Variety*, 8 January 1975, p. 133.
3 Ian Jack, 'How a 1960s actor shopping in a junk shop foretold the future', *The Guardian,* 31 May 2008, https://www.theguardian.com/commentisfree/2008/may/31/1968theyearofrevolt.past
4 Tara H. Saunders, 'Basking in Second-hand Glory: Resale Consumerism in the Twentieth-Century United States' (Ph.D. dissertation, Indiana University, 2006), p. 232.
5 Diane K. Shah et al., 'The New Junk Trade', *Newsweek*, 94(4), 23 July 1979, pp. 90–1, p. 90.
6 Ibid.
7 Ibid., pp. 90–1, p. 92.
8 'Nostalgia: Treasures from the Past', *Newsweek*, 76(26), 28 December 1970, p. 34.
9 Ibid.
10 Display Ad 446, The *New York Times*, 17 November 1974, p. 253.
11 Charles Michener, 'Cooling the Jazz Age', *Newsweek*, 83(13), 1 April 1974, p. 72.
12 'Surviving Black October', *The New York Times,* 30 September 1979, p. 120.
13 Ibid.

14   Sol Weinstein, 'Nostalgia Quiz', *Variety*, 265(8), 5 January 1972, p. 84.

15   'Nostalgia I.Q. Test', *Billboard*, 86(18), 4 May 1974, N17.

16   John Rockwell, 'Beach Boys Riding Crest of New Popularity', *The New York Times*, 27 August 1976, p. 54.

17   Bernadine Morris, 'Nostalgia for Old Days at the Rome Shows', *The New York Times*, 26 January 1974, p. 20.

18   Russell Baker, 'The Nostalgia Affair', *The New York Times*, 14 August 1973, p. 33.

19   Fred Davis, *Yearning for Yesterday: A Sociology of Nostalgia* (New York, NY: The Free Press, 1979), p. x.

20   Baker, 'The Nostalgia Affair', p. 33.

21   Display Ad 446, *The New York Times*, 17 November 1974, p. 253.

22   Otto L. Bettmann, *The Good Old Days: They Were Terrible!* (New York, NY: Random House, 1974).

23   Martin Hillman, 'The New Nostalgia and other escapism', *Tribune*, 38(18), 3 May 1974, pp. 6–7.

24   Alan Brien, 'Nostalgia, the Ostrich', *New Statesman*, 1 January 1971, p. 304.

25   Colin McArthur, 'Dangers of Nostalgia', *Tribune*, 6 January 1978, p. 7.

26   Hillman, 'The New Nostalgia and other escapism', p. 6.

27   McArthur, 'Dangers of Nostalgia', p. 7.

28   Margaret Richards, 'Forties Art: Nostalgia, Foreshadowings', *Tribune*, 10 November 1972, p. 7.

29   'Dream of Victorian Childhood', *The Observer*, 1 April 1962, p. 30.

30   James Collins, 'Rags to Riches', *The Guardian*, 20 February 1976, p. 8.

31   'Nostalgia Wave Hits in France', *Billboard*, 25 January 1975, p. 46.

32   Geoffrey Weston, 'Historic Spa Bubbles Along Merrily on Wave of Nostalgia', *The Times*, 22 June 1977, p. xii.

33   Craig R. Whitney, 'In West Germany, Real Bread by Real Bakers', *The New York Times*, 17 July 1975, p. 34.

34   'Last word', *The Times Higher Education Supplement*, 12, 1 February 1974, p. 4.

35   David Beresford, 'Tills Ring as Nazi Nostalgia Grows in Britain', *The Guardian*, 17 July 1978, p. 5.

36   John Frazer, 'War Nostalgia, German Style', *New Statesman*, 8 July 1977, p. 43

37   Beresford, 'Tills Ring as Nazi Nostalgia Grows in Britain', p. 5.

38   Frazer, 'War Nostalgia, German Style', p. 43.

39   Ibid.

40   Ibid.

41   Beresford, 'Tills Ring as Nazi Nostalgia Grows in Britain', p. 5.

42   Ibid.

43   'Jews' Org in Germany Warns of Possible "Hitler Nostalgia Wave"', *Variety*, 31 August 1977, p. 37.

44 Beresford, 'Tills Ring as Nazi Nostalgia Grows in Britain', p. 5.

45 Dan Glaun, 'Germany's Laws on Hate Speech, Nazi Propaganda & Holocaust Denial: An Explainer', Frontline, PBS (website), 1 July 2021, https://www.pbs.org/wgbh/frontline/article/germanys-laws-antisemitic-hate-speech-nazi-propaganda-holocaust-denial/

46 Frazer, 'War Nostalgia, German Style', p. 43.

47 John Vinocur, 'Bonn Says Neo-Nazis are Growing More Millitant', The New York Times, 1 May 1978, p. 7.

48 Glaun, 'Germany's Laws on Hate Speech, Nazi Propaganda & Holocaust Denial: An Explainer'.

49 Hillman, 'The New Nostalgia and other escapism', p. 6.

50 Ibid.

51 'Appeasement 1977 Style', British Medical Journal, 2, 1977, p. 1619.

52 Guy Ortolano, Thatcher's Progress: From Social Democracy to Market Liberalism Through an English New Town (Cambridge: Cambridge University Press, 2019), p. 20.

53 Hillman, 'The New Nostalgia and other escapism', Tribune, p. 6.

54 McArthur, 'Dangers of Nostalgia', p. 7.

55 Ibid.

56 Davis, Yearning for Yesterday, pp. 107–8.

57 Ibid., p. ix.

58 Ibid., p. 104.

59 Ibid., p. x.

60 Ibid., p. 110.

61 Ibid., p. 104.

CHAPTER SIX

1 Hovis Commercial, 'Our Dad', dir. Ridley Scott, 1974, https://www.hatads.org.uk/catalogue/record/e3e0afc4-54ea-4655-a316-d9b66dab86e0

2 'The Two Ronnies – their classic 1978 "Hovis" Advert', YouTube, https://www.youtube.com/watch?v=DJi_5TojSnA

3 Hovis Commercial, 'Bike', dir. Ridley Scott, 1973, 'Hovis "Bike" advert 1973 (Britain's favourite TV ad)', YouTube, https://www.youtube.com/watch?v=6Mq59ykPnAE

4 Paul Harris, 'Star of the Hovis ad returns to the cobbled hill 40 YEARS on from climbing it with his loaves and bicycle', Daily Mail, 4 December 2013, https://www.dailymail.co.uk/news/article-2517410/Hovis-advert-bakers-boy-Carl-Barlow-returns-cobbled-hill-40-YEARS.html

5 'Hovis "Bike" advert 1973 (Britain's favourite TV ad)', YouTube, https://www.youtube.com/watch?v=6Mq59ykPnAE

6 Harris, 'Star of the Hovis ad returns to the cobbled hill'.

7 Ashley Rodriguez, 'Watch: The First TV Commercial, which Aired 75 Years

Ago Today', Quartz (website), 1 July 2016, https://qz.com/721431/ watch-the-first-tv-commercial-which-aired-75-years-ago-today/

8 Quoted in Alison Alexander et al., '"We'll Be Back in a Moment": A Content Analysis of Advertisements in Children's Television in the 1950s', *Journal of Advertising*, 27(3), 1998, pp. 1–9, p. 2.

9 Kori Wallace, 'The History and Future of Television Advertising', Oracle Advertising Blog, 11 July 2019, https://blogs.oracle.com/advertising/ post/the-history-and-future-of-television-advertising

10 Alexander et al., '"We'll Be Back in a Moment": A Content Analysis of Advertisements in Children's Television in the 1950s', p. 2.

11 'A Short History of British TV Advertising', Science + Media Museum (website), 5 November 2020, https://www.scienceandmediamuseum. org.uk/objects-and-stories/short-history-british-tv-advertising

12 'What Caused the Advertising Industry Boom in the 1950s?', Chron. (website), *Houston Chronicle*, 4 September 2020, https://smallbusiness. chron.com/caused-advertising-industry-boom-1950s-69115.html

13 'The Wheel', *Mad Men* (season 1, episode 13), written by Matthew Weiner and Robin Veith, dir. Matthew Weiner, AMC, 2007.

14 Cadbury's Cake Range Commercial, 'The Years to Remember', 1966, https://www.hatads.org.uk/catalogue/record/03a94431e-07f0-4f49-ad26-481cad8c7a16

15 Heinz Cream of Tomato Soup Commercial, 'Nostalgia', 1981, https:// www.hatads.org.uk/catalogue/record/4425795c-43cc-4f5d-a934-f09d-280f1efd

16 Ribena Commercial, 'Memories', 1970, https://www.hatads.org.uk/ catalogue/record/fb0f9cd2-7dc4-4efa-ac97-9bf2e7c2f66f

17 Anchor Butter Commercial, 'Car Rides', 1983, https://www.hatads.org. uk/catalogue/record/516ad295-3666-4727-974a-12ffadof533f

18 Weetabix Commercial, 'Picnic', 1970, https://www.hatads.org.uk/cata-logue/record/d05420dc-0745-476e-9097-595d96722c4f

19 Darrel D. Muehling and David E. Sprott, 'The Power of Reflection: An Empirical Examination of Nostalgia Advertising Effects', *Journal of Advertising*, 33(3), 2004, pp. 25–35, p. 25.

20 Ibid., p. 25.

21 Barbara B. Stern, 'Historical and Personal Nostalgia in Advertising Text: The *Fin de siècle* Effect', *Journal of Advertising*, 21(4), 1992, p. 13.

22 Ibid.

23 Ibid., p. 16.

24 Ibid., p. 17.

25 Raphaëlle Lambert-Pandraud and Gilles Laurent, 'Why Do Older Consumers Buy Older Brands? The Role of Attachment and Declining Innovativeness', *Journal of Marketing*, 74(5), 2010, pp. 104–21, p. 105.

26 Ibid., p. 104.

27 Ibid.
28 Stern, 'Historical and Personal Nostalgia in Advertising Text', *Journal of Advertising*, 21(4), p. 15.
29 Olof Brunninge and Benjamin Julien Hartmann, 'Inventing a Past: Corporate Heritage as Dialectical Relationships of Past and Present', *Marketing Theory*, 19(2), 2018, pp. 229–34.
30 Benjamin J. Hartmann and Katja H. Brunk, 'Nostalgia Marketing and (Re-) enchantment', *International Journal of Research in Marketing*, 36(4), 2019, pp. 669–86, p. 670.
31 Lambert-Pandraud and Laurent, 'Why Do Older Consumers Buy Older Brands?', p. 105.
32 Muehling and Sprott, 'The Power of Reflection', pp. 25–35, p. 25.
33 Owen Hatherley, *The Ministry of Nostalgia* (London: Verso Book, 2016).
34 Ibid., p. 15.
35 Thomas Dixon, *Weeping Britannia: Portrait of a Nation in Tears* (Oxford: Oxford University Press, 2015).
36 Hatherley, *The Ministry of Nostalgia*, p. 31.
37 Ibid., p. 21.
38 Ibid., p. 16.
39 Alexander Fury, 'The Case for Déjà Vu', *Financial Times*, 16 September 2022.
40 Ibid.
41 Jack Neff, 'America's Hottest Brands 2022: 20 Brands that are Having a Marketing Moment', *Advertising Age*, 93(11), 2022, p. 8.
42 'Mint Explainer: Campa Cola and the power of nostalgia', *Mint*, 1 September 2022.
43 Erich Schwartzel, 'The 1990s Are Back, Putting Nostalgic Viewers to Sleep', *The Wall Street Journal*, 29 Apr 2022.
44 Ally Burnie, 'How tapping into nostalgia solidified Booking.com in the local community', *The Australian*, 17 July 2022.
45 'I Believe in Yesterday: Why Nostalgia Keeps Coming Back', Spotify Advertising (website), June 2019, https://ads.spotify.com/en-GB/news-and-insights/i-believe-in-yesterday-why-nostalgia-keeps-coming-back/
46 Eloise Hendy, 'Were the Nineties Really so Good?', *The Independent*, 21 January 2023, https://www.independent.co.uk/life-style/90s-nostalgia-best-decade-b2265400.html
47 Alex Hawgood, 'Why Does '90s Nostalgia Feel So Good Right Now?', *W* magazine, 31 January 2022, https://www.wmagazine.com/culture/90s-fashion-revival-trend-music-tv
48 Quoted in Hawgood, 'Why Does '90s Nostalgia Feel So Good Right Now?'.
49 Hendy, 'Were the Nineties Really so Good?'.

50 Hawgood, 'Why Does '90s Nostalgia Feel So Good Right Now?'.
51 Ibid.

CHAPTER SEVEN

1   Mark Girouard, *The Return to Camelot* (London: Yale University Press, 1981), p. 88.
2   Florence S. Boos, 'Introduction', in Florence S. Boos (ed.), *History and Community: Essays in Victorian Medievalism* (New York, NY & London: Garland Publishing Inc., 1992), pp. xi–xii.
3   Charles Dellheim, 'Interpreting Victorian Medievalism', in Boos (ed.), *History and Community*, pp. 47–8.
4   Ibid., p. 48.
5   Angela Bartie et al., *Restaging the Past: Historical Pageants, Culture and Society in Modern Britain* (London: UCL Press, 2020).
6   Ibid., p. 9
7   Ibid., p. 161.
8   Tison Pugh and Angela Jane Weisl, *Medievalisms* (Abingdon: Routledge, 2012), p. 1.
9   Ibid.
10 Lev Grossman, 'Feeding on Fantasy. Forward into the Past! At a Time of Uncertainty, American Culture Looks Backward for Comfort', *Time*, 2 December 2002, pp. 90–6.
11 Ibid., p. 90.
12 Ibid., p. 94.
13 Pugh and Weisl, *Medievalisms*, p. 1.
14 Society for Creative Anachronism (website), https://www.sca.org/; Michael A. Cramer, *Medieval Fantasy as Performance: The Society for Creative Anachronism and the Current Middle Ages* (Lanham, MD: Scarecrow Press, 2009).
15 Pugh and Weisl, *Medievalisms*, p. 9.
16 Ibid.
17 Ibid., p. 113.
18 Grossman, 'Feeding on Fantasy', p. 96.
19 Ibid.
20 Cramer, *Medieval Fantasy as Performance*, p. 23.
21 Ibid.
22 Ibid., p. xi.
23 Dellheim, 'Interpreting Victorian Medievalism', p. 48.
24 Carolyn Dinshaw, *How Soon is Now? Medieval Texts, Amateur Readers, and the Queerness of Time* (Durham, NC, Duke University Press, 2012), p. 34.
25 Raphael Samuel, *Theatres of Memory* (London: Verso, 1994), p. 139.

26 Charter on the Built Vernacular Heritage, ICOMOS, October 1999, https://www.icomos.org/en/particiaper/179-articles-en-francais/ressources/charters-and-standards/164-charter-of-the-built-vernacular-heritage

27 'Case Study: The Canterbury Tales', Continuum Attractions (website), https://www.continuumattractions.com/case_studies/the-canterbury-tales/

28 Jorvik Viking Centre (website), https://www.jorvikvikingcentre.co.uk/

29 Medieval Times (website), https://www.medievaltimes.com/

30 Pugh and Weisl, *Medievalisms*, p. 128.

31 Ibid, pp. 128–9.

32 Ibid., p. 128.

33 Medieval Times careers (website), apply.jobappnetwork.com/medieval-times/

34 Pugh and Weisl, *Medievalisms*, p. 130.

35 Ibid.

36 Ibid.

37 Melody Ward Leslie, 'Medieval Studies and the Viking Feast', Around the O, University of Oregon (website), 2 October 2019, https://around.uoregon.edu/content/medieval-studies-and-viking-feast

38 Erin McCann, 'Civil War Veterans at Gettysburg Anniversary in 1913, In Pictures', *The Guardian*, 1 July 2013, https://www.theguardian.com/world/gallery/2013/jul/01/civil-war-gettysburg-anniversary-pictures

39 Daniel Arnold, 'The Decline of the Civil War Re-enactor', *The New York Times*, 28 July 2018.

40 John Skow, Beth Austin and Joseph J. Kane, 'Bang, Bang! You're History, Buddy', *Time*, 8 November 1986.

41 Ibid.

42 'Blists Hill Victorian Town', Ironbridge (website), https://www.ironbridge.org.uk/visit/blists-hill-victorian-town/

43 'Blists Hill Victorian Town', TripAdvisor (website), https://www.tripadvisor.co.uk/Attraction_Review-g186366-d261211-Reviews-or20-Blists_Hill_Victorian_Town-Ironbridge_Ironbridge_Gorge_Telford_Shropshire_Eng.html

44 Lara Rutherford-Morrison, 'Playing Victorian: Heritage, Authenticity, and Make-Believe in Blists Hill Victorian Town, the Ironbridge Gorge', *The Public History*, 37(3), 2015, pp. 76–101.

45 Tom Paulin, 'Question of Real Value', *The Independent*, 5 October 1993, quoted in Samuel, *Theatres of Memory*, p. 260; Robert Hewison, *The Heritage Industry: Britain in a Climate of Decline* (London: Methuen, 1987), p. 141.

46 Patrick Wright, *On Living in an Old Country* (London: Verso, 1985), p. 70.

47 Samuel, *Theatres of Memory*, p. 260.

48 Ibid.

49 Bob West, 'The Making of the English Working Past: a Critical View of the Ironbridge Gorge Museum', in Robert Lumley (ed.), *The Museum Time-Machine* (Abingdon: Routledge, 1988), p. 57.

50 Harry Cheadle, 'Why Would You Ever Want to Live in 2019?', *Vice*, 7 October 2019, https://www.vice.com/en/article/qvgw3x/gabriel-sarah-chrisman-victorian-couple-profile

51 Ibid.

52 Eloise Hendy, 'Were the Nineties Really so Good?', *The Independent*, 21 January 2023, https://www.independent.co.uk/life-style/90s-nostalgia-best-decade-b2265400.html

53 Johann Hari, *Stolen Focus: Why You Can't Pay Attention, And How to Think Deeply Again* (London: Bloomsbury, 2023).

54 Sean Illing, 'Why you (probably) won't finish reading this story', Vox, 8 February 2022, https://www.vox.com/vox-conversations-podcast/2022/2/8/22910773/vox-conversations-johann-hari-stolen-focus

55 Stephanie Vozza, 'Three Reasons you Can't Focus Right Now (and why it's not your fault)', *Fast Company*, 27 January 2022, https://www.fastcompany.com/90715607/3-reasons-you-cant-focus-right-now-and-why-its-not-your-fault

56 Post by @DrMatthewSweet, Twitter (website), 6 January 2022, https://twitter.com/drmatthewsweet/status/1479125910896975877

57 Grossman, 'Feeding on Fantasy', p. 96.

58 Kevin McSpadden, 'You Now Have a Shorter Attention Span Than a Goldfish', *Time*, 14 May 2015.

59 Post by @DrMatthewSweet, Twitter (website), 6 January 2022, https://twitter.com/DrMatthewSweet/status/1479125923119214597?s=20&t=QeXKWSinqYEaP9GgoWbQZQ

60 Evita March, 'When Too Much News is Bad News: Is the Way We Consume News Detrimental to Our Health?', *The Conversation*, 20 October 2020.

61 Yehuda Wacks and Aviv M. Weinstein, 'Excessive Smartphone Use Is Associated With Health Problems in Adolescents and Young Adults', *Frontiers in Psychiatry*, 12, 2021.

62 Diseases of Modern Life, University of Oxford (website), accessed 25 August 2017, https://diseasesofmodernlife.org/

63 John Marshall, 'Overwork of the Brain', *The Spectator*, 1 July 1854, p. 701.

64 'Hurried to Death', *The Medical Times and Gazette*, 22 February 1868, pp. 204–6, p. 204.

65 Ibid., pp. 204–6, p. 205.

66 Ibid., pp. 204–6.

67 'A Medical Lecture on the Railway Mania', *Punch*, 22 November 1845, p. 228.

68 'Hurried to Death', *The Medical Times and Gazette*, 22 February 1868, pp. 204–6.

69 W. M. Ewart, 'Abstract Of The Harveian Lectures. On Disease And Its Treatment, And The Profession Of Medicine In The Year 1899', *British Medical Journal*, 2(1981), 1898, pp. 1801–5, p. 1805.

70 'Letters, Notes, And Answers To Correspondents', *British Medical Journal*, 2(1765), 1894, pp. 963–4.

71 Ewart, 'Abstract Of The Harveian Lectures. On Disease And Its Treatment, And The Profession Of Medicine In The Year 1899', p. 1805.

72 Daniel Pick, *Faces of Degeneration: A European Disorder, c.1848 – c.1918* (Cambridge: Cambridge University Press, 1989).

73 See J. E. Chamberlin and S. Gilman (eds.), *Degeneration: The Dark Side of Progress* (New York, NY: Columbia University Press, 1985) and George Stocking, *Victorian Anthropology* (London: Simon and Schuster, 1991).

74 Post by @DrMatthewSweet, Twitter (website), 6 January 2022, https://twitter.com/DrMatthewSweet/status/1479125949480382469?s=20&t=odbhaVQzqQLqHrQI6kogtw

75 *The Diary of Samuel Pepys*, 13 May 1665, https://www.pepysdiary.com/diary/1665/05/13/

76 Sarah A. Chrisman, 'What Millennial Women Can Learn From Victorian Ladies', Refinery29 (website), 1 October 2015, https://www.refinery29.com/en-us/victorian-living-millennial-women

77 Cheadle, 'Why Would You Ever Want to Live in 2019?'.

CHAPTER EIGHT

1 Grafton Tanner, *The Hours Have Lost Their Clock: The Politics of Nostalgia* (London: Watkins Media Limited, 2021).

2 Jennifer Rankin, 'EU chief negotiator blames Brexit on "nostalgia for the past"', *The Guardian*, 30 May 2019, https://www.theguardian.com/politics/2019/may/30/eu-chief-negotiator-blames-brexit-on-nostalgia-for-the-past-michel-barnier

3 Yiannis Gabriel, 'Organisational Nostalgia: Reflections on the Golden Age', in S. Fineman (ed.), *Emotions in Organisations* (London: Sage Publications Ltd, 1993), pp. 118–41.

4 George K. Behlmer, 'Introduction', in George K. Behlmer and F. M. Leventhal (eds.), *Singular Continuities: Tradition, Nostalgia, and Identity in Modern British Culture* (Stanford, CA: Stanford University Press, 2000), p. 7.

5 Ibid.

6 Nick Cohen, 'Our politics of nostalgia is a sure sign of present-day decay', *The Observer*, 26 June 2021.

7 Sophie Gaston and Sacha Hilhorst, *Nostalgia as a Cultural and Political Force in Britain, France and Germany* (London: Demos, 2018), p. 11.

8   Catherine E. de Vries and Isabell Hoffmann, 'The Power of the Past:
    How Nostalgia Shapes European Public Opinion', Eupinions (website), 5
    November 2018, https://eupinions.eu/de/text/the-power-of-the-past/
9   Ibid.
10 David Olusoga, 'Empire 2.0 is dangerous nostalgia for something that
    never existed', *The Observer*, 19 March 2017, https://www.theguardian.
    com/commentisfree/2017/mar/19/empire-20-is-dangerous-nostalgia-
    for-something-that-never-existed
11 Ben Judah, 'England's Last Gasp of Empire', *The New York Times,* 12 July
    2016, https://www.nytimes.com/2016/07/13/opinion/englands-last-
    gasp-of-empire.html
12 Nandine El-Enany, 'Europe's colonial embrace and the Brexit nostalgia
    for empire are two sides of the same coin', LSE Blog, 29 April 2020,
    https://blogs.lse.ac.uk/brexit/2020/04/29/europes-colonial-embrace-
    and-brexit-as-nostalgia-for-empire-are-part-of-the-same-story/
13 Ibid.
14 Quoted in Sathnam Sanghera, *Empireland: How Imperialism Has Shaped
    Modern Britain* (London: Penguin, 2021), p. 113.
15 Kojo Koram, 'Britain's Blindness', *Dissent* magazine, 6 February 2019,
    https://www.dissentmagazine.org/online_articles/britains-brexit-
    blindness
16 El-Enany, 'Europe's colonial embrace and the Brexit nostalgia for empire
    are two sides of the same coin', LSE Blog, 29 April 2020.
17 Jon Stone, 'British people are proud of colonialism and the British
    Empire, poll finds', *The Independent*, 19 January 2016, https://www.
    independent.co.uk/news/uk/politics/british-people-are-proud-of-
    colonialism-and-the-british-empire-poll-finds-a6821206.html#
    commentsDiv
18 El-Enany, 'Europe's colonial embrace and the Brexit nostalgia for empire
    are two sides of the same coin', LSE Blog, 29 April 2020.
19 Ibid.
20 Peter Mitchell, *Imperial Nostalgia: How the British Conquered Themselves*
    (Manchester: Manchester University Press, 2021), p. 6.
21 Paul Gilroy, *Postcolonial Melancholia* (New York, NY: Columbia University
    Press, 2006).
22 Anna Maria C. Behler et al., 'Making America Great Again? National
    Nostalgia's Effect on Outgroup Perceptions', *Frontiers in Psychology*, 12,
    2021, https://www.frontiersin.org/articles/10.3389/fpsyg.2021.555667/
    full
23 Ibid.
24 Ronald Brownstein, 'Trump's Rhetoric of White Nostalgia', *The Atlantic*,
    2 June 2016, https://www.theatlantic.com/politics/archive/2016/06/
    trumps-rhetoric-of-white-nostalgia/485192/

25   Ibid.

26   Joseph C. Harsch London, 'Britain's Conservatives – And Ours', *The New York Times*, 14 June 1959.

27   Anthony Lewis, 'Convention Moods Reflects a Historic Change', *The New York Times*, 19 July 1964.

28   Josh Greenfeld, 'The Conservatives Are Out to Beat – "Rockeberg, Goldfeller, Ottindell and Goodinger"', *The New York Times*, 19 October 1970.

29   Richard Jobson, '"The ghost of Keir Hardie": Nostalgia and the modern Labour Party', LSE Blog, 23 September 2015, https://blogs.lse.ac.uk/politicsandpolicy/the-ghost-of-keir-hardie-nostalgia-and-the-modern-labour-party/

30   Robert Saunders, 'The Myth of Brexit as Imperial Nostalgia', *Prospect*, 7 January 2019, https://www.prospectmagazine.co.uk/world/the-myth-of-brexit-as-imperial-nostalgia

31   Ibid.

32   Ibid.

33   Jenkins was also president of the European Commission from 1977 to 1981.

34   Saunders, 'The Myth of Brexit as Imperial Nostalgia'.

35   Raymond Plant, *Citizenship, Rights and Socialism* (Fabian Society, no. 531, 1988), p. 2.

36   Quoted in Bridget Phillipson, 'Labour Loves Nostalgia. But we Succeed when our Politics is about the Future', *New Statesman,* 23 October 2019.

37   'Socialism in London', *The New York Times*, 4 April 1881, p. 2.

38   Barbara Tuchman, 'Myth and Revolution', *The New York Times*, 30 January 1966, p. 24.

39   Louis Stark, 'The Paris Commune in Socialist History', *The New York Times*, 31 May 1931, p. 2.

40   Jack Raymond, 'Yugoslavia Plans Commune System: Her Experiment in Socialism Calls for Self-Governing Local Political Unites', *The New York Times*, 16 June 1955, p. 6.

41   Tuchman, 'Myth and Revolution', p. 24.

42   Charles Mohr, 'Leftists in China Score Mao Policy: Demand Return to Initial Paris Commune Aims', *The New York Times*, 14 June 1968, p. 3.

43   Laura C. Forster, 'Radical Commemoration, the Politics of the Street, and the 150th Anniversary of the Paris Commune of 1871', *History Workshop Journal*, 92, 2021, pp. 83–105, p. 84.

44   'Most Russians Say Soviet Union "Took Care of Ordinary People" – Poll', *The Moscow Times*, 24 June 2019.

45   Christine Esche, Rosa Katharine Mossiah and Sandra Topalska, 'Lost and Found: Communism Nostalgia and Communist Chic among Poland's Old and Young Generations', Humanities in Action (website), September

2010, https://www.humanityinaction.org/knowledge_detail/lost-and-found-communism-nostalgia-and-communist-chic-among-polands-old-and-young-generations/

46 Ibid.

47 Ekaterina Kalinina, 'Multiple Faces of the Nostalgia Channel in Russia', *Journal of European Television History & Culture*, 3(5), 2014, pp. 108–18, p. 108.

48 Anna Kutor, 'Milking the Communist Cow', *Discover Poland Magazine*, 1 April 2008. Quoted in Esche, Mossiah and Topalska, 'Lost and Found: Communism Nostalgia and Communist Chic among Poland's Old and Young Generations', Humanities in Action (website), September 2010.

49 Katarzyna Pabijanek, 'Art of Nostalgia', *The Nosztalgia Encyclopedia*, 2007. Quoted in Esche, Mossiah and Topalska, 'Lost and Found: Communism Nostalgia and Communist Chic among Poland's Old and Young Generations', Humanities in Action (website), September 2010.

50 Esche, Mossiah and Topalska, 'Lost and Found: Communism Nostalgia and Communist Chic among Poland's Old and Young Generations', Humanities in Action (website), September 2010.

51 Ibid.

52 Enzo Traverso, *Left-Wing Melancholia: Marxism, History, and Memory* (New York, NY: Columbia University Press, 2021), p. 2.

53 Virginia Heffernan, 'Commie Chic', *New York Magazine*, 23 February 1998.

54 Ibid.

55 Jennifer Crane, '"Save our NHS": Activism, Information-based Expertise and the "New Times" of the 1980s', *Contemporary British History*, 33, 2019, pp. 52–74.

56 Steven Kettell and Peter Kerr, 'The Brexit Religion and the Holy Grail of the NHS', *Social Policy and Society*, 20(2), 2021, pp. 282–95, p. 291.

57 Ian Birrell, 'The London 2012 Opening Ceremony, and a Night that Set NHS Reform Back Years', *Mail on Sunday*, 3 August 2012.

58 Ibid.

59 Catherine Baker, 'Beyond the Island Story?: The Opening Ceremony of the London 2012 Olympic Games as Public History', *Rethinking History: The Journal of Theory and Practice*, 19(3), 2015, pp. 409–28.

60 'Bassetlaw Hospital Patient Recounts his Experiences as the Hospital's Chef in the 1950s', *Doncaster and Bassetlaw Teaching Hospitals,* 18 July 2019.

61 'Come and join in the celebration', NHS Tayside (website), https://www.nhstayside.scot.nhs.uk/OurServicesA-Z/NHSScotland70thAnniversary/PROD_302830/index.htm

62 *Spectra*, 73, NHS Tayside, September–October, https://www.nhstaysid-ecdn.scot.nhs.uk/NHSTaysideWeb/idcplg?IdcService=GET_SECURE_FILE&dDocName=PROD_210894&Rendition=web&RevisionSelectionMethod=LatestReleased&noSaveAs=1

63 Post by @SueSuezep, Twitter (website), 17 September 2022, https://
twitter.com/SueSuezep/status/1571146757865869312?s=20&t=GZryC-
2q1mSCgd_YMyTnXNQ

64 Graeme Culliford, 'Back in the Good Old Days of the NHS', News
Shopper (website), 17 October 2002, https://www.newsshopper.co.uk/
news/6291359.back-in-the-good-old-days-of-the-nhs/

65 Meg Henderson, Letters, *Sunday Times*, 17 June 2007.

66 Jill Parkin, 'Carry on Matron', *Daily Mail*, 12 November 2005.

67 Claire Rayner, 'Stop your Gossiping Nurse', *Daily Mail*, 22 April 2008.

68 Dr Max Gammon, Letters, *The Times*, 19 January 1999.

69 Agnes Arnold-Forster, 'Ordinary People and the 1979 Royal Commission
on the NHS', *Twentieth Century British History*, 34(2), June 2023, https://
doi.org/10.1093/tcbh/hwac043

70 Alec Merrison, *Royal Commission on the National Health Service: Report*
(London: HMSO, 1979), p. 1.

71 Ibid., p. 13.

72 The National Archives (TNA) BS6/12, Letter from Keith A. Mallinson
to A. Merrison, 7 May 1976.

73 Ibid, p. 31.

74 Wellcome Library, History and Origins of the NHS, GC/201/A/1/63

75 Ibid.

76 Ibid.

77 Ibid.

78 TNA BS6/26, Letter from Dr Librach to A. Merrison, 12 May 1976.

79 Pamela M. Jefferies, 'Personal View', *British Medical Journal*, 3(5770),
1971, p. 367.

CHAPTER NINE

1 Oliver W. Sacks and M. Kohl, 'Incontinent Nostalgia Induced by
L-Dopa', *The Lancet*, 1970, p. 1394.

2 Oliver Sacks, *The Man who Mistook His Wife for a Hat* (London: Picador,
2014).

3 Nostalgia Inventory, CBS News (website), https://www.cbsnews.com/
htdocs/pdf/Batcho_Nostalgia_Inventory.pdf

4 Krystine I. Batcho, 'Personal Nostalgia, World View, Memory, and
Emotionality', *Perceptual and Motor Skills*, 87(2), 1998, pp. 411–32.

5 Fred Davis, *Yearning for Yesterday: A Sociology of Nostalgia* (New York, NY:
The Free Press, 1979), p. ix.

6 'Speaking of Psychology: Does Nostalgia have a Psychological Purpose?',
American Psychological Association (podcast), episode 93, https://
www.apa.org/news/podcasts/speaking-of-psychology/nostalgia

7 Ziyan Yang et al, 'Patterns of brain activity associated with nostalgia: a

social-cognitive neuroscience perspective', *Social Cognitive and Affective Neuroscience*, 17:12 (2022): pp. 1131–44.

8   Cherry Norton, 'Odours Best to Evoke Memories', *The Independent*, 17 April 2000.

9   Ibid.

10 Heini Saarimäki et al., 'Distributed Affective Space Represents Multiple Emotion Categories across the Human Brain', *Social Cognitive and Affective Neuroscience*, 13(5), 2018, pp. 471–82; Hedy Kober et al., 'Functional grouping and cortical-subcortical interactions in emotion: a meta-analysis of neuroimaging studies', *NeuroImage*, 42(2), 2008, pp. 998–1031.

11 Lisa Feldman Barrett and Ajay B. Satpute, 'Historical Pitfalls and New Directions in the Neuroscience of Emotion', *Neuroscience Letters*, 693, 2019, pp. 9–18, p. 18.

12 Leonard Mlodinow, *Emotional: The New Thinking About Feeling* (London: Penguin, 2022).

13 Constantine Sedikides, 'Nostalgia: Past, Present, and Future', *Current Directions in Psychological Science*, 17(5), 2008, pp. 304–7.

14 Tim Wildschut, Constantine Sedikides and Clay Routledge, 'Nostalgia: From Cowbells to the Meaning of Life', *The British Psychological Society*, (3 January 2008) https://www.bps.org.uk/psychologist/nostalgia-cowbells-meaning-life

15 Ibid

16 D. G. Hertz, 'Trauma and nostalgia: New aspects of the coping of aging holocaust survivors', *Israeli Journal of Psychiatry and Related Sciences*, 27 (1990): pp. 189–98.

17 Wijnand A. P. Van Tilburg, Constantine Sedikides and Tim Wildschut, 'Adverse Weather Evokes Nostalgia', *Personality and Social Psychology Bulletin*, 44(7), 2018, pp. 984–95.

18 Davis, *Yearning for Yesterday*, p. 420.

19 Bin Li et al., 'Can Good Memories of the Past Instil Happiness? Nostalgia Improves Subjective Well-Being by Increasing Gratitude', *Journal of Happiness Studies*, 24, 2023, pp. 699–715.

20 Krystine I. Batcho, 'Nostalgia: The bittersweet history of a psychological concept', *History of Psychology*, 16(3), 2013, pp. 165–76.

21 Tetsuya Yamagami et al., 'Effect of Activity Reminiscence Therapy as Brain-Activating Rehabilitation for Elderly People with and without Dementia', *Psychogeriatrics*, 7(2), 2007, pp. 69–75.

22 Ernst Bohlmeijer et al., 'The effects of reminiscence on psychological well-being in older adults: A meta-analysis', *Aging & Mental Health*, 11(2), 2007, pp. 291–300.

23 Kai-Jo Chiang et al., 'The effects of reminiscence therapy on psychological well-being, depression, and loneliness among the institutionalized aged', *Geriatric Psychiatry*, 25(4), 2010, pp. 380–8.

24   Marie A. Mills and Peter G. Coleman, 'Nostalgic Memories in Dementia: A Case Study', *The International Journal of Aging & Human Development*, 38(3), 1994, pp. 203–19.

25   Krystine I. Batcho, 'When Nostalgia Tilts to Sad: Anticipatory and Personal Nostalgia', *Frontiers in Psychology*, 11(1186), 2020.

26   Yiannis Gabriel, 'Organizational Nostalgia: Reflections on "The Golden Age"', in S. Fineman (ed.), *Emotion in Organizations* (London: Sage, 1993), pp. 118–41.

27   M. Van Dijke et al., 'Nostalgia Buffers the Negative Impact of Low Procedural Justice on Cooperation', *Organizational Behavior and Human Decision Processes*, 127, 2015, pp. 15–29.

28   Marius Van Dijke and Joost M. Leunissen, 'Review: Nostalgia in Organizations', *Current Opinion in Psychology*, 49, 2023.

29   O. H. Ylijoki, 'Academic Nostalgia: A Narrative Approach to Academic Work', *Human Relations*, 58, 2005, pp. 555–76.

30   Ruth McDonald et al., 'At the Cutting Edge? Modernization and Nostalgia in a Hospital Operating Theatre Department', *Sociology*, 40, 2006, pp. 1097–115.

31   Van Dijke and Leunissen, 'Review: Nostalgia in Organizations'.

32   E. Stephan et al., 'The Mnemonic Mover: Nostalgia Regulates Avoidance and Approach Motivation', *Emotion*, 14(3), 2014, pp. 545–61.

33   T. Wildschut et al., 'Collective Nostalgia: A group-level emotion that confers unique benefits on the group', *Journal of Personal and Social Psychology*, 107, 2014, pp. 844–63.

34   J. M. Leunissen et al., 'Organizational Nostalgia Lowers Turnover Intentions by Increasing Work Meaning: The Moderating Role of Burnout', *Journal of Occupational Health Psychology*, 23, 2018, pp. 44–57.

35   Tim Strangleman, 'The Nostalgia of Organisations and the Organisation of Nostalgia: Past and Present in the Contemporary Railway Industry', *Sociology*, 33, 1999, pp. 725–46.

36   Anthony Toft, 'Has Humanity disappeared from the NHS?', *British Medical Journal*, 320(7247), 2000, p. 1483.

37   Quoted in McDonald et al., 'At the Cutting Edge?', p. 1103.

38   Correspondence with author.

CHAPTER TEN

1   Robert Saunders, 'Brexit and Empire: "Global Britain" and the Myth of Imperial Nostalgia', *The Journal of Imperial and Commonwealth History*, 48(6), 2020, pp. 1140–74, p. 1141.

2   Eleanor Newbigin, 'Brexit, nostalgia and the Great British fantasy', Open Democracy (website), 15 February 2017, https://eprints.soas.ac.uk/25232/1/newbigin-opendemocracy.net-brexit-nostalgia-and-the-

great-british-fantasy.pdf; Samuel Earle, 'The Toxic Nostalgia of Brexit', *The Atlantic*, 5 October 2017, https://www.theatlantic.com/international/archive/2017/10/brexit-britain-may-johnson-eu/542079/; Michael Goldfarb, 'Brexit has been driven by England's nostalgia for an imagined past', *The National*, 26 February 2019, https://www.thenationalnews.com/world/brexit/brexit-has-been-driven-by-england-s-nostalgia-for-an-imagined-past-1.821625; Tony Barber, 'Nostalgia and the promise of Brexit', *Financial Times*, 19 July 2018, https://www.ft.com/content/bf70b80e-8b39-11e8-bf9e-8771d5404543

3   Cheryl Thompson, 'Trump has made America nostalgic again for a past that never existed', *The Conversation*, 4 November 2020, https://theconversation.com/trump-has-made-america-nostalgic-again-for-a-past-that-never-existed-149449

4   Ronald Brownstein, 'Trump's Rhetoric of White Nostalgia', *The Atlantic*, 2 June 2016, https://www.theatlantic.com/politics/archive/2016/06/trumps-rhetoric-of-white-nostalgia/485192/

5   Emily St James, 'Stranger Things, La La Land, and Donald Trump: Empty Nostalgia Dominated 2016', Vox, 4 June 2017, https://www.vox.com/culture/2017/1/4/14048076/nostalgia-2016-trump

6   Vanessa Thorpe, 'Rewriting History: How Imperfect Costume Dramas make the Past Relevant', *The Observer*, 27 June 2021, https://www.theguardian.com/tv-and-radio/2021/jun/27/rewriting-history-how-imperfect-costume-dramas-make-the-past-relevant

7   Emily Robinson, 'Touching the Void: Affective History and the Impossible', *Rethinking History: The Journal of Theory and Practice*, 14(4), 2010, pp. 503–20, p. 506.

8   Ibid., p. 520.

9   Ibid.

10   Ibid., p. 507.

11   Ibid.

12   Alex Von Tunzelmann, *Fallen Idols* (London: Headline, 2021); Dan Hicks, *The Brutish Museums: The Benin Bronzes, Colonial Violence and Cultural Restitution* (London: Pluto Press, 2020); Colonial Countryside Project, National Trust (website), https://www.nationaltrust.org.uk/who-we-are/research/colonial-countryside-project; Corinne Fowler, *Green Unpleasant Land: Creative Responses to Rural England's Colonial Connections* (Leeds: Peepal Tree Press Limited, 2020); Jamie Doward, 'I've Been Unfairly Targeted, says Academic at Heart of National Trust "Woke" Row', *The Observer*, 20 December 2020, https://www.theguardian.com/uk-news/2020/dec/20/ive-been-unfairly-targeted-says-academic-at-heart-of-national-trust-woke-row; 'The 1619 Project', *The New York Times*, https://www.nytimes.com/interactive/2019/08/14/magazine/1619-america-slavery.html

13   Hannah Rose Woods, *Rule, Nostalgia: A Backwards History of Britain* (London: Random House, 2022).

14   Emily Keightley and Michael Pickering, *The Mnemonic Imagination: Remembering as Creative Practice* (London: Palgrave Macmillan, 2012), p. 127.

15   Svetlana Boym, *The Future of Nostalgia* (New York, NY: Basic Books, 2001), p. xvi.

16   Ibid.

17   Tim Strangleman, 'The Nostalgia of Organisations and the Organisation of Nostalgia: Past and Present in the Contemporary Railway Industry', *Sociology*, 33, 1999, pp. 725–46.

18   Enzo Traverso, *Left-Wing Melancholia: Marxism, History, and Memory* (New York, NY: Columbia University Press, 2021).

INDEX